Language Change: Progress or Decay?

Fourth edition

How and why do languages change? Where does the evidence of language change come from? How do languages begin and end? This introduction to language change explores these and other questions, considering changes through time.

The central theme of this book is whether language change is a symptom of progress or decay. This book will show you why it is neither, and that understanding the factors surrounding how language change occurs is essential to understanding why it happens.

This updated edition remains non-technical and accessible to readers with no previous knowledge of linguistics.

After many years lecturing at the University of London, (London School of Economics), Jean Aitchison was Professor of Language and Communication at the University of Oxford (1993–2003), and is now an Emeritus Professor. She is the author of a number of books on language, including *The Language Web* (Cambridge University Press, 1997).

Cambridge Approaches to Linguistics

General editor: Jean Aitchison, *Emeritus Rupert Murdoch Professor of Language and Communication, University of Oxford*

In the past twenty-five years, linguistics – the systematic study of language – has expanded dramatically. Its findings are now of interest to psychologists, sociologists, philosophers, anthropologists, teachers, speech therapists and numerous others who have realized that language is of crucial importance in their life and work. But when newcomers try to discover more about the subject, a major problem faces them – the technical and often narrow nature of much writing about linguistics.

Cambridge Approaches to Linguistics is an attempt to solve this problem by presenting current findings in a lucid and non-technical way. Its object is twofold. First, it hopes to outline the 'state of play' in key areas of the subject, concentrating on what is happening now, rather than on surveying the past. Secondly, it aims to provide links between branches of linguistics that are traditionally separate.

The series will give readers an understanding of the multi-faceted nature of language, and its central position in human affairs, as well as equipping those who wish to find out more about linguistics with a basis from which to read some of the more technical literature in books and journals.

Also in the series

Language Change: Progress or Decay?

Fourth edition

JEAN AITCHISON

Emeritus Professor,
University of Oxford

CAMBRIDGE
UNIVERSITY PRESS

CAMBRIDGE UNIVERSITY PRESS
Cambridge, New York, Melbourne, Madrid, Cape Town,
Singapore, São Paulo, Delhi, Mexico City

Cambridge University Press
The Edinburgh Building, Cambridge CB2 8RU, UK

Published in the United States of America by Cambridge University Press, New York

www.cambridge.org
Information on this title: www.cambridge.org/9781107678927

First published by Fontana Press in 1981
Second edition published by Cambridge University Press in 1991
Sixth printing 1998
Third edition 2001
Tenth printing 2011
Fourth edition 2013

Printed and bound in the United Kingdom by the MPG Books Group

A catalogue record for this publication is available from the British Library

Library of Congress Cataloguing in Publication data
Aitchison, Jean, 1938–
Language change : progress or decay? / Jean Aitchison. – 4th ed.
    p.   cm. – (Cambridge approaches to linguistics)
Includes bibliographical references and index.
ISBN 978-1-107-02362-8
1. Linguistic change.   I. Title.
P142.A37   2012
417′.7 – dc23   2012027127

ISBN 978-1-107-02362-8 Hardback
ISBN 978-1-107-67892-7 Paperback

Contents

v

Preface

Language change is a topic which, perhaps more than most others, spreads itself over a wide range of areas. For this reason, the literature often seems disjointed and contradictory, since many scholars, like Jane Austen, prefer to polish their own square inch of ivory, rather than tackle the whole vast subject. This book is an attempt to pull the various strands together into a coherent whole, and to provide an overview of the phenomenon of human language change. It discusses where our evidence comes from, how changes happen, why they happen, and how and why whole languages begin and end. It does this within the framework of one central question. Is language change a symptom of either progress or decay?

The study of language change – often labelled 'historical linguistics' – has altered its character considerably in recent years. Traditionally, scholars concerned themselves with reconstructing the earliest possible stages of languages, and with describing sound changes as they unrolled through the ages. In this, they paid relatively little attention to changes currently taking place, to syntactic change, to meaning change, to pidgins and creoles, to dying languages, or to the sociolinguistic factors which underlie many alterations. In the second half of the twentieth century, these neglected topics rose one by one to the forefront of attention. This book is an attempt to draw together the old and the new into an integrated whole. In short, it tries to combine old-style historical linguistics with more recent approaches, so as to give an overview of the field as it stands at the moment.

The flow of new books and articles on historical linguistics has become a flood since the third edition of this book was published in

2001. This fourth edition tries to reflect the torrent of new work. I have deleted one chapter (on child language and aphasia) since I, and others, have become convinced that these topics do not significantly affect language change. This has provided space for additions to other chapters (for example, new evidence on the previously maligned Bishop Lowth, and information on text messaging). Numerous books and articles have been added to the 'Notes and suggestions for further reading'. Hopefully, the book provides an up-to-date 'bird's-eye view' of what is happening in historical linguistics.

Symbols and technical terms have been kept to a minimum. Those that are essential have been explained in the text as they occur, but since several common ones crop up more than once, a brief glossary has been added for those not familiar with linguistics.

As in previous editions, I would like to remember with thanks those teachers from my past who fired my enthusiasm for the subject when I was a student, in particular Professor W. S. Allen and Dr J. Chadwick, Professor O. Szemerényi, Professor R. Jakobson and Professor C. Watkins. I would also like to thank all those colleagues, students and friends who both in discussions and by their writing have helped me to clarify my thoughts on language change. Thank you, also, to all those who have sent me books, papers and offprints. Please continue to do so!

Thanks go to the publishers at Cambridge University Press, especially Sarah Green, Editor of Language and Linguistics, who answers email queries with astonishing promptness and efficiency. Finally, I want to give particular thanks to my husband, the lexicographer John Ayto, whose loving kindness and helpful books made my task an easier one.

I have not always followed the advice and suggestions made to me by others (though I certainly considered them seriously at the time), so I alone am responsible for any oversimplifications or inaccuracies which may remain.

Acknowledgments

For kind permission to quote from copyright material the author is grateful to the following: André Deutsch and Little, Brown and Company, for 'Laments for a dying language', *Everyone but thee and me*, © 1960 Ogden Nash, renewed 1985 by Frances Nash, Isabel Nash Eberstadt and Linell Nash Smith, 'Baby, what makes the sky blue?', © 1940 Ogden Nash, *Family reunion* (first appeared in the *New Yorker*) and 'Thunder over the nursery', *Verses from 1929 on*, © 1935 Ogden Nash; ATV Music, for 'Getting better', © 1969 words and music by John Lennon and Paul McCartney; Tom Lehrer, for 'When you are old and gray', © 1953 Tom Lehrer; Lawrence & Wishart, for *Selections from the prison notebooks of Antonio Gramsci*, Q. Hoare and G. Nowell-Smith (eds.); Grove Weidenfeld and Harmony Music Ltd, for *Alice's restaurant* by Arlo Guthrie; Faber and Faber Ltd and Harcourt Brace Jovanovitch Inc., for 'Burnt Norton' from 'Four Quartets', *The collected poems 1909–1962*, © 1943 T. S. Eliot, renewed 1971 by Esme Valerie Eliot; The Bodley Head, for *Zen and the art of motorcycle maintenance* by Robert Pirsig; Allen Lane, Penguin, and the executors of the estate of Stevie Smith, for 'The jungle husband', *The collected poems of Stevie Smith*, James MacGibbon (ed.) (Penguin 20th Century Classics); Harper Collins Publishers Ltd and Sterling Lord Literistic Inc., for *The phantom tollbooth* by Norton Juster.

Every effort has been made to acknowledge and secure copyright permissions for quoted material. The publishers apologize for any inadvertent omissions or errors, and would welcome information regarding them.

Symbols and technical terms

Most symbols and technical terms are explained in the text the first time they occur, in cases where an explanation seems necessary. But since several common ones occur more than once, this glossary has been added for the benefit of those readers not familiar with them.

General

[ ]   Square brackets indicate sounds. For example, the pronunciation of the English word *kissed* may be represented by the phonetic transcription [kɪst].

*   An asterisk indicates a non-permitted sequence of sounds or words in the language concerned. For example, English does not permit a word with the sound sequence *[tpet], or a sentence *Augusta roses wants*.

→   An arrow means 'changed into historically', as in [e] → [i], which means [e] changed into [i].

Phonetic symbols

When a phonetic symbol is essential, this book uses IPA (International Phonetic Alphabet) symbols, which are conventionally put between square brackets. However, since phonetic symbols make a text more difficult to read, the standard written form is used whenever possible, even though the spoken form is under discussion.

Phonetic symbols which are not explained are either obvious from the context, or have a value similar to that in the standard written form, e.g. [m] symbolizes the sound at the beginning of the word *men*.

The following list gives some of the less obvious terms and symbols.

Consonants

[θ]	The sound at the beginning of English *thick*.
[ð]	The sound at the beginning of *then*.
[ʃ]	The sound at the beginning of *shock*.
[ʒ]	The sound at the end of *beige* or in the middle of *leisure*.
[tʃ]	The sound at the beginning and end of *church*.
[ʤ]	The sound at the beginning and end of *judge*.
[ŋ]	The sound at the end of *bang* (**velar nasal**).
[ʔ]	A **glottal stop** – see explanation below.

Stop: a consonant involving a complete stoppage of the airstream at some point in the vocal tract, as [p], [t], [k]. A glottal stop [ʔ] is a complete stoppage of the airstream in the glottis (lower part of the throat), as at the end of Cockney or Glaswegian *pit* [pɪʔ].

Fricative: a consonant in which the airstream is never completely cut off, resulting in audible friction, as in [f], [v], [s], [z].

Affricate: a combination of a stop and a fricative, as in [tʃ], [ʤ].

Sibilant: a hissing or hushing sound, as in [s], [z], [ʃ].

Voiced: a voiced sound is one whose production involves vibration of the vocal cords, as in [b], [d], [g], [v], [z].

Voiceless: a voiceless sound is one whose production does not involve the vibration of the vocal cords, as in [p], [t], [k], [f], [s]. Technically, it involves 'late voice onset', that is, some voicing, but delayed.

Vowels

: A colon added to a vowel indicates length, as in [tiː] *tea*.

~ A wavy line over a vowel indicates nasalization, as in French [bɔ̃] *bon* 'good'.

[ə] **Schwa:** a short indeterminate vowel, like that at the beginning of *ago*, or the end of *sofa*.

[iː] a vowel somewhat like that in *meet*, *bee*.

[ɪ] a vowel like that in *hit*.

Other vowel symbols are mostly explained as they occur. Key words are less useful for vowels, since there is so much variation in accent in the English-speaking world.

Diphthong: a sequence of two vowels which glide into one another, as in *play* [pleɪ].

Part 1
Preliminaries

1 The ever-whirling wheel
The inevitability of change

Since 'tis Nature's Law to change.
Constancy alone is strange.

John Wilmot, Earl of Rochester,
A dialogue between Strephon and Daphne

Introduction

This chapter notes that language change is inevitable, yet points out that there is a puzzling, long-standing custom of moaning about it. The complaint tradition is outlined and some reasons for it are pointed out, such as an admiration for Latin, and a long-lasting, but unjustified preference for written language forms over spoken. But finding that some complaints are groundless does not answer the central question: is our language progressing, decaying, or standing still? This is the topic of the whole book. The chapter then discusses the meaning of the word *grammar*, distinguishing between old-style prescriptive grammars which tried to lay down outdated 'rules', and modern descriptive grammars which describe actual usage. The main components of a modern grammar are outlined. Finally, the chapter explains the organization of the book, listing the main sections, and the outline content of each.

Everything in this universe is perpetually in a state of change, a fact commented on by philosophers and poets through the ages. A flick through any book of quotations reveals numerous statements about the fluctuating world we live in: 'Everything rolls on, nothing stays still,' claimed the ancient Greek philosopher Heraclitus in the sixth century BC. In the sixteenth century, Edmund Spenser speaks of 'the ever-whirling wheel of change, the which all mortal things doth sway', while 'time and the world are ever in flight' is a statement by the twentieth-century Irish poet William Butler Yeats – to take just a few random examples.

Language, like everything else, joins in this general flux. As the German philosopher–linguist Wilhelm von Humboldt noted in 1836: 'There can never be a moment of true standstill in language, just as little as in the ceaseless flaming thought of men. By nature it is a continuous process of development.'[1]

Even the simplest and most colloquial English of several hundred years ago sounds remarkably strange to us. Take the work of Robert Mannyng, who wrote a history of England in the mid fourteenth century. He claimed that he made his language as simple as he could so that ordinary people could understand it, yet it is barely comprehensible to the average person today:

> In symple speche as I couthe,
> That is lightest in mannes mouthe.
> I mad noght for no disours,
> Ne for no seggers, no harpours,
> Bot for the luf of symple men
> That strange Inglis can not ken.[2]

A glance at any page of Chaucer shows clearly the massive changes which have taken place in the last millennium. It is amusing to note that he himself, in *Troylus and Criseyde*, expressed his wonderment that men of long ago spoke in so different a manner from his contemporaries:

> Ye knowe ek, that in forme of speche is chaunge
> Withinne a thousand yer, and wordes tho
> That hadden prys now wonder nyce and straunge
> Us thenketh hem, and yet they spake hem so,
> And spedde as wel in love as men now do.[3]

Language, then, like everything else, gradually transforms itself over the centuries. There is nothing surprising in this. In a world where humans grow old, tadpoles change into frogs, and milk turns into cheese, it would be strange if language alone remained unaltered. As the famous Swiss linguist Ferdinand de Saussure noted: 'Time changes all things: there is no reason why language should escape this universal law.'[4]

In spite of this, large numbers of intelligent people condemn and resent language change, regarding alterations as due to unnecessary sloppiness, laziness or ignorance. More accurately, perhaps, they accept that language changes, but disapprove of particular alterations, namely those that they personally dislike. Letters are written to newspapers and indignant articles are published, all deploring the fact that words acquire new meanings and new pronunciations. The following is a representative sample taken from the last half-century or so. In the late 1960s we find a columnist in a British newspaper complaining about the 'growing unintelligibility of spoken English', and maintaining that 'English used to be a language which foreigners couldn't pronounce but could often understand. Today it is rapidly becoming a language which the English can't pronounce and few foreigners can understand.'[5] At around the same time, another commentator declared angrily that 'through sheer laziness and sloppiness of mind, we are in danger of losing our past subjunctive'.[6] A third owned to a 'queasy distaste for the vulgarity of "between you and I", "these sort", "the media is" . . . precisely the kind of distaste I feel at seeing a damp spoon dipped in the sugar bowl or butter spread with the bread-knife'.[7]

In 1972 the writer of an article emotively entitled 'Polluting our language' condemned the 'blind surrender to the momentum or inertia of slovenly and tasteless ignorance and insensitivity'.[8] A reviewer discussing the 1978 edition of the *Pocket Oxford Dictionary* announced that his 'only sadness is that the current editor seems prepared to bow to every slaphappy and slipshod change of meaning'.[9] The author of a book published in 1979 compared a word which changes its meaning to 'a piece of wreckage with a ship's name on it floating away from a sunken hulk': the book was entitled *Decadence*.[10]

In 1980, the literary editor of *The Times* complained that the grammar of English 'is becoming simpler and coarser'.[11] In 1982, a newspaper article commented that 'The standard of speech and pronunciation in England has declined so much . . . that one is almost ashamed to let foreigners hear it.'[12] In 1986, a letter written to an evening paper complained about 'the abuse of our beautiful language by native-born English speakers . . . We go out of our way to promulgate incessantly . . . the very ugliest sounds and worst possible grammar.'[13] In 1988, a journalist bemoaned 'pronunciation lapses' which affect him 'like a blackboard brushed with barbed wire'.[14] In 1990, a well-known author published an article entitled: 'They can't even say it properly now', in which he grumbled that 'We seem to be moving . . . towards a social and linguistic situation in which nobody says or writes or probably knows anything more than an approximation to what he or she means.'[15] In 1999, a writer in a Sunday newspaper coined the label 'Slop English' for the 'maulings and misusages' of 'Teletotties' (young television presenters).[16]

In 2004, a journalist wrote a book with the emotive subtitle 'The mangling and manipulating of the English language'.[17] He explained his worries as follows: 'Ugly language can ruin your day . . . I love words . . . Sometimes there is a real thrill of pleasure. It is like walking in the surf, letting the waves lap over your bare feet. Then you step on something nasty. Ugly language is the detritus washed up on the beach.'[18] The same journalist became quite apoplectic over text messaging. He described 'texters' (those who 'text') as 'vandals who are doing to our language what Genghis Khan did to his neighbours eight hundred years ago. They are destroying it: pillaging our punctuation; savaging our sentences; raping our vocabulary. And they must be stopped.'[19]

The above views are neatly summarized in Ogden Nash's poem 'Laments for a dying language' (1962):

> Coin brassy words at will, debase the coinage;
> We're in an if-you-cannot-lick-them-join age,
> A slovenliness provides its own excuse age,
> Where usage overnight condones misusage.
> Farewell, farewell to my beloved language,
> Once English, now a vile orangutanguage.

Some questions immediately spring to mind. Are these objectors merely ludicrous, akin to fools who think it might be possible to halt the movement of the waves or the course of the sun? Are their efforts to hold back the sea of change completely misguided? Alternatively, could these intelligent and well-known writers possibly be right? Is it indeed possible that language change is largely due to lack of care and maintenance on our part? Are we simply behaving like the inhabitants of underdeveloped countries who allow tractors and cars to rot after only months of use because they do not understand the need to oil and check the parts every so often? Is it true that 'we need not simply accept it, as though it were some catastrophe of nature. We all talk and we all listen. Each one of us, therefore, every day can break a lance on behalf of our embattled English tongue, by taking a little more trouble', as a *Daily Telegraph* writer claimed?[20] Ought we to be actually doing something, such as starting a Campaign for Real English, as one letter to a newspaper proposed?[21] Or, in a slightly modified form, we might ask the following. Even if eventual change is inevitable, can we appreciably retard it, and would it be to our advantage to do so? Furthermore, is it possible to distinguish between 'good' and 'bad' changes, and root out the latter?

These questions often arouse surprisingly strong feelings, and they are not easy to answer. In order to answer them satisfactorily, we need to know considerably more about language change, how it happens, when it happens, who initiates it, and other possible reasons for its occurrence. These are the topics examined in this book. In short, we shall look at how and why language change occurs, with the ultimate aim of finding out the direction, if any, in which human languages are moving.

In theory, there are three possibilities to be considered. They could apply either to human language as a whole, or to any one language in particular. The first possibility is slow decay, as was frequently suggested in the nineteenth century. Many scholars were convinced that European languages were on the decline because they were gradually losing their old word endings. For example, the popular German writer Max Müller asserted that, 'The history of all the Aryan languages is nothing but a gradual process of decay.'[22]

Alternatively, languages might be slowly evolving to a more efficient state. We might be witnessing the survival of the fittest, with existing languages adapting to the needs of the times. The lack of a complicated word-ending system in English might be a sign of streamlining and sophistication, as argued by the Danish linguist Otto Jespersen in 1922: 'In the evolution of languages the discarding of old flexions goes hand in hand with the development of simpler and more regular expedients that are rather less liable than the old ones to produce misunderstanding.'[23]

A third possibility is that language remains in a substantially similar state from the point of view of progress or decay. It may be marking time, or treading water, as it were, with its advance or decline held in check by opposing forces. This is the view of the Belgian linguist Joseph Vendryès, who claimed that 'Progress in the absolute sense is impossible, just as it is in morality or politics. It is simply that different states exist, succeeding each other, each dominated by certain general laws imposed by the equilibrium of the forces with which they are confronted. So it is with language.'[24]

In the course of this book, we shall try to find out where the truth of the matter lies.

The search for purity

Before we look at language change itself, it may be useful to consider why people currently so often disapprove of alterations. On examination, much of the dislike turns out to be based on social-class prejudice which needs to be stripped away.

Let us begin by asking why the conviction that our language is decaying is so much more widespread than the belief that it is progressing. In an intellectual climate where the notion of the survival of the fittest is at least as strong as the belief in inevitable decay, it is strange that so many people are convinced of the decline in the quality of English, a language which is now spoken by an estimated half a billion people or more – a possible hundredfold increase in the number of speakers during the past millennium.

One's first reaction is to wonder whether the members of the anti-slovenliness brigade, as we may call them, are subconsciously reacting to the fast-moving world we live in, and consequently resenting change in any area of life. To some extent this is likely to be true. A feeling that 'fings ain't wot they used to be' and an attempt to preserve life unchanged seem to be natural reactions to insecurity, symptoms of growing old. Every generation inevitably believes that the clothes, manners and speech of the following one have deteriorated. We would therefore expect to find a respect for conservative language in every century and every culture and, in literate societies, a reverence for the language of the 'best authors' of the past. We would predict a mild nostalgia, typified perhaps by a native speaker of Kru, one of the Niger-Congo group of languages. When asked if it would be acceptable to place the verb at the end of a particular sentence, instead of in the middle where it was usually placed, he replied that this was the 'real Kru' which his father spoke.[25]

In Europe, however, the feeling that language is on the decline seems more widely spread and stronger than the predictable mood of mild regret. On examination, we find that today's laments take their place in a long tradition of complaints about the corruption of language. Similar expressions of horror were common in the nineteenth century. In 1858 we discover a certain Reverend A. Mursell fulminating against the use of phrases such as *hard up, make oneself scarce, shut up.*[26] At around the same time in Germany, Jacob Grimm, one of the Brothers Grimm of folk-tale fame, stated nostalgically that 'six hundred years ago every rustic knew, that is to say practised daily, perfections and niceties in the German language of which the best grammarians nowadays do not even dream'.[27]

Moving back into the eighteenth century, we find the puristic movement at its height. Utterances of dismay and disgust at the state of the language followed one another thick and fast, expressed with far greater urgency than we normally find today. Famous outbursts included one in 1710 by Jonathan Swift. Writing in the *Tatler*, he launched an attack on the condition of English. He followed this up two years later with a letter to the Lord Treasurer urging the formation of an academy to regulate language usage, since even the best authors of the age, in his opinion, committed 'many gross improprieties which . . . ought to be discarded'.[28] In 1755, Samuel Johnson's famous dictionary of the English language was published. He stated in the preface that 'Tongues, like governments, have a natural tendency to degeneration', urging that 'we retard what we cannot repel, that we palliate what we cannot cure'. In 1762, Robert Lowth, Bishop of London, complained that 'the English Language hath been much cultivated during the last 200 years . . . but . . . it hath made no advances in Grammatical accuracy'.[29]

In short, expressions of disgust about language, and proposals for remedying the situation, were at their height in the eighteenth century. Such widespread linguistic fervour has never been paralleled. Let us therefore consider what special factors caused such obsessive worry about language at this time.

Around 1700, English spelling and usage were in a fairly fluid state. Against this background, two powerful social factors combined to convert a normal mild nostalgia for the language of the past into a quasi-religious doctrine. The first was a long-standing admiration for Latin, and the second was powerful class snobbery.

The admiration for Latin was a legacy from its use as the language of the church in the Middle Ages, and as the common language of European scholarship from the Renaissance onwards. It was widely regarded as the most perfect of languages – Ben Jonson spoke of it as 'queen of tongues' – and great emphasis was placed on learning to write it 'correctly', that is, in accordance with the usage of the great classical authors such as Cicero. It was taught in schools, and Latin grammar was used as a model for the description of all other languages – however dissimilar – despite the fact that it was no longer anyone's native tongue.

This had three direct effects on attitudes towards language. First, because of the emphasis on replicating the Latin of the 'best authors', people felt that there ought to be a fixed 'correct' form for any language, including English. Secondly, because Latin was primarily written and read, it led to the belief that the written language was in some sense superior to the spoken. Thirdly, even though our language is by no means a direct descendant of Latin, more like a great-niece or great-nephew, English was viewed by many as having slipped from the classical purity of Latin by losing its endings. The idea that a language with a full set of endings for its nouns and verbs was superior to one without these appendages was very persistent. Even in the twentieth century, we find linguists forced to argue against this continuing irrational attachment to Latin: 'A linguist that insists on talking about the Latin type of morphology as though it were necessarily the high water mark of linguistic development is like the zoologist that sees in the organic world a huge conspiracy to evolve the racehorse or the Jersey cow,' wrote Edward Sapir in 1921.[30]

Against this background of admiration for a written language which appeared to have a fixed correct form and a full set of endings, there arose a widespread feeling that someone ought to adjudicate among the variant forms of English, and tell people what was 'correct'. The task was undertaken by Samuel Johnson, the son of a bookseller in Lichfield. Johnson, like many people of fairly humble origin, had an illogical reverence for his social betters. When he attempted to codify the English language in his famous dictionary he selected middle- and upper-class usage. When he said that he had 'laboured to refine our language to grammatical purity, and to clear it from colloquial barbarisms, licentious idioms, and irregular combinations',[31] he meant that he had in many instances pronounced against the spoken language of the lower classes, and in favour of the spoken and written forms of groups with social prestige. He asserted, therefore, that there were standards of correctness which should be adhered to, implying that these were already in use among certain social classes, and ought to be acquired by the others. Johnson's dictionary rightly had enormous influence, and its publication has been called 'the most important linguistic event of the eighteenth century'.[32] It was considered a worthwhile undertaking both by his contemporaries and by later generations since it paid fairly close attention to actual usage, even if it was the usage of only a small proportion of speakers.

However, there were other eighteenth-century writers whose influence may have equalled that of Johnson. The best known of these was Robert Lowth, Bishop of London. A prominent Hebraist and theologian, he wrote *A short introduction to English grammar* (1762). Lowth's book title was possibly based on that of a well-known Latin grammar, *A short introduction to grammar*, by William Lily.[33] This grammar was several centuries old. Reportedly, it had been authorized as a grammar of Latin by Henry VIII in 1640, and remained in long-term use in English schools. It was possibly the grammar used by Lowth in his youth: he may even have been forced to memorize it.[34]

Lowth claimed he had written his grammar 'for the use of my little boy', his young son Thomas. He believed he could prepare his son for the hard task of learning Latin, if he taught him the rudiments of English grammar before he went to school. As he stated: 'if children were first taught the principles of Grammar by some short and clear system of *English* grammar, ... they would have some notion of what they were going about when they should enter into *Latin* grammar'.[35] Lowth's grammar was not really suitable for children, but it became widely used.

Lowth is thought to have owned a copy of Johnson's dictionary, yet he disagreed with Johnson's procedure, which had been to describe the usages of the best authors. In contrast, Lowth wanted to show that 'our best Authors for want of some rudiments [of grammar] have sometimes fallen into mistakes and been guilty of palpable errors of Grammar'.[36] He also wanted to promote study of his own grammar in order to remedy the situation. Lowth's use of speech samples showing errors was an innovation in grammar writing. Only later did such behaviour become associated with pedantry. He appears to have found his samples somewhat at random in order to illustrate the points he wished to make. In some ways he was ahead of his time in that he distinguished everyday usage from elevated or written usage, tending to prefer the latter, as in his treatment of prepositions at the end of sentences:

> The Preposition is often separated from the Relative which it governs, and joined to the verb at the end of the Sentence . . . as, 'Horace is an author, whom I am much delighted with' . . . This is an Idiom which our language is strongly inclined to; it prevails in common conversation, and suits very well with the familiar style of writing; but the placing of the Preposition before the Relative is more graceful, as well as more perspicuous; and agrees much better with the solemn and elevated style.[37]

As a result, the notion that it is somehow 'wrong' to end a sentence with a preposition is nowadays widely held. In addition, Lowth insisted on the pronoun *I* in phrases such as *wiser than I*, condemning lines of Swift such as 'she suffers hourly more than me', regardless of the fact that many languages, French and English included, prefer a different form of the pronoun when it is detached from its verb: compare the French *plus sage que moi* 'wiser than me', not **plus sage que je*. In consequence, many people nowadays mistakenly believe that a phrase such as *wiser than I* is 'better' than *wiser than me*. To continue, Lowth may have been the first to argue that a double negative is wrong, on the grounds that one cancels the other out. Those who support this point of view fail to realize that language is not logic or mathematics, and that the heaping up of negatives is very common in the languages of the world. It occurs frequently in Chaucer (and in other pre-eighteenth-century

English authors). For example, in the Prologue to the *Canterbury tales*, Chaucer heaps up negatives to emphasize the fact that the knight was never rude to anyone:

> He nevere yet no vileynye ne sayde
> In all his lyf unto no maner wight.
> He was a verray, parfit gentil knyght.[38]

Today, the belief that a double negative is wrong is perhaps the most widely accepted of all popular convictions about 'correctness', even though stacked-up negatives occur in several varieties of English, without causing any problems of understanding: 'I didn't know nothin' bout gettin' no checks to (= for) nothin', no so (= social) security or nothin'.' This 65-year-old black woman originally from the Mississippi River area of America was clearly not getting the social security payments due to her.[39]

In the nineteenth century, prominent church dignitaries continued to make well-intentioned, but bizarre pronouncements. An influential Archbishop of Dublin, Richard Chenevix Trench, promoted his belief that the language of 'savages' (his word) had slithered down from former excellence, due to lack of care: 'What does their language on close inspection prove? In every case what they are themselves, the remnant and ruin of a better and a nobler past. Fearful indeed is the impress of degradation which is stamped on the language of the savage.'[40] He urged English speakers to preserve their language, quoting with approval the words of a German scholar, Friedrich Schlegel: 'A nation whose language becomes rude and barbarous, must be on the brink of barbarism in regard to everything else.'[41]

We in the twenty-first century are the direct descendants of this earlier puristic passion. Statements very like those of Bishop Lowth are still found in books and newspapers, often reiterating the points he made – points which are still being drummed into the heads of the younger generation by some parents and schoolteachers who misguidedly think they are handing over the essential prerequisites for speaking and writing 'good English'.

Not only are the strictures set on language often arbitrary but, in addition, they cannot usually be said to 'purify' the language in any way. Consider the journalist mentioned earlier who had a 'queasy distaste' for *the media is* (in place of the 'correct' form, *the media are*). To an impartial observer, the treatment of *media* as a singular noun might seem to be an advantage, not a sign of decay. Since most English plurals end in *-s*, it irons out an exception. Surely it is 'purer' to have all plurals ending in the same way? A similar complaint occurred several centuries back over the word *chicken*. Once, the word *cicen* 'a young hen' had a plural *cicenu*. The old plural ending *-u* was eventually replaced by *-s*. Again, surely it is an advantage to smooth away exceptional plurals? Yet we find a seventeenth-century grammarian stating, 'those who say *chicken* in the singular and *chickens* in the plural are completely wrong'.[42]

Purism, then, does not necessarily make language 'purer'. Nor does it always favour the older form, merely the most socially prestigious. A clear-cut example of this is the British dislike of the American form *gotten*, as in *he's gotten married*. Yet this is older than British *got*, and is seen now in a few relic forms only, such as *ill-gotten gains*.

In brief, the puristic attitude towards language – the idea that there is an absolute standard of correctness which should be maintained – has its origin in a natural nostalgic tendency, supplemented and intensified by social pressures. It is illogical and impossible to pin down to any firm base. Purists behave as if there was a vintage year when language achieved a measure of excellence which we should all strive to maintain. In fact, there never was such a year. The language of Chaucer's or Shakespeare's time was no better and no worse than that of our own – just different.

Of course, the fact that the puristic movement is wrong in the details it complains about does not prove that purists are wrong overall. Those who argue that language is decaying may be right for the wrong reasons, they may be entirely wrong, or they may be partially right and partially wrong. All we have discovered so far is that there are no easy answers, and that social prejudices simply cloud the issue.

Rules and grammars

It is important to distinguish between the 'grammar' and 'rules' of old-fashioned purists, and those of linguists. (A linguist here means someone professionally concerned with linguistics, the study of language.) In Bishop Lowth's view, 'the principal design of a Grammar of any Language is to teach us to express ourselves with propriety in that Language, and to be able to judge of every phrase and form of construction, whether it be right or not. The plain way of doing this is to lay down rules.'[43]

Any grammar which lays down artificial rules in order to impose some arbitrary standard of 'correctness' is a **prescriptive** grammar, since it prescribes what people should, in the opinion of the writer, say. It may have relatively little to do with what people really say, a fact illustrated by a comment of Eliza Doolittle in Bernard Shaw's play *Pygmalion*: 'I don't want to talk grammar, I want to talk like a lady.' The artificial and constraining effect of pseudo-rules might be summarized by lines from the Beatles' song 'Getting better':

> I used to get mad at my school
> the teachers who taught me weren't cool
> holding me down, turning me round,
> filling me up with your rules.

The grammars and rules of linguists, on the other hand, are not prescriptive but **descriptive**, since they describe what people actually say. For linguists, rules are not arbitrary laws imposed by an external authority, but a codification of subconscious principles or conventions followed by the speakers of a language. Linguists also regard the spoken and written forms of language as separate, related systems, and treat the spoken as primary.[44]

Let us consider the notion of **rules** (in this modern sense) more carefully. It is clear that it is impossible to list all the sentences of any human language. A language such as English does not have, say, 7,123,541 possible sentences which people gradually learn, one by one. Instead, the speakers of a language have a finite number of principles or 'rules' which enable them to understand and put together a potentially infinite number of sentences. These rules vary from language to language. In English, for example, the sounds [b], [d], [e] can be arranged as [bed], [deb], or [ebd] as in *ebbed*. *[bde], *[dbe] and *[edb] are all impossible, since words cannot begin with [bd] or [db], or end with [db], though these sequences are pronounceable. (An asterisk indicates a non-permitted sequence of sounds or words in the language concerned. Also, sounds are conventionally indicated by square brackets.) Yet in ancient Greek, the sequence [bd] was allowable at the beginning of a word, as in *bdeluros* 'rascal', while a sequence [sl], as in *sleep*, was not permitted.

Rules for permissible sequences exist also for segments of words, and words. In English, for instance, we find the recurring segments *love, -ing, -ly*. These can be combined to form *lovely, loving,* or *lovingly*, but not **ing-love, *ly-love,* or **love-ly-ing*. Similarly, you could say *Sebastian is eating peanuts*, but not **Sebastian is peanuts eating, *Peanuts is eating Sebastian,* or **Eating is Sebastian peanuts* – though if the sentence was translated into a language such as Latin or Dyirbal, the words for 'Sebastian' and 'peanuts' could occur in a greater variety of positions.

In brief, humans do not learn lists of utterances. Instead, they learn a number of principles or rules which they follow subconsciously. These are not pseudo-rules invented by pedants, but real ones which codify the actual patterns of the language. Although people use the rules all the time, they cannot normally formulate them, any more than they could specify the muscles used when riding a bicycle. In fact, in day-to-day life, we are so used to speaking and being understood that we are not usually aware of the rule-governed nature of our utterances. We only pause to think about it when the rules break down, or when someone uses rules which differ from our own, as when Alice in Looking-Glass Land tried to communicate with the Frog, whose subconscious language rules differed from her own. She asked him whose business it was to answer the door:

> 'To answer the door?' he said. 'What's it been asking of?'
> 'I don't know what you mean,' she said.
> 'I speaks English, doesn't I?' the Frog went on. 'Or are you deaf?'

The sum total of the rules found in any one language is known as a **grammar**, a term which is often used interchangeably by linguists to mean two different things: first, the rules applied subconsciously by the speakers of a language; secondly, a linguist's conscious attempt to codify these rules. A statement such as 'In English, you normally put an *-s* on plural nouns' is an informal statement of a principle that is known by the speakers of a language, and is also likely to be expressed in a rather more formal way in a grammar written by a linguist. There are, incidentally, quite a number of differences between a native speaker's grammar and a linguist's grammar. Above all, they differ in completeness. All normal native speakers of a language have a far more comprehensive set of rules than any linguist has yet been able to specify, even though the former are not consciously aware of possessing any special skill. No linguist has ever yet succeeded in formulating a perfect grammar – an exhaustive summary of the principles followed by the speakers of a language when they produce and understand speech.

The term **grammar** is commonly used nowadays by linguists to cover the whole of a language: the **phonology** (sound patterns), the **syntax** (word patterns) and the **semantics** (meaning patterns).

An important subdivision within syntax is **morphology**, which deals with the organization of segments of words as in *kind-ness*, *kind-ly, un-kind*, and so on.

The comprehensive scope of the word *grammar* sometimes causes confusion, since in some older books it is used to mean only the syntax, or occasionally, only the word endings. This has led to the strange claim that English has practically no grammar at all – if this were really so nobody would be able to speak it!

Grammars fluctuate and change over the centuries, and even within the lifetime of individuals. In this book, we shall be considering both how this happens, and why. We shall be more interested in speakers' subconscious rules than in the addition and loss of single words. Vocabulary items tend to be added, replaced, or changed in meaning more rapidly than any other aspect of language. Any big dictionary contains numerous words which have totally disappeared from normal usage today, such as *scobberlotch* 'to loaf around doing nothing in particular', *ruddock* 'robin', *dudder* 'to deafen with noise', as well as an array of relatively new ones such as *atomizer, laser, transistorize*. Other words have changed their meaning in unpredictable ways. As Robin Lakoff has pointed out,[45] because of the decline in the employment of servants, the terms *master* and *mistress* are now used to signify something rather different from their original meaning. *Master* now usually means 'a person supremely skilful in something', while *mistress*, on the other hand, often refers to a female lover:

> He is a master of the intricacies of academic politics
> Rosemary refused to be Harry's mistress and returned to her husband.

The different ways in which these previously parallel words have changed are apparent if we try to substitute one for the other:

> She is a mistress of the intricacies of academic politics
> Harry refused to be Rosemary's master and returned to his wife.

This particular change reflects not only a decline in the master or mistress to servant relationship, but also, according to Lakoff, the lowly status of women in our society.

The rapid turnover in vocabulary and the continual changes in the meaning of words often directly reflect social changes. As Samuel Johnson said in the preface to his dictionary (1755): 'As any custom is disused, the words that expressed it must perish with it; as any opinion grows popular, it will innovate speech in the same proportion as it alters practice.' Alongside vocabulary change, there are other less obvious alterations continually in progress, affecting the sounds and the syntax. These seemingly mysterious happenings will be the main concern of this book, though vocabulary change will also be discussed (Chapter 9).

The chapters are organized into four main sections. Part 1, 'Preliminaries', deals mainly with the ways in which historical linguists obtain their evidence. Part 2, 'Transition', explains *how* language change occurs. Part 3, 'Causation', discusses possible reasons *why* change takes place. Part 4, 'Beginnings and endings', examines how languages begin and end. The final chapter tries to answer the question posed in the title of the book: are languages progressing? decaying? or maintaining a precarious balance?

2 Collecting up clues
Piecing together the evidence

> There was no light nonsense about Miss Blimber . . . She
> was dry and sandy with working in the graves of deceased
> languages. None of your live languages for Miss Blimber.
> They must be dead – stone dead – and then Miss Blimber
> dug them up like a Ghoul.
>
> Charles Dickens, *Dombey and Son* (1847–8)

Introduction

This chapter looks at ways of collecting evidence for studying
language change. How old pronunciations are reconstructed is
explained. Then other methods of finding out about the linguistic past are described. Comparative historical linguistics builds up
a picture of a 'proto-language', the parent language from which a
group of related languages are descended. Internal reconstruction
deduces facts about the previous history of one language by looking at irregularities in structure which have been brought about
by change. Typological reconstruction is based on the insight that
languages can be divided into a number of different types, and
knowledge of the characteristics of these types enables gaps in the
evidence to be filled. Population typology explores constructions
which diffuse across different language types via contact. Computerized text corpora can now provide reliable evidence for all these
historical methods. (A **corpus** – plural **corpora** – is a body of
spoken and/or written language for linguistic study.)

A Faroese recipe in a cookbook explains how to catch a puffin before
you roast it.[1] Like a cook, a linguist studying language change must
first gather together the basic ingredients. In the case of the linguist,
the facts must be collected and pieced together before they can be
interpreted. How is this done?

There are basically two ways of collecting evidence, which we
may call the 'armchair method' and the 'tape recorder method'

respectively. In the first, a linguist studies the written documents of bygone ages, sitting in a library or at a computer, and in the second he or she slings a tape recorder over one shoulder and studies change as it happens. Both methods are important, and complement one another. The armchair method enables a large number of changes to be followed in outline over a long period, whereas the tape recorder method allows a relatively small amount of change to be studied in great detail. These days, advances made in the field of corpus linguistics have allowed these two methods to be successfully combined, as will be explained later.

The armchair method is the older, and the basic techniques were laid down in the nineteenth century – as is shown by the quotation above from Dickens' novel *Dombey and Son* which was published in the mid nineteenth century. Let us therefore deal with it first.

To a casual onlooker, an afternoon spent sitting in a library studying old documents sounds like an easy option. In practice, it presents numerous problems. The data are inevitably variable in both quantity and quality, since some centuries and cultures are likely to be well represented, others sparsely. Our knowledge of early Greek, for instance, might be rather different if Greece, like Egypt, had a sandy soil in which papyri can lie preserved for centuries. In all probability, the documents which survive will be from various regions, may represent a range of social classes, and are likely to have been written for different purposes. The letters of Queen Elizabeth I, for example, are rather different from the plays of William Shakespeare, even though they date from around the same time. Furthermore, a certain amount of the information will be damaged. Old tablets get chipped, and manuscripts are sometimes chewed by rats or coated in mildew. The data will be further obscured by the use of conventional orthography, which is often far from the spoken pronunciation. As the linguist Saussure noted, 'Written forms obscure our view of language. They are not so much a garment as a disguise.'[2]

It is the task of historical linguists to rectify, as far as possible, these shortcomings in the data. In brief, they must discover how the language of their documents was pronounced as a first priority, then go on to fill in the gaps by reconstructing what happened during periods for which there are no written records.

Let us look at each of these tasks in turn.

Making old documents speak

Going behind the written form and making old documents 'speak' is a fascinating but time-consuming task. The reconstruction of pronunciation resembles the work of a detective, in that linguists must seek out and piece together a vast assemblage of minute clues. They must follow the advice of Sherlock Holmes, who claimed that, 'It has long been an axiom of mine that the little things are infinitely the most important.'[3] As in detective work, each individual piece of evidence is of little value on its own. It is the cumulative effect which counts. When several clues all point in the same direction, a linguist can be more confident that the reconstruction is a plausible one.

The type of clue used varies from language to language. English is perhaps simpler to deal with than a number of others because it traditionally uses rhyme in its poetry:

> You spotted snakes with double tongue,
> Thorny hedge-hogs, be not seen;
> Newts, and blind-worms, do no wrong;
> Come not near our fairy queen.[4]

These lines from Shakespeare's *A midsummer night's dream* suggest that in the sixteenth century, *tongue* rhymed with *wrong*, rather than with *rung* as it would today. By itself, this piece of evidence is unconvincing, since Shakespeare may have been using poetic licence and forcing words to rhyme which did not in fact do so. Or his pronunciation may have been an old or idiosyncratic one. Or he may have been mimicking a French accent, or *tongue* might have had alternative pronunciations. On the other hand, it may be the word *wrong* which has changed, not *tongue*. Whatever the truth of the matter, this is the type of clue which linguists must seize and check up on. They will look for further examples, and for other types of corroborating evidence. In this case, the rhyme is supported by a play on words between *tongues* and *tongs* in *Twelfth night*.[5]

Puns provide similar information to rhymes: for example, in Shakespeare's *The merchant of Venice*, Shylock starts to sharpen his knife on his shoe, preparing to cut a pound of flesh away from his victim's breast. At this point a bystander says:

> Not on thy sole, but on thy soul, harsh Jew,
> Thou mak'st the knife keen[6]

indicating that the words *sole* and *soul* were pronounced similarly by the late sixteenth century (their spelling shows they once differed). Puns are particularly useful when they occur in languages where rhymes are not normal, such as classical Latin. For instance, the Roman general Marcus Crassus was preparing to go on a military expedition which later proved disastrous. As he was about to board his ship, a fig-seller approached him saying *Cauneas* 'figs from Caunea'. Cicero, the narrator of this episode, pointed out that Crassus was foolish to have proceeded with his expedition, since the fig-seller was uttering a cryptic warning and was really saying *cave ne eas* 'don't go'.[7] The confusion of *Cauneas* with *cave ne eas* shows clearly that Latin *v* was indistinguishable from *u* at this point in time, and that unstressed vowels were often omitted.

Representations of animal noises may also be informative. In some fragments of ancient Greek comedy, the bleating of sheep is represented by the sequence βῆ βῆ. A modern Greek would read this as *vee-vee* [vi: vi:].[8] Since sheep are unlikely to have changed their basic *baa-baa* cry in 2,000 years, we may be fairly confident that the ancient and modern Greek pronunciations of the sequence βῆ βῆ are rather different.

Social climbers can also inadvertently provide clues. In the first century BC the Roman poet Catullus laughs gently at a man who said *hinsidias* 'hambush' instead of the correct *insidias* 'ambush' – a word which had never had an *h*.[9] This indicates that *h* was still pronounced in fashionable circles, but had been lost in less prestigious types of speech. Consequently, social climbers attempted to insert it, but sometimes made mistakes and added an aspirate where one never existed. A similar example occurs in Charles Dickens' *Pickwick papers*, when Mr Pickwick's servant Sam Weller speaks of 'gas microscopes of hextra power'.[10]

Spelling mistakes may provide useful information. The Romans, for example, had an official known as a *consul* and another called a *censor*. These titles were sometimes misspelt on inscriptions as *cosul* and *cesor*, indicating that the *n* was probably omitted in casual speech.[11]

Indirect clues of the type discussed so far can sometimes be supplemented by statements from old grammarians. A number of ancient treatises on language still exist, perhaps more than most people realize. Some are vague, but others are informative. For example, in the sixteenth century, a court official named John Hart wrote a fairly clear account of the English pronunciation of his time, noting among other things that *a* was produced 'with a wyde opening of the mouth as when a man yauneth',[12] indicating that *a* in his time was probably similar to that in the standard British English pronunciation of *father*.

Detailed accounts exist also of ancient Greek and Latin pronunciation. Read the following phonetic description, and try to work out the sound specified by the Roman grammarian Victorinus: 'We produce this letter by pressing the lower lip on the upper teeth. The tongue is turned back towards the roof of the mouth, and the sound is accompanied by a gentle puff of breath.' This is a fairly accurate description of the pronunciation of the sound [f].[13]

The clues mentioned above are only a selection of the total possible ones. We have also ignored the extra problems which arise when the linguist is dealing with a syllabary – a writing system which uses one sign per syllable – or how a linguist might attempt to decipher an unknown script. But the general picture is clear: linguists, like detectives or archaeologists, patiently search for and piece together fragmentary clues. Bit by minute bit, they build up a complete picture. When they feel that they have satisfactorily reconstructed the pronunciation of the words in their documents, they can proceed to the next stage – the filling in of gaps. At this point, they attempt to reconstruct what the language was like during the periods for which they have no written evidence.

Filling the gaps

> There are certain areas of scholarship, early Greek history is one and Roman law is another, where the scantiness of the evidence sets a special challenge to the disciplined mind. It is a game with very few pieces where the skill of the player lies in complicating the rules. The isolated and uneloquent fact must be exhibited within a tissue of hypothesis subtle enough to make it speak, and it was the weaving of this tissue which fascinated Ducane.[14]

Ducane is a character in Iris Murdoch's novel *The nice and the good* and his interest was in Roman Law. But the quotation also applies particularly well to anyone involved in piecing together linguistic evidence from old documents.

Essentially, we need to fill two kinds of gap. On the one hand, our knowledge of the language must be pushed back to a point prior to that of our first written records. On the other hand, the gaps between documents must be bridged. In this way, we may build up a picture of the development of a language over a span of hundreds or even thousands of years.

Pushing back into the past is a topic which has long been the concern of linguists. In the nineteenth century, scholars regarded the task of reconstructing the hypothetical language spoken by our Indo-European ancestors some 5,000 years ago as one of major importance, so much so that a number of people today have the mistaken impression that such a preoccupation is the backbone of linguistics. Nowadays it is simply one smallish branch of the subject.

The hypothetical ancestor of a group of related languages is known as a **proto-language**. Proto-Indo-European, for example, is the presumed parent language from which a number of present-day languages such as Greek, German, English, Welsh, Hindi, etc., subsequently developed.[15] Building up a picture of a protolanguage is a major part of comparative historical linguistics, so called because conclusions are reached by comparing a number of different languages.[16] The old name for the subject, comparative philology, tends to be avoided because of the confusion it creates in America and continental Europe where 'philology' more usually refers to the scholarly study of literary texts.

In brief, comparative reconstruction involves comparing corresponding words from a number of related languages and drawing conclusions about their common ancestor, in the same way that one might be able to draw up a reasonable physical description of a man or woman from a close examination of his or her grandchildren. It is most successful in cases where languages have split up cleanly because groups of speakers have migrated in different directions. It works particularly well with Polynesian languages (such as Hawaiian, Samoan, Tongan), since speakers of a single Proto-Polynesian language split up and sailed off to different Pacific islands. In contrast, it may be impossible where quite different languages have come into contact and intermingled.[17]

Comparative historical linguistics relies on two basic assumptions. The first is that language is essentially arbitrary in the sense that there is no intrinsic connection between a linguistic symbol and what it represents. Onomatopoeic words, which imitate different types of sounds, are an exception, and need to be excluded. Typically, these cover inanimate noises, such as *bang*, *splash*, *plop*; animal cries, such as *baa*, *moo*; bird names coined from their calls, such as *cuckoo*, *whippoorwill*; and human burps and grunts, words for 'hiccough', 'snore', 'sneeze', 'kiss' and so on.[18] Words for parents, such as *papa*, *mama*, must be ignored, because these represent adult over-interpretations of children's early babbles.[19] Sound symbolism is another confusing factor, when particular languages adopt idiosyncratic sound–meaning patterns, as with the English *fl-* set, *flash*, *flare*, *flicker*, which all describe light emission, possibly influenced by *flame*. So linguists must be on their guard.

But mostly, the arbitrariness assumption holds. For example, there is no deep reason for the word *squid* to represent a particular type of marine animal described by dictionaries as a 'ten-armed cephalopod', since there is no essential 'squiddiness' in the sound sequence [skwɪd]. It is a purely conventional label, as are the names for this animal in other languages, such as *calmar* (French), *tauka* (Tok Pisin).

The second basic assumption of comparative historical linguistics is that sound changes are to a large extent consistent or 'regular' rather than haphazard. Just as tulips which are planted in the same area and exposed to similar soil and weather conditions tend to flower and wither at around the same time, so a sound change is likely to affect comparable instances of the same sound within the dialect affected. Take the word *leisure*. There used to be a genuine [s] in the middle of this word which changed first to [z] and then to its present-day sound [ʒ]. But this was not an isolated happening, limited to one word: the change also occurred in *pleasure*, *treasure*, *measure* and so on – though some amendments to this blanket regularity assumption will be discussed in Chapter 5.

These basic assumptions of arbitrariness and regularity allow us to make the following deduction. If we find consistent sound correspondences between words with similar meanings in languages where borrowing can be ruled out, the correspondences cannot be due to chance. We therefore infer that the languages concerned are so-called 'daughter languages' descended from one 'parent'. For example, English repeatedly has *f* where Latin has *p* in words with similar meaning such as *father:pater, foot:pedem, fish:pisces*, and so on. There is no evidence of a Latin–English cultural bond. When the Romans first came to Britain, the woad-painted natives they found did not yet speak English, which was brought from across the Channel at a later date. So borrowing can be eliminated as the source of the regular *f:p* correspondence. We conclude therefore that Latin and English are both descended from the same parent, which must have existed at some earlier age. Of course, one single set of correspondences, such as the *f:p* set, is too frail a foundation on which to set any firm conclusions, so this must be backed up with others such as *s:s* in *six:sex, seven:septem, salt:sal, sun:sol*, and *t:d* in *two:duo, ten:decem, tooth:dens*, and so on. The more correspondences we find, the more certain we become that the languages concerned are genetically related.

Chance resemblances between languages intermittently pop up: Jaqaru, an American-Indian language, has a word *aska* meaning the same as English *ask*. Japanese *furo* 'hot bath' resembles French *four* 'oven', and French *palais* 'palace' looks a bit like Balinese *balay* 'house'. But these are flukes, and should be ignored: they are not backed up by any consistent correspondences. Statistical data can be a further aid in guarding against chance. For example, around 15 per cent of English vocabulary begins with an *s*, but less than 10 per cent begins with *w*. Consequently, more chance resemblances are likely to be found involving words beginning with *s* than those beginning with *w*, especially if the other language also has a high level of initial *s*.[20]

When we have assembled correspondences from two or more related languages, we can begin to draw conclusions about the parent from which they sprang. The methods are similar to those of any other type of historian. Suppose we were reconstructing the physical characteristics of grandparents from a group of grandchildren. We might begin by considering eye colour. If we found that all the grandchildren had blue eyes except one, we would probably suggest that the grandparents had blue eyes too, and would discount the odd one out. The only thing that would alter our decision might be the knowledge that we had proposed something physically impossible, but in this case, there seems no reason to change our hypothesis, since blue-eyed grandparents could quite easily have grandchildren with brown or blue eyes. Linguistic reconstruction works in the same way. We take the majority verdict as our major guideline, and then check that we have not proposed anything that is phonetically implausible. For example, a number of Indo-European languages have *s* at the beginning of certain words. English has *six, seven, sun, salt, sow* 'female pig'. Latin has *sex, septem, sol, sal, sus*, and so on. Greek, however, has an *h* in place of the expected *s*, with *hex, hepta, helios, hals, hus*. Since Greek is the odd one out, we conclude that the original sound was probably *s*, and that Greek changed an original *s* to *h*. We confirm that *s* to *h* is a fairly common development (and note that the reverse, *h* to *s*, is unheard of). Our hypothesis can therefore stand. We shall of course look for further corroborative evidence, and amend our theory if we find any counterevidence.

If a majority verdict leads us to a conclusion that is phonetically improbable, we would revise our original suggestion. For example, faced with the Spanish, Italian and Sardinian words for 'smoke', which are *humo, fumo* and *ummu* respectively, the majority verdict would lead us to suggest that the word originally began with the vowel *u*, and that Italian had inserted an *f* at the beginning. However, there are no recorded examples of *f* spontaneously appearing in front of a vowel, though the disappearance of *f* at the beginning of a word is common, usually with an intermediate stage of *h* (*f* → *h* → zero). Here, then, phonetic probability overrules the majority verdict, and we propose *f* as the sound at the beginning of the word 'smoke' at an earlier stage – an assumption we can in this case check, since we know that Latin, the ancestor of the three languages in question, had a word *fumus* for 'smoke'.

Consider another example, from Polynesian languages.[21] The words *tapu* 'forbidden' and *taŋata* 'man' occur in Tongan, Samoan and Raratongan, which is spoken in the Cook Islands, near Tahiti. Hawaiian, on the other hand, has *kapu* and *kanaka*. Majority verdict suggests that Hawaiian is the innovator, and the other languages preserve an older form.

But take the word for 'fish', which is *ika* in Tongan and Raratongan, *iʔa* in Samoan and Hawaiian – and the word for 'octopus' behaves in a similar way, with a *k* in the middle of Tongan *feke* and Raratongan *ʔeke*, but a glottal stop [ʔ] (a stoppage of breath with no actual sound uttered) in Samoan *feʔe* and Hawaiian *heʔe*. At this point, phonetic probability must be taken into account. It is quite common for *k* to become a glottal stop, and is even occasionally heard in the word *soccer* in British English. But it is most unlikely that a glottal stop would turn into *k*. So Tongan and Raratongan preserve a form that is likely to be the older.

A final stage in this type of reconstruction is to consider whether the reconstructed sounds fit together into a patterned sound system. If the proposed reconstruction is a higgledy-piggledy muddle, then the evidence needs to be re-checked.

The examples above are straightforward ones, but in practice the situation is often messier. Usually the behaviour of a sound varies, depending on its position in a word. Or it might be necessary to reconstruct a sound which did not occur in any of the daughter languages. Or an influx of invaders speaking a totally different language might have obscured the situation. Or variant forms might represent different dialects of the parent tongue. Borrowing might have complicated the picture. Or unexpected social customs may muddy the situation, as in areas of New Caledonia, where brides may be imported into a new community with a different language.[22] Linguists must be aware of all these possibilities, and must constantly be on the lookout for new evidence and be prepared to revise their hypotheses about the proto-language. Certainty is impossible, and there are subtleties and complications in the use of comparative reconstruction which cannot be discussed here. But the basic principles of majority verdict followed by a probability check on the proposed changes and the overall system are likely to remain the main methodological foundations of this type of reconstruction.

The method has been applied in most detail to the Indo-European language family, and quite a lot is now known about the probable appearance of Proto-Indo-European, the ancestor of a large number of Indian, Iranian and European languages, which probably flourished around 2500 BC. More recently, useful work has been done on other language families such as Sino-Tibetan (which includes Chinese), Semitic (which includes Hebrew and Arabic), Polynesian and various American-Indian groups. In some of these cases, the correspondences have been drawn up from our knowledge of the current-day languages, rather than from written records.

Reconstruction does not lead back to any kind of 'primitive language'. Pooh-Bah in the comic opera *The Mikado* claimed that he could trace his ancestry back 'to a protoplasmal primordial atomic globule'. The same is not true of reconstruction. Reconstructed Indo-European is a fully fledged language, not a system of primordial grunts. A total of 8,000 years, or at most 10,000, is the furthest back this type of reconstruction can take us[23] – and human language arose at least 80,000 years ago.[24]

A few optimists have tried to link several existing language families together into an umbrella family known as 'Nostratic', from the Latin word for 'our (language)'.[25] The whole topic is one of debate, and even the languages covered are under discussion. According to one (disputed) view, Nostratic covers Indo-European, the Dravidian languages of India, the Kartvelian languages of the Caucasus, the Uralic family which includes Finnish and Hungarian, Altaic which takes in Turkish and Mongolian, and Afro-Asiatic which includes Arabic and Berber. Beyond this, Super-Nostratic has been proposed, which links Nostratic to Arctic Indian languages in the north, and to other African languages in the south. Discussions continue on this controversial topic, in which facts are struggling to emerge from the mists of time.[26]

Comparative reconstruction has proved most useful in the reconstruction of sound systems and inflectional endings. Some scholars have attempted to draw tentative conclusions about stress and accent,[27] and also syntax. For example, in the earliest documents most Indo-European languages have objects preceding their verbs. That is, simple sentences have the order *Pigs apples eat* rather than *Pigs eat apples*. Majority verdict in this case indicates that verbs were normally placed at the end of sentences in the parent language. Even archaic formulae can occasionally be reconstructed: a phrase requesting protection for people and livestock crops up in several languages.[28]

Sometimes, the comparative method can be used to reach negative conclusions, if proven daughter languages disagree totally on some point. Take the Iroquoian language family, which is represented by various American-Indian languages spoken in the eastern USA. The daughter languages each have a different word for 'and'. Mohawk has *tanu*, Seneka *kho*, Cayuga *hniʔ* and so on. This suggests that Proto-Iroquoian managed without such a word, probably because it was a spoken language, with no literary tradition, so intonation was originally used to join items. Words for 'and' gradually crept in as these speakers of American-Indian languages came into contact with English.[29]

A further well-established method of pushing back the past is **internal reconstruction**. This involves making a detailed study of one language at a single point in time, and deducing facts about a previous state of that language. Essentially, we assume that irregularities in structure are likely to have been brought about by language change. We therefore try to peel these away, in order to reconstruct an earlier, more regular state of affairs.[30]

Here is an example. Consider the chorus of the Tom Lehrer song 'When you are old and gray':

> An awful *debility*, a lessened *utility*,
> a loss of *mobility* is a strong *possibility*.
> In all *probability*, I'll lose my *virility*,
> and you your *fertility* and *desirability*.

> And this *liability* of total *sterility*
> will lead to *hostility* and a sense of *futility*.
> So let's act with *agility* while we still have *facility*,
> for we'll soon reach *senility* and lose the *ability*.

This song shows clearly that abstract nouns ending in *-ity* are common in English, and dozens more could be added to the above list, such as *purity, obscurity, serenity, virginity, profanity, obscenity, sanity* and so on. Many of these nouns in *-ity* are paired with adjectives, as in *mobile/mobility, possible/possibility, pure/purity, serene/serenity, sane/sanity* and numerous others. In the spoken language a number of these nouns are formed simply by adding *-ity* [iti:] on to the end of the adjective, as in *obscure/obscurity, pure/purity, passive/passivity*. In others, however, the pronunciation of the vowels in the noun and corresponding adjective differ, as in *senile/senility, sane/sanity, serene/serenity*.

What causes this difference? Why can we not simply add *-ity* on to the adjective for all of them? Following the principles of internal reconstruction, we suggest that this was the situation at some unspecified time in the past, and that the pairs which fail to match up have undergone change. It is not immediately clear whether it is the adjective which has undergone change, or the form to which *-ity* is attached, or both. As in external reconstruction, phonetic probability guides us in our reconstruction, as well as (in this case) the clues given by the spelling. The most plausible suggestion is that a pair such as *serene/serenity* originally had [e:] in the second syllable, rather like the vowel in *bed* somewhat lengthened. [e:] then changed to [i:] in *serene* [səri:n], and was shortened to [e] in *serenity* [səreniti:]. In English there are copious written records, and this hypothesis can be checked. Sure enough, there was a time in Middle English when *serene/serenity* both had [e:] in the second syllable. Similarly, pairs such as *profane/profanity* had a common vowel [a:], rather like the [a] in *father*, and pairs such as *hostile/hostility* had a common [i:] like the vowel in the second syllable of *machine* – so confirming these reconstructed forms.

A second example of internal reconstruction is a less obvious one, and relates to the sounds [θ] as in *thin* and [ð] as in *then*. These are separate phonemes, not variants (allophones) of one, because they sometimes distinguish between words, e.g. *thigh/thy*; *wreath/writhe*. If we examine the distribution of these sounds in modern English, we find a curious imbalance. [ð] hardly ever occurs at the beginning of words, apart from a smallish group of related words such as *the*, *this*, *that*, *those*, *then*, *there*. Yet it is very common inside words, as in *father*, *mother*, *feather*, *heather*, *weather*, *bother*, *rather* and so on. The [θ] situation is just the opposite. There are numerous words beginning with [θ], such as *thick*, *thin*, *thigh*, *thank*, *think*, *thaw*, *thimble*, *thief*, *thorn*, *thistle* and many others. Yet [θ] hardly ever occurs in the middle of words. It is possible to find a few scattered examples such as *breathy*, *pithy*, *toothy*, but not many. Why? This uneven distribution suggests that at an earlier stage of English, [θ] and [ð] were variants of the same basic sound, which was pronounced as [θ] at the beginning of a word, and [ð] inside it – as is now thought to have been the case.

This type of reconstruction is not really needed for a language such as English, for which we already have copious data. It is indispensable, however, in cases where there are no earlier written records, or where there is a big gap in the evidence, especially as we can sometimes work back into the past for quite a long way. Once we have peeled off one layer, we are then likely to find new irregularities revealed.

Inevitably, the method has problems, especially in a language such as Chinese, which tends not to have neat pairs of related words such as *mobile/mobility*. In addition, we are in danger of getting the chronology very muddled, since we cannot always tell how long ago the pairs we are working from formed a single unit. Nevertheless, internal reconstruction is a valuable tool if no others are available.

Relatively recently, further methods of reconstruction have been developed. **Typological reconstruction** may be the most important. This is based on the insight that languages can be divided into a number of basic types, each with its own set of characteristics. We have known for a long time that it is possible to divide humans physically into a number of racial types – Caucasian, Negroid, and so on – and can list the characteristics associated with each type. Linguists have realized that we can do the same for languages. English, for example, can be categorized as a verb–object (VO) language, since it places its object after the verb, as in *Bears eat honey*.

One fairly predictable characteristic of VO languages is that they place extra or auxiliary verbs before the main verb, as in *Bears may eat honey*. The reverse happens in object–verb (OV) languages such as Turkish, Hindi, Japanese, which place auxiliaries after the verb, and say, as it were, *Bears honey eat may*.[31]

Typological reconstruction can also be applied to sounds. The best-known case, perhaps, is that of Proto-Indo-European stop consonants (sounds such as [p], [b], [t], [d], produced with a complete stoppage of air). According to the 'standard' reconstruction based on the comparative method, the proto-language lacked [b]. However, it is somewhat odd for a language to have [d] and [g] but not [b]. Statistically, languages with a missing labial (sounds produced with the lips, such as [b], [p]) are those with 'glottalic sounds', which make use of a pocket of air trapped between the vocal cords deep in the throat and a point further up in the mouth. Some researchers therefore argue that it would be better to reconstruct [t'], [k'] which are 'ejectives' (sounds spoken on an outgoing glottalic airstream), in place of ordinary [d], [g].[32] Such sounds are heard (for example) in Amharic in Ethiopia, and in the Caucasian languages, but they are somewhat exotic to English ears. These proposals are still being evaluated. This is hard to do, because we do not yet know enough about the sound systems of the world to assess probabilities in any reliable way, especially as at least one language, Kelabit (spoken in Borneo), has been reported to have a system similar to the supposedly unlikely Proto-Indo-European one.

If, therefore, we are able partially to reconstruct a language by means of comparative reconstruction, we can then infer more detailed knowledge about it by assigning it to its probable language type. Our knowledge of the characteristics associated with its type will allow us to predict facts for which we have no direct evidence. Typological reconstruction is still controversial. Problems arise because few languages seem to represent 'pure' types – most are a mixture with one type predominating. In addition, people still argue about what the 'pure' types should look like, or even whether we are looking at the right kind of criteria when we assign languages to types. But taken alongside other evidence, typological reconstruction allows us to push back further into the past than we otherwise could.

An offshoot of typological studies is a growing understanding of which sections of a language are liable to turn into which others: for example, verbs of wishing typically over time are converted into future tenses. Such conversions will be discussed in Chapter 8.

Tracing diffusion of linguistic changes across different geographical areas is another type of reconstruction. Dialect geographers have long tried to do this for scattered individual words. But they mostly ignored more sweeping changes. The problem is to obtain enough data. But patient chasing up of geographical records of who said what in which region have started to provide solutions to some old linguistic puzzles.[33]

So-called **population typology** is a newish variant of these diffusion studies.[34] As its starting point, Joanna Nichols, its pioneer, a linguist from the University of California at Berkeley, notes that words are easily borrowed, but linguistic constructions are not (Chapter 8). They creep across from one language to another very, very slowly, usually via bilingual speakers. Nichols plotted construction-types shared by different language families. These, she hypothesized, must have come about via contact. In a number of cases, she found an eastward increase: that is, more languages which had these constructions were in the east than in the west.

For this purpose, American-Indian languages are regarded as being 'eastern', since America was originally populated by immigrants moving westward via the Bering Strait. Nichols argued that these 'eastern' features reflect a very ancient layer, which is slowly being erased by newer, western language characteristics, as these spread eastwards.

In Nichols' sample of the world's languages, for example, 89 per cent of those furthest east, mostly Australian languages, distinguish between *we* inclusive and *we* exclusive, that is, between 'we, including you the addressee' and 'we, excluding you the addressee', as in Tok Pisin (Papua New Guinea):

yumi painim pukpuk (*we* inclusive)
'We (including you) found a crocodile'

mipela painim pukpuk (*we* exclusive)
'We (excluding you) found a crocodile.'

This distinction occurs in 56 per cent of South and Southeast Asian languages, but in only 10 per cent of European and Asian languages. Another feature which showed an eastward increase was a tendency to mark only verbs for plurality, not nouns. Yet another 'eastern' characteristic was a preference for distinguishing between alienable possession (something from which an owner may be separated, such as 'my dog') and inalienable possession (something which is firmly linked to its owner, such as 'my hand'). These eastward features are not primitive, she pointed out, even though they may represent a layer of language earlier than any other we can reconstruct, maybe up to 60,000 years old.

Of course, not all constructions are equally likely to endure. Ideally, linguists try to assess the survival probability of different linguistic features.[35] They can now to some extent distinguish persistent (dominant) features in languages from unstable (recessive) characteristics – though this type of work is inevitably controversial.

Overall, reconstructing past linguistic forms requires endless patient scrabbling, and no reliable short cuts have been found.

Historical corpora

But in recent years, it is not only the refinement of linguistic techniques which has allowed historical linguists to make progress, but also the development of historical corpora.

A steady stream of hard-working, practical linguists have built up machine-readable (computerized) text corpora, which have become widely available to students and researchers.[36] At first, mainly vocabulary was explored. Then historical corpora enabled the history of different constructions to be charted, together with their associated vocabulary items.

For example, in modern English *that* and zero are interchangeable in sentences such as:

I know that he is ill/I know he is ill.

A historical corpus showed that the interchange of *that* and zero was/is not random, but each occurred/occurs in connection with particular vocabulary items.[37] As early as the fifteenth century *think* has favoured zero, and still does so today, but *say* shows more variation, with *that* gaining favour, particularly in more formal styles of writing. Undoubtedly, similar detailed syntactic and lexical findings are waiting to be found by tomorrow's linguists.

3   Charting the changes
Studying changes in progress

> The crisis consists precisely in the fact that the old is dying
> and the new cannot be born; in this interregnum a great
> variety of morbid symptoms appear.
>
> Antonio Gramsci, *Prison notebooks*

Introduction

This chapter describes how linguists realized they needed to study ongoing changes. In the early part of the twentieth century, language change was assumed to happen too slowly to be observable. In their grammars, linguists had unwittingly omitted the variations which indicated that changes were under way. The American linguist William Labov was the key figure in this twentieth-century linguistic breakthrough. He made a preliminary ingenious attempt to study current changes in a now-famous department store survey in New York. Later, he proceeded to other New York changes. He found he could reliably predict the percentage of the features he was investigating in the speech of different ethnic groups, sexes, ages and socio-economic classes, in different speech styles. In his later work, he has refined his early techniques and produced a solid methodological framework for future researchers. His later work in Philadelphia again proved groundbreaking. Meanwhile, in Northern Ireland, Jim and Leslie Milroy explored speech varieties in different social networks. These seminal studies, on each side of the Atlantic, kick-started work on ongoing changes, which are now a standard part of language change investigations.

Until relatively recently, the majority of linguists were convinced that language change was unobservable. Most of them simply accepted that it happened, but could never be pinpointed.

A popular assumption was that language change was a continuous but very slow process, like the rotation of the earth, or the creeping up of wrinkles, or the opening of flowers. It happened so slowly and over so many decades that it was quite impossible to detect its occurrence. You could only look at it beforehand and afterwards, and realize it had happened, just as you might glance at a watch at four o'clock, and then at ten past four. You could note that ten minutes had passed by, but you would probably not have seen the hands actually moving. Leonard Bloomfield, sometimes called 'the father of American linguistics', stated in 1933 that 'the process of linguistic change has never been directly observed – we shall see that such observation, with our present facilities, is inconceivable'.[1] As recently as 1958, another influential American linguist, Charles Hockett, claimed that 'No one has yet observed sound change; we have only been able to detect it via its consequences . . . A more nearly direct observation would be theoretically possible, if impractical, but any ostensible report of such an observation so far must be discredited.'[2]

Why should intelligent men who spent their whole lives working on language be so convinced that change was unobservable? The answer is simply that they did not know where to look. They looked in the wrong direction because they uncritically adopted certain methodological guidelines laid down for the study of language at the beginning of the nineteenth century.

In the early twentieth century, many linguists consciously turned their backs on the 'absurdities of reasoning'[3] and non-rigorous approach of their nineteenth-century predecessors. They attempted to lay down a 'scientific' framework for the study of language which led to the making of a number of useful, but oversimplified, distinctions.

One much-praised methodological principle was the strict separation of **diachronic** linguistics, the study of language change, from **synchronic** linguistics, the study of the state of a language at a given point in time. This principle dated from the time of Ferdinand de Saussure (1857–1913), who has been labelled 'the father of modern linguistics'. His statements about the necessity of separating the two aspects of linguistics were dogmatic and categorical: 'The opposition between the two viewpoints – synchronic and diachronic – is absolute and allows of no compromise.'[4] He likened the two viewpoints to cuts through the trunk of a tree (see Figure 3.1). Either one made a horizontal cut, and examined a language at

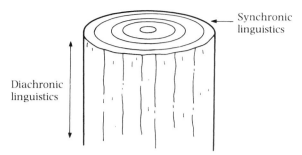

Figure 3.1   The tree trunk analogy of Saussure

a single point in time, or one made a vertical cut, and followed the development of selected items over the course of a number of years.

For most of the twentieth century, synchronic linguistics was considered to be prior to diachronic linguistics. Historical linguists were expected to gather together descriptions of a language at various points in time, relying to a large extent on the previous work of synchronic linguists. Then they studied the changes which had taken place by comparing the various synchronic states. They behaved somewhat like a photographer trying to work out a continuous sequence of events from a series of separate snapshots – on the face of it, a sensible enough procedure. The problem was simply this: linguists making the synchronic descriptions were, without realizing it, simply leaving out those aspects of the description that were essential for an understanding of language change. How did this happen? Let us consider why they unwittingly omitted the crucial evidence.

The missing evidence

In the first chapter, we noted that there is a set of underlying rules which people who know a language subconsciously follow, the sum total of which constitutes a grammar. This statement implies that it is, in principle, possible for a linguist to write a perfect grammar, to formulate a complete set of rules which will account for all the well-formed sentences of a language and reject all the ill-formed

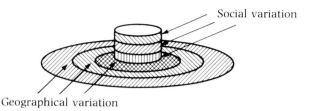

Figure 3.2   Social and geographical dialect variation

ones. In practice, this optimistic aim faces a number of problems involving **language variation** on the one hand, and **language fuzziness** on the other.

Consider, first, the question of language variation. The most obvious type is geographical variation. Everybody is aware that people from different geographical areas are likely to display differences in their speech, as Ivy, a character in John Steinbeck's novel *The grapes of wrath*, points out:

> 'Ever'body says words different,' said Ivy. 'Arkansas folks says 'em different, and Oklahomy folks says 'em different. And we seen a lady from Massachusetts, an' she said 'em differentest of all. Couldn' hardly make out what she was sayin'.'

This type of variation does not present any insuperable problems. We simply note that the grammatical rules of a language are likely to alter slightly from region to region, and then try to specify what these alterations are – though we must not expect abrupt changes between areas, more a gradual shifting with no clear-cut breaks.

Parallel to geographical variation, we find social variation. As we move from one social class to another, we are likely to come across the same types of alterations as from region to region, only this time co-existing within a single area. Once again, this second type of variation does not surprise us, and we simply need to specify the minor rule alterations which occur between the different strata of society. Here also, there is likely to be a certain amount of overlap between the different classes.

These fairly straightforward types of variation are represented in Figure 3.2, which shows social variation as a number of slightly different dialects, heaped on top of one another, and geographical variation as a number of slightly different dialects spread out side by side.

So far, so good. More problematical, however, are the variations in style which exist within the speech of individual speakers. These variations have somewhat facetiously been likened to the two clocks which are reputed to exist on Ballyhough railway station, which disagree by some six minutes. One day a helpful Englishman pointed this fact out to the porter, whose reply was 'Faith Sir, if they was to tell the same time, why should we be having two of them?'[5]

These stylistic variations are not, in fact, as random as the above anecdote suggests. Almost all speakers of a language alter their speech to fit the casualness or formality of the occasion, though they are often unaware of doing so. For example, in informal situations a London schoolboy will drop his aitches, alter the *t* in the middle of words such as *football*, or the end of the word *what* to a glottal stop – a stoppage of outgoing breath with no actual *t* pronounced – and change the *l* at the end of a word such as *thistle*, *drizzle* into a *u*-like sound. But in an interview with his headmaster, or a visit to a fastidious grandmother, the schoolboy might pronounce the words more slowly and carefully, and put in the consonants omitted in casual speech. Variations occur not only in pronunciation, but also in syntax and vocabulary. Contractions such as *wanna, I'd, we've, ain't* are likely to be common in casual situations, but replaced by *want to, I would, we have, haven't* in more formal ones. A man might say 'Shut up and sit down' to his young son when he wants him to sit down and eat, but 'Gentlemen, please be seated' to colleagues at a formal dinner. Or, to take another example, the linguist Robin Lakoff points out that in some social situations euphemisms are common, whereas in scientific literature they are completely out of place.[6] She notes that at a certain type of party, someone might conceivably say 'Harold has gone to the little boys' room', whereas in the anthropological literature, we might find a sentence such as: 'When the natives of Mbanga wish to defecate, first they find a large pineapple leaf.' It would, however, be very strange to find an anthropologist saying: 'When the natives of Mbanga wish to use the little boys' room, they first find a large pineapple leaf,' or to find someone announcing at a party that 'Harold has gone to defecate' unless her intention was to shock or antagonize the other partygoers.

In brief, it is normal for speakers to have a variety of different forms in their repertoire, and to vary them according to the needs of the occasion. It is difficult to reconcile this fluctuation with the notion that there is a fixed set of rules which speakers follow. It is not surprising, therefore, that many conscientious linguists felt it was their duty to ignore this 'purely social' variation and concentrate on the more rigid 'central core' of the language.

Language fuzziness received similar treatment. Consider the following sentences, and try to decide whether each is a 'normal' or 'good' English sentence.

> I saw a man scarlet in the face.
> Who did the postman bring the letter?
> Did you see anyone not pretty in Honolulu?
> He promised me to come.
> He donated the charity ten dollars.

What is your opinion? Most people would judge them to be borderline cases, and make comments such as, 'They sound a bit odd, but I can't really lay my finger on what's wrong.' 'I wouldn't say them myself, but they're probably possible.' 'I don't think they are really English, but I'm not sure.' So, are these sentences well formed or not? If a linguist is writing a set of rules which distinguish well-formed from ill-formed sentences, it is important to make a decision about cases such as those above. How should this be done when the speakers of the language seem unable to judge? Once again, it seemed best to many linguists writing grammars to deal first and foremost with the clear-cut cases. In the opinion of many, borderline messiness was perhaps unsolvable, and so best left alone.

To summarize, descriptive linguists aim to write a set of rules which tell us which sequences of a language are permissible, and which not. When faced with social fluctuations and unsolvable fuzziness, the majority of linguists have, in the past, made the understandable decision to concentrate on the clear-cut cases and ignore the messy bits. 'All grammars leak,' said the insightful anthropologist–linguist Edward Sapir in 1921.[7] Yet, for the first two-thirds of the twentieth century, most linguists tried to pretend that grammars could be watertight. Since diachronic linguists based their studies of language change on these watertight grammars, it is not surprising that they failed to identify changes in progress, which are signalled by the frayed edges of languages. These frayed edges must be examined, not snipped away and tidied up. To return to the words of Gramsci quoted at the beginning of this chapter, these are the 'morbid symptoms' which occur when 'the old is dying and the new cannot be born'. But perhaps the phrase 'morbid symptoms' gives the wrong impression. Language change is not a disease, any more than adolescence, or autumn, are illnesses. Human language, like human life, is not static, and periods of change can appear turbulent. But such undulation is normal. Let us now go on to consider how this fluctuation can be charted.

Charting fluctuations

Since the 1970s, linguists have realized that language change is observable, provided one knows where to look. As already mentioned, the pioneer in this field was William Labov, an American at the University of Pennsylvania. Labov recognized clearly one important fact: the variation and fuzziness which so many linguists tried to ignore were quite often indications that changes were in progress.

This insight was not, of course, entirely new, and the observation that changes involve periods of fluctuation had occurred in several places in the literature – even though no one had paid much attention to it. Labov's essential contribution to linguistics was that he showed that variation and fuzziness are amenable to strict observation and statistical analysis. Indeed, according to at least one linguist, the study of change in progress 'might be the most striking single accomplishment of contemporary linguistics'.[8]

Another important innovation was Labov's highlighting of 'real time' versus 'apparent time' differences.[9] Real time is of course what it sounds like, documentation of the exact pronunciation at particular points in time. Labov suggested that linguistic differences between the speech of different generations (apparent time differences) mirror a genuine diachronic difference in speakers' use of these features. And this turns out to be the case. As a result, linguists are able to make reliable inferences about real-time changes from their observations of apparent time changes.

But to turn back to Labov's early work, in which he considered the fluctuating *r* in New York speech. Sometimes New Yorkers pronounce an *r* in words such as *car, bear, beard* and sometimes they do not. Early reports of the phenomenon suggested that the insertion or omission of *r* was a purely chance affair, with no rhyme or reason to it. The following report was typical: 'The speaker hears both types of pronunciation about him all the time, both seem almost equally natural to him, and it is a matter of pure chance which one comes to his lips.'[10] Labov rejected this notion of randomness. He had a hunch that the presence or absence of *r* would not be mere chance, but would be correlated with social status. Let us consider how he set about testing this hunch and how he developed methodology for dealing with linguistic fluctuation in an objective and reliable way.

Labov made a preliminary check on his hunch that New York *r* was related to social status by an ingenious and amusing method. He checked the speech of sales people in a number of New York stores.[11] Sociologists have found that salesgirls in large department stores subconsciously mimic their customers, particularly when the customers have relatively high social status. Labov hoped, therefore, that if he picked three Manhattan department stores from the top, middle and bottom of the price and fashion range, the sales people would reflect this social pattern in the pronunciation or non-pronunciation of *r* in their speech. Therefore, he picked first Saks Fifth Avenue, which was near the centre of the high-fashion shopping district. It was a spacious store with carpeted floors, and on the upper floors very few goods on display. His second store was the middle-ranking Macy's, which was regarded as a middle-class, middle-priced store. His third was Klein's, a cheap store seemingly cluttered with goods, not far from the Lower East Side – a notoriously poor area. Compared with Saks, Klein's was a 'maze of annexes, sloping concrete floors, low ceilings – it had the maximum amount of goods displayed at the least possible expense'.[12] Comparative prices also showed the difference: women's coats in Saks cost on average over three times as much as women's coats in

Klein's, while prices in Macy's were about twice as high as those in Klein's.

The technique used was surprisingly simple. Labov pretended to be a customer. He approached one of the staff and asked to be directed to a particular department, which was located on the fourth floor. For example, 'Excuse me, where are the women's shoes?' When the answer was given, he then leaned forward as if he had not heard properly, and said 'Excuse me?' This normally led to a repetition of the words 'Fourth floor', only this time spoken more carefully and with emphatic stress.

As soon as he had received these answers, Labov then hastily moved out of sight and made a note of the pronunciation, recording also other factors such as the sex, approximate age, and race of the shop assistant. On the fourth floor, of course, he asked a slightly different question: 'Excuse me, what floor is this?' In this way, 264 interviews were carried out in the three stores.

As Labov had hypothesized, there was variation in the use of *r* in each store: the overall percentage of *r*-inclusion was higher in Saks than in Macy's and higher in Macy's than in Klein's. And, interestingly, the overall percentage of *r*-inclusion was higher on the *upper* floors at Saks than on the ground floor. The ground floor of Saks looked very like Macy's, with crowded counters and a considerable amount of merchandise on display. But the upper floors of Saks were far more spacious: there were long vistas of empty carpeting, and on the floors devoted to high fashion, there were models who displayed the individual garments to the customers. Receptionists were stationed at strategic points to screen out the casual spectators from the serious buyers.

So far, then, Labov's hunch was confirmed. His results suggested that there was social stratification in New York which was reflected in language: the higher socio-economic groups tended to insert *r* in words such as *beard, bear, car, card,* while the lower groups tended to omit it. But what evidence was there that an actual *change* was taking place?

A pointer that a change was occurring was the difference between the casual speech and the emphatic speech in the data from Klein's. At Klein's, there was a significantly higher proportion of *r*s inserted in the more careful, emphatic repetition of 'fourth floor' than in the original casual response to Labov's query. It seemed as if these assistants had at least two styles of speech: a casual style, in which they did not consciously think about what they said, and a more careful, formal style in which they tried to insert elements which they felt were socially desirable. Labov suggested, then, that the reinsertion of *r* was an important characteristic of a prestige pattern which was being superimposed upon the native New York pattern. This was supported by descriptions of New York speech in the early part of the century, which suggested that *r* was virtually absent at this time – as observable in films made in New York in the 1930s.

A follow-up study to Labov's department-store survey was carried out over twenty years later.[13] This found more examples of *r* overall, but the same general pattern. As in the original study, more examples of *r* were found in Saks than in Macy's, and more in Macy's than in May's, a lower-class department store which in the new study replaced Klein's, which no longer existed. But the percentage of speakers who used *r* all the time had increased in all three stores. The greatest increase was in Saks, the highest-status store, and the lowest in May's.

In the next chapter we shall consider where such changes start, and how they spread. We shall also look at changes which are not moving in the direction of a socially acceptable pronunciation. In this chapter we shall continue to concern ourselves with Labov's methodology: how he observed and charted language variation.

Labov's successful department store survey encouraged him to make a more detailed survey of pronunciation habits in New York City. He examined a number of other fluctuating sounds, or **linguistic variables**, as they are usually called. Apart from a further analysis of *r*, he looked at the sounds at the beginning of *the, this, that* [ð], which in New York were sometimes pronounced *de, dis, dat* [d]. He also scrutinized the wide range of vowels used in words such as *dog, coffee, more, door, bad, back*. In order to do this, he conducted long interviews with a balanced population-sample whose social position, age, ethnic group, occupation and geographic history were known. But he faced one major problem. His department-store survey showed that he needed to elicit a *range* of speech styles from each person. Often, it was the variation between styles which indicated that a change was taking place. How should he set about eliciting these different styles?

Samples of careful speech were relatively easy to obtain. Labov and his assistants interviewed selected individuals, and asked them about themselves and their use of language. Since the interviewers were well-educated strangers, those interviewed tended to speak fairly carefully. The speech used was less formal than in a job interview, but more formal than in casual conversation with the family. Samples of even more careful speech were obtained by asking people to read a prose passage, and of extra-careful speech by asking them to read word lists.

The chief difficulty arose with obtaining samples of casual speech. As Labov noted: 'We must somehow become witnesses to the everyday speech which the informant will use as soon as the door is closed behind us: the style in which he argues with his wife, scolds his children, or passes the time of day with his friends. The difficulty of the problem is considerable.'[14]

Labov found there was no one method which he could use. Within the interview situation, he devised one ingenious way of eliciting casual style, and this was to say to people: 'Have you ever been in a situation where you thought you were in serious danger of being killed – where you thought to yourself, "This is it"?' As the narrators became emotionally involved in remembering and recounting a dramatic incident of this type, they often moved without realizing it into a more casual style of speech. For example, nineteen-year-old Eddie had been reserved and careful in his replies until he described how he had been up a ship's mast in a strong wind, when the rope tied round him to stop him from falling had parted, and left him 'just hanging there by my fingernails'. At this point, his breathing became heavy and irregular, his voice began to shake, sweat appeared on his forehead, small traces of nervous laughter appeared in his speech, and his pronunciation changed noticeably: 'I never prayed to God so fast and so hard in my life . . . Well, I came out all right . . . Well, the guys came up and they got me . . . Yeah, I came down, I couldn't hold a pencil in my hand. I couldn't touch nuttin'. I was shaking like a leaf.'[15]

In another interview, a woman named Rose described a road accident she had had in her childhood. Thirteen of them had piled into one car, a wheel fell off, and the car turned over. As she recounted the incident, her speech became rapid and colloquial:

> It was upside down – you know what happened, do you know how I felt? I don't remember anything. This is really the truth . . . All I remember is – I thought I fell asleep, and I was in a dream . . . I actually saw stars . . . you know, stars in the sky – y'know, when you look up there . . . and I was seein' stars. And then after a while, I felt somebody pushing and pulling – you know, they were all on top of each other – and they were pulling us out from the bottom of the car, and I was goin' 'Ooooh'. And when I came – you know – to, I says to myself, 'Ooooh, we're in a car accident,' – and that's all I remember.[16]

But 'danger of death' memories were not the only way in which Labov elicited informal speech. He was sometimes able to overhear casual speech when the person being interviewed turned away and spoke to her children or answered the phone. He gave an example of this in connection with an informant called Dolly. In the interview Dolly talked to him in a seemingly informal style, and was friendly and relaxed. For example, talking about the meaning of various words she said: 'Smart? Well, I mean, when you use the word *intelligent* an' *smart* I mean . . . you use it in the same sense? . . . (laughs). Some people are pretty witty – I mean – yet they're not so intelligent.' However, a phone conversation which interrupted the interview showed just how different Dolly's really casual speech was: 'Huh? . . . Yeah, go down 'ere to stay. This is. So you know what Carol Ann say, "An' then when papa die, can we come back?" . . . Ain't these chillun sump'm? . . . An' when papa die, can we come back?'[17]

Another woman, a thirty-five-year-old black widow with six children, was speaking about her husband, who was killed in an uprising in Santo Domingo: 'I believe that those that want to go and give up their life for their country, let them go. For my part, his place was here with the children to help raise them and give them a good education . . . that's from my point of view.' This careful, quiet controlled style of conversation contrasted sharply with an interruption caused by one of the children: 'Get out of the refrigerator, Darlene! Tiny or Teena, or whatever your name is! . . . Close the refrigerator, Darlene! . . . What pocketbook? I don't have no pocketbook – if he lookin' for money from me, dear heart, I have no money!'[18]

Sometimes street rhymes or nursery rhymes evoked a casual style. Labov found the following one useful for his study of the vowels in *more* and *door*:

> I won't go to Macy's any more, more, more
> There's a big fat policeman at the door, door, door,
> He pulls you by the collar
> And makes you pay a dollar,
> I won't go to Macy's any more, more, more.[19]

Another way of eliciting casual speech was to allow a speaker to digress. Whenever a subject showed signs of wanting to talk, the interviewers let him or her go ahead. The longer the digression, the better chance they had of hearing natural speech. This worked particularly well with older speakers. Labov notes:

> Some older speakers, in particular, pay little attention to the questions they are asked. They may have certain favorite points of view that they want to express, and they have a great deal of experience in making a rapid transition from the topic to the subject that is closest to their hearts.[20]

By these and similar means, Labov was able to build up a detailed picture of the fluctuating pronunciation of the sounds he examined in New York City. He found that, within the area he worked on, he could reliably predict for each ethnic group, sex, age, and socio-economic group the overall percentage of occurrence of a linguistic variable in each of four styles – casual, careful, reading prose, reading word lists. For example, he found that the upper middle class pronounced *r* in words such as *car, beard* just under 20 per cent of the time in casual speech, but over 30 per cent of the time in careful speech, and around 60 per cent of the time when they read word lists. For the working class the comparable figures were under 10 per cent for casual speech, just over 10 per cent for careful speech, and around 30 per cent for reading word lists.[21]

Labov's methods have become widely used for studying change in progress. They have also been extended to old documents, where change within different styles can be examined.[22]

In his recent work, Labov has paid great attention to methodology, explaining, for example, how to obtain a representative sample for analysis:

A truly representative sample of the speech community must be based on a random sample in which each one of several million speakers has an equal chance of being selected. Such a sample requires an enumeration of those individuals, the selection by random number, and a rigorous pursuit of the individuals selected. This is a formidable task, but not outside the capacity of a single investigator.[23]

In addition, as will be explained in the next chapter, he has made important steps forward in finding out where changes typically begin.

However, initially, there were two problems with large-scale investigations of the type conducted in New York by Labov. First, they give more information about formal than casual speech, because people tend to be extra polite in interviews with strangers. Second, they imply that society is a fairly simple layer-cake with upper class, middle class and working class heaped on top of one another. In practice, humans are more like stars than sponge-cakes, since they group themselves into loose-knit clusters. Study of these **social networks** can reveal the intricate interlacing of human contacts. Potentially, they can show who influences who. So ideally, broad, outline surveys need to be supplemented by smaller-scale studies of speech within networks.

Social networks vary in density. Sometimes they are close-knit, when the same group of people live, work, and spend their free time together. Or they can be loose-knit, as with neighbours who chat occasionally, colleagues who meet only at work, or a choir which gets together once a week for singing practice. Quite often a person is most closely associated with one network, but has weaker links with several others (see Figure 3.3). All these links potentially affect a person's language.

The study of language change within social networks was pioneered in a project in Belfast, Northern Ireland, where Jim and Lesley Milroy studied three working-class communities in the inner city.[24] Here, community ties were strong. This led to dense, multi-stranded networks, in which people work, play and live in the same group.

The Milroys acquired their evidence by joining networks as a 'friend of a friend'. The fieldworker (Lesley) entered one area by mentioning the name of a student who had once lived there. The first person she approached was a middle-aged man (the janitor

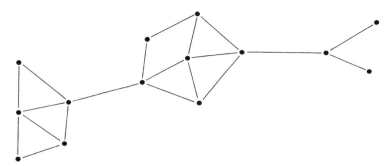

Figure 3.3   Social networks (dots represent people, lines the links between them)

of a public building) to whom she identified herself as 'a friend of Sam's'. She was introduced to others in this way, and later as 'a friend of Ted's', Ted being the local person who gave most help.[25] She therefore became a 'participant observer', someone who joined in as a friend, and collected data at the same time. This guaranteed trust and acceptance as an insider, and made speakers less likely to put on extra-special 'polite' behaviour. The fieldworker needs to collect enough data from different ages and sexes to make a useful statistical analysis, but the emphasis is on acquiring a rounded picture of the speech of a smallish group, rather than on semiformal samples of a wide range of people.

The 'participant observer' style involves fitting in with local customs, and trying not to intrude. Lesley sometimes had to be very patient. She notes:

A fairly familiar (but not necessarily intimate) visitor entering a working-class house in Belfast may sit in total silence without the host feeling the slightest obligation to say anything to him at all. For his own part, the visitor may settle down in his host's kitchen without uttering a word or giving an explanation for his visit. I adopted a similar behaviour pattern, on one occasion sitting for nearly two hours in complete silence while two brothers completed their football pools in the same room. Two more people (both women well known to me) came in during this period, nodded a greeting and remained silent. Interaction was finally initiated by the brothers arguing over the ownership of a pair of socks.[26]

Recordings were often made in the presence of others, which guaranteed relatively 'normal' speech. For example, one youth in a noisy group of five suddenly altered his tone and accent, and 'self-consciously fingered his hair and straightened his clothes. One of his friends punched him and shouted "Come on, you're not on television you know". The others laughed mockingly. Next time the boy spoke, his style had shifted markedly.'[27]

A detailed study of three social networks enabled the Milroys to explain some puzzling features of Belfast speech which might have remained hidden in a more formal study, as will be discussed in Chapter 5.

A broad-range survey, therefore, can show the general outlines of a change. But network analysis can sometimes narrow this down to understanding the mechanisms of language spread in more detail. This will be the topic of the next part of the book, 'Transition' (Chapters 4–9).

Part 2

Transition

4 Spreading the word
From person to person

> You know, if one person, just one person, does it, they
> may think he's really sick . . . And if two people do it . . .
> they may think they're both faggots . . . And if three
> people do it! . . . They may think it's an organization! . . .
> And can you imagine fifty people a day? I said fifty people
> a day . . . Friends, they may think it's a movement, and
> that's what it is.
>
> Arlo Guthrie, Alice's restaurant

Introduction

This chapter explains how language changes spread from person
to person, a once mysterious process. As elsewhere, William Labov
was the key innovator. His research papers on New York [r] and
Martha's Vineyard diphthongs are considered linguistic 'classics',
essential reading for anyone studying language change. He found
that insertion of [r] in words such as *bear, beard* was considered
a prestige feature, an item which speakers felt should be there in
good speech. The lower middle class and upper working class had
many more *r*-sounds in their careful speech than in their casual
conversation. This over-insertion of [r] was a sure sign that a partially conscious change was in progress. Speakers were less aware
of the ongoing change in Martha's Vineyard diphthongs. Subconsciously, those who wanted to remain on the island had been trying
to sound more like some respected old fishermen, who represented
traditional values: the change was less established in those who
were planning to move away. These findings highlight the importance of social issues in the spread of change. In his most recent
work, Labov has promoted the label 'the curvilinear hypothesis',
which is a description of a diagram which shows changes radiating
from speakers in the middle of the social scale.

At one time, the origin and spread of language change were as
obscure to the majority of linguists as the sources of disease still are

to some primitive communities around the world. The following is a typical comment by an early twentieth-century writer on the seemingly mysterious origins of sound change:

> No records have ever been kept of these first beginnings of regular changes of sound . . . We know that English *wah* has changed to *waw*, and we can give approximate dates for some stages of this process; but we do not know when or where or in whose pronunciation the first impulse towards the change occurred.[1]

This statement was made around a century ago. It is still true that, for the majority of past changes, we are unlikely to know who started them, and where they began. However, thanks to the work of scholars such as Labov, whose methods were discussed in the last chapter, we are now in a position to observe changes happening with far greater accuracy than ever before. We can see how they spread, and, in some cases, trace them to their point of origin. This is what we shall be considering in this and the next three chapters.

Before looking at the changes in detail, we need to distinguish between conscious and unconscious change, since this difference is likely to affect the way a change spreads. On the one hand, we find changes which people realize are happening, and actively encourage. On the other hand, we also find changes which people do not notice, which are below the level of conscious awareness.[2] This is a useful preliminary distinction, even though it is not always possible to categorize changes neatly into one or the other type. In this chapter, we will look at one conscious and one unconscious one.

New York City

New Yorkers wished they did not talk like New Yorkers. Labov commented: 'In general New Yorkers show a strong dislike for the sound of New York City speech. Most have tried to change their speech in one way or another, and would be sincerely complimented to be told that they do not sound like New Yorkers.'[3] This 'sink of negative prestige'[4] was an ideal situation in which to find consciously cultivated changes, provided one could find a method

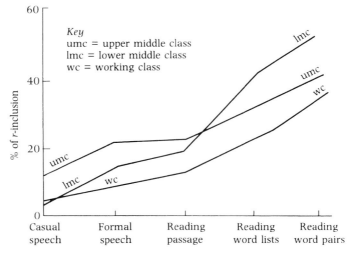

Figure 4.1   Labov's findings on *r*-inclusion, according to socio-economic class (based on Labov, 1972a)

of charting the apparently 'thoroughly haphazard'[5] language variation.

In the last chapter, we described how Labov tackled the problem of New York *r*. After a preliminary department-store survey, he went on to a more comprehensive analysis of *r*-usage in certain areas of New York City. Using survey techniques developed by sociologists, he obtained systematic speech samples from different socio-economic, ethnic, age and sex groups, in a variety of language styles.

Let us begin by looking at Figure 4.1, which shows some of Labov's findings.[6] The diagram shows the percentage of *r*-inclusion in words such as *bear, beard* in upper-middle-class (umc), lower-middle-class (lmc) and working-class (wc) speakers for each of five speech styles: casual speech, formal speech, reading connected prose, reading word lists, and reading word pairs.

What could this chart tell us? First, it confirmed the findings of the department-store survey in that it showed that *r*-insertion in words such as *bear, beard* was socially prestigious, since it occurred more frequently in the casual and formal speech of the upper middle class than of the lower social classes. A further indication of social prestige was that the more careful the speech style, the more likely *r* was to be pronounced. Obviously, when people spoke slowly and carefully, they remembered to insert an *r* which they felt should be there. Further evidence of its prestige value was provided by the finding that, when questioned about whether they pronounced *r*, New Yorkers claimed to insert *r* more often than they actually did. It is a common observation that many people think that they speak in a more socially prestigious way than they really do.

The most interesting feature on the chart, however, was the speech behaviour of the lower middle class. There was an enormous difference between the percentage of *r*s used in casual speech (under 10 per cent) and those inserted in reading word lists (around 60 per cent). When they read word lists, lower-middle-class New Yorkers used even more *r*s than the upper middle class! What was the significance of this strange over-use of *r*, or **hypercorrection**, as Labov called it?

Labov claimed that 'the hypercorrect behaviour of the lower middle class is seen as a synchronic indicator of linguistic change in progress'.[7] He suggested that members of the lower middle class tended to be socially and linguistically insecure, and anxious to improve their low status. More than other socio-economic classes, they were likely to be aware of which speech forms were 'classy' prestige ones, and would tend to insert these forms in careful speech. The more they inserted these forms in careful speech, the more they would get into the habit of inserting *r* in casual speech. In this way, the proportion of *r*s would gradually creep upwards. Labov noted: 'Middle-aged, lower-middle-class speakers tend to adopt the formal speech patterns of the younger, upper-middle-class speakers. This tendency provides a feed-back mechanism which is potentially capable of accelerating the introduction of any prestige feature.'[8] Lower-middle-class youths, he pointed out, would be in contact with the new prestige pronunciation on two fronts. On the one hand, they would be familiar with the speech of those who are going to college, whether or not they belonged to this group. On the other hand, their parents and teachers would also use this prestige pattern in formal circumstances. He noted furthermore that hypercorrection seemed to be commoner in women than in men: 'Hypercorrectness is certainly strongest in women – and it may be that the lower-middle-class mother, and the grade school teacher, are prime agents in the acceleration of this type of linguistic change.'[9]

In brief, a change seemed to be in progress in New York City, in that *r* was being increasingly inserted into words such as *beard, bear*. This change seemed to be strongest in the language-conscious lower middle class, particularly lower-middle-class women, who were imitating and, in some cases, exaggerating a prestige feature found in the speech of the upper middle class.

But how did *r* come to be in the speech of the upper middle class in New York in the first place? We find, on examination, that *r* has a strange, fluctuating history in American speech. We know, from spelling and other sources, that both British and American speech once had an *r* in words such as *car, card*. By the end of the eighteenth century, this *r* had disappeared from the speech of London and Boston. Then New York, apparently following the lead of these fashionable cities, lost its *r* also. There are reports that it was *r*-less by the mid nineteenth century, when, for example, a New York poet rhymed *shore* with *pshaw*.[10] It remained *r*-less in the early twentieth century, as is confirmed by Edward Sturtevant, a linguist writing in 1917, who noted that an inserted *r* was characteristic of the western parts of the USA and likely to be a disadvantage to someone in the east: 'A strong western *r* is a distinct hindrance to a man who is trying to make his way in the East or the South of the United States.'[11] According to Sturtevant, not only was New York *r*-less, but the *r*-less pronunciation characteristic of New York was in the process of spreading to nearby districts: 'Another gradually spreading sound change may be observed in the neighbourhood of New York City . . . this [*r*-less] pronunciation is gradually spreading to the southwest . . . There is little doubt that soon the whole district tributary to New York City will pronounce "caht", etc.'[12] *R*-less speech was still the norm in the 1930s, then *r* was reported to be on the increase in the 1950s and 1960s. When and how did this sudden change come about?

The reintroduction of *r*, which brought New York in line with the use of *r* in most other American dialects, seems to have occurred around the time of the Second World War. Labov suggested that 'one might argue that the experience of men in the services was somehow involved',[13] though he admits that it would be difficult to prove this suggestion. One possibility is that around this time New Yorkers had a growing awareness of themselves as American, and picked a non-British style of speech on which to model themselves. But this is speculation. All we can say is that the *r*-less pronunciation began to lose ground from the 1940s onwards.

This New York change, then, was a conscious one, in which the lower middle class played a prominent role. The change progressed as New Yorkers inserted a greater proportion of *r*s in their speech, starting consciously with the most formal speech styles. We note further that *r* did not arrive 'out of the blue'. It was always present in some dialects of American English. The change occurred when these *r* dialects were taken as a prestige model by the rest of America.

New York is, in many ways, an extraordinary city. To what extent is this New York change typical of language changes in general? We will discuss this question by considering further examples of change. We will next look at a change which is rather different. It occurred on a small island, Martha's Vineyard, rather than in a large city, and it took place for the most part below the level of conscious awareness.

Martha's Vineyard

One of the problems of studying sound change in a busy city like New York is that people's lives are extremely complex. Every socio-economic class, age group or ethnic group meets so many different people, and has so many conflicting influences, that it is hard to know where to begin. For this reason, Labov in his early work tried to find an area which was relatively self-contained.

He chose the island known as Martha's Vineyard, which is part of the state of Massachusetts.[14] It is an island lying about three miles off the east coast of mainland America, with a permanent population of about 6,000. However, this charming and picturesque island is not left undisturbed, and, much to the disgust of a number of

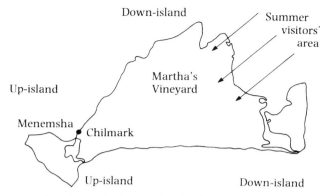

Figure 4.2   Martha's Vineyard (based on Labov, 1972a)

locals, over 40,000 visitors, known somewhat disparagingly as the 'summer people', flood in every summer. More people are familiar with the appearance of Martha's Vineyard than they realize, since it was the location of the film *Jaws*. The island itself is shaped roughly like a gigantic shark, with its head lying to the east, and its tail to the west (see Figure 4.2).

The eastern part of the island is more densely populated by the permanent residents, and is the area mostly visited by the summer visitors, who have bought up almost the entire northeast shore, a fact deeply resented by some of the old inhabitants. As one said, 'You can cross the island from one end to the other without stepping on anything but "No Trespassing" signs.'[15] This heavily populated end of the island is generally referred to as Down-island. The western third of the island is known as Up-island. It is strictly rural, and, apart from a few villages, contains salt ponds, marshes, and a large central area of uninhabited pine barrens. It is in this western part that most of the original population of the island live.

Labov made an exploratory visit to the island in order to decide which aspect of the islanders' language to study. He noted that, approximately thirty years earlier, a linguist had visited Martha's Vineyard, and had at that time interviewed members of the old families of the island. When Labov compared this thirty-year-old record with his own preliminary observations, he discovered that the vowel in words such as *out, trout, house* seemed to be changing, and so, to a lesser extent, was the vowel in words such as *white, pie, night, like.*

The vowel in each of these words is a diphthong, which is actually two overlapping vowels, one gliding imperceptibly into the other: [a] + [u] making [au] in the case of *house*, and [a] + [i] making [ai] in the case of *night*. In each case, the first part of the diphthong seemed to be shifting from a sound somewhat like [a] in the word *car*, towards a vowel [ə] like that at the beginning of the word *ago* or in the American pronunciation of *but*:

[au] → [əu]
[ai] → [əi]

Labov then interviewed a cross-section of the islanders, excluding the summer visitors, after devising questions which were likely to elicit a large number of [ai] and [au] forms. For example, he asked them: 'When we speak of the *right* to *life*, liberty and the pursuit of happiness, what does *right* mean?' He also asked people to read a passage which contained further examples of the crucial sounds: 'After the *high* winds last Thursday, we went *down* to the mooring to see *how* the boat was making *out* . . . ' In this way he recorded sixty-nine formal interviews, as well as making numerous informal observations in diners, restaurants, bars, stores and docks.

When he had obtained his results, he plotted them on a series of charts showing age, geographical distribution, ethnic group and occupation. He found that, as regards this particular change, there was no conscious awareness on the part of the islanders that it was happening. And, as a consequence of this finding, that there was no significant stylistic variation within individual speakers.

Labov's Martha's Vineyard study is deservedly famous, and 'is one of the best-known examples of empirical investigation of language variation and change in the entire world',[16] it has been claimed. Let us now consider what he found. He discovered that the change was least in evidence in the over-75-year-olds, and was most prominent in the 31 to 45 age group. Somewhat surprisingly, the speech of the 30 and under group was less affected than that of the 40-year-olds. Geographically, the change was far more widespread in rural, western Up-island than in the more populous Down-island.

It was particularly notable in an area known as Chilmark, which formed the centre of the island's fishing activities. Martha's Vineyard had once been a prosperous centre of the whaling industry, but Labov noted that only around 2.5 per cent of the islanders were still occupied in full-time fishing. This 2.5 per cent mostly lived around the Up-island village of Menemsha in Chilmark. In Down-island, on the other hand, most of the population was involved in service industries, looking after the summer visitors in various ways. When occupational groups were considered, it was the fishermen whose speech contained the highest proportion of 'local' diphthongs. The difference between ethnic groups was not so noticeable: those of English descent showed more evidence of the local pronunciation than people from Portuguese and Indian backgrounds, though not by much.

To summarize, Labov found that, compared with mainland America, a change was taking place in certain diphthongs on Martha's Vineyard. This change seemed to be most advanced in the speech of people in their thirties and early forties, and was particularly far advanced in the speech of a number of fishermen in Up-island.

Labov's survey, therefore, suggested that the change under observation possibly radiated from a small group of fishermen living in Up-island, and had then spread to people of English descent, particularly those in the 31 to 45 age group.

These findings raised a number of puzzling questions. First, where did the fishermen get the change from in the first place? Did one fisherman suddenly decide to alter his vowels and persuade the rest to follow him? Or what happened? Secondly, why should the adult population of Martha's Vineyard suddenly start subconsciously imitating the speech of a small and apparently insignificant bunch of fishermen?

When Labov considered these problems, he uncovered some interesting facts. He discovered that the fishermen had not suddenly altered the way they talked, as one might suppose. Instead, they had simply started to exaggerate a tendency which was already there. The 'new' diphthongs had, as far as could be ascertained, always been present to some extent in the fishermen's speech. Far from representing an innovation, the vowels in question appeared to be

Time (centuries)

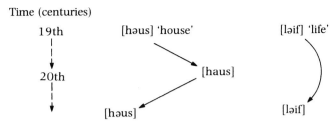

Figure 4.3   Vowel changes on Martha's Vineyard

a conservative, old-fashioned feature in the fishermen's pronunciation, which in certain ways resembled that of mainland America in the eighteenth and nineteenth centuries. One of them even prided himself on preserving old values, and speaking differently from the rest of America:

> You people who come down here to Martha's Vineyard don't understand the background of the old families of the island . . . strictly a maritime background and tradition . . . and what we're interested in, the rest of America, this part over here across the water that belongs to you and we don't have anything to do with, has forgotten all about . . . I think perhaps we use entirely different . . . type of English language . . . think differently here on the island . . . it's almost a separate language within the English language.[17]

Why had the original inhabitants clung to their old speech habits, and not brought their pronunciation into line with that of the people around them? Oddly enough, there was some evidence that, some time previously, Martha's Vineyarders *had* started to lose their old diphthongs, and *had* begun to bring their vowel sounds into line with those of neighbouring mainland areas. The vowel in words such as *house* and *south* had become almost 'normal', though the vowel in *life* and *night* had lagged behind. Later, however, the almost-completed change had suddenly reversed itself. The vowel in *house* had not only reverted to its original pronunciation, but it had actually gone farther and become more extreme. This strange episode is illustrated in Figure 4.3.

Why did the change which would have brought Martha's Vineyarders in line with mainland Americans suddenly reverse itself, and move in the opposite direction in an exaggerated way? And why did such a backwards move catch on among the inhabitants of the island, particularly among those of English descent between the ages of 31 and 45?

The answer, Labov suggests, is connected with the rise in popularity of the island as a tourist resort, and the disapproval of the summer people by the old inhabitants. The Chilmark fishermen, Labov noted, formed the most close-knit social group on the island, the most independent, the one which was the most stubbornly opposed to the incursions of the summer people. The next generation down admired these old fishermen, who appeared to exemplify the virtues traditional to Martha's Vineyard: they were viewed as independent, skilful, physically strong, courageous. They epitomized the good old Yankee virtues, as opposed to the indolent consumer-oriented society of the summer visitors. This led a number of Vineyarders to subconsciously imitate the speech characteristics of the fishermen, in order to identify themselves as 'true islanders'. This hypothesis is supported by Labov's finding that the local pronunciation was far stronger in those inhabitants who were planning to stay on the island permanently. These were mostly in the 31- to 45-year-old age group. Those who planned to leave and live on the mainland had vowels which were more standard, and so did those who were as yet uncommitted to their future. In one case, a mother whose son had recently returned from college actually noted the change in her son, who, she suggested, was consciously adopting the speech of the fishermen. She commented: 'You know, E. didn't always speak that way . . . it's only since he came back from college. I guess he wanted to be more like the men on the docks.'[18]

Labov's seminal study is now almost half a century old. So are his original results still valid today? His findings have recently been challenged.[19] This set up a flurry of interest into whether the situation had changed. It turned out that those querying Labov's findings had not followed his methodology in all its details, and had inadvertently included many more 'summer visitors' in their survey. Later, more careful replication revealed results that paralleled Labov's original claims.[20] At the current time, then, Labov's findings still stand. Of course, old research needs constant rechecking, but subsequent work needs to be careful to pay close attention to

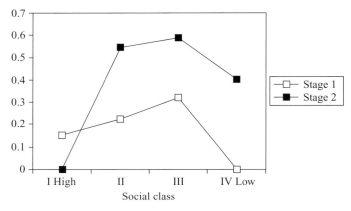

Figure 4.4   Curvilinear pattern, based on Labov, 2001: 32

the original methodology. Labov himself has continued rechecking, and has also done considerable work on a different community, in Philadelphia, USA.[21]

His most interesting new insight is a realization of who, in any group initiating a change, are likely to be leading that change. Under a somewhat pompous label, 'the curvilinear hypothesis', which is a summary of a diagram type showing the change (Figure 4.4), he comes to the following conclusion: in general, changes seem to radiate from lower-middle-class or upper-working-class members. In short, they do not climb downwards from the top, or upwards from the bottom: they start in the middle.[22]

Let us now summarize what we have found out so far. On Martha's Vineyard a small group of fishermen began to exaggerate a tendency already existing in their speech. They did this seemingly subconsciously, in order to establish themselves as an independent social group with superior status to the despised summer visitors. A number of other islanders regarded this group as one which epitomized old virtues and desirable values, and subconsciously imitated the way its members talked. For these people, the new pronunciation was an innovation. As more and more people came to speak in the same way, the innovation gradually became the norm for those living on the island.

We may therefore divide the spread of a change such as this into a series of overlapping stages:

Stage 1   An aspect of the speech of a particular social group differed from that of the 'standard' dialect of the area. In this case, the speech of the Chilmark fishermen contained certain 'old' diphthongs which no longer existed in the standard speech of the area.

Stage 2   A second social group admired and modelled itself on the first group, and subconsciously adopted and exaggerated certain features in the speech of the former. In this case, Chilmark fishermen were regarded as representing traditional virtues and 'true' values by those who lived permanently on the island. The fishermen's diphthongs were subconsciously copied and exaggerated as a sign of solidarity against the despised 'summer visitors'.

Stage 3   The new speech feature gradually took hold among those who had adopted it, and became the norm. In this case, the local diphthongs were adopted as the standard pronunciation by those of English descent in the 31 to 45 age group.

Stage 4   The process repeated itself as a new social group started to model itself on the group which had now adopted the linguistic innovation as the norm. In this case, those of English descent in the 31 to 45 age range were taken as models by other age groups and ethnic groups on Martha's Vineyard.

The change on Martha's Vineyard is instructive for two reasons. First, it occurred in a relatively simple social situation, where the relevant factors could be isolated without too much difficulty. Secondly, as noted above, the inhabitants of Martha's Vineyard were for the most part unaware that a change was occurring in their speech.

Superficially the New York *r*-change was quite different from the one on Martha's Vineyard. Nevertheless, the changes have two notable features in common. First, they did not come 'out of the blue'. The *r* adopted by New Yorkers was always present in the speech of some if not the majority of Americans, just as the Martha's Vineyard fishermen had always retained certain 'old' vowels. Secondly, in both places the changes took hold when one group adopted another as its model. The New York *r*-change occurred when New Yorkers imitated other Americans around the time of the Second World War, perhaps because of a growing awareness of themselves as being American, and requiring an American standard on which to model themselves. This *r* gradually spread among the upper middle class, who were in turn taken as a model by the socially and linguistically insecure lower middle class.

The main difference between the New York and Martha's Vineyard changes is that the New York one was above the level of conscious awareness and the Martha's Vineyard one below it. The difference may be related to how long the change had been going on. A change tends to sneak quietly into a language, like a seed, which enters the soil and germinates unseen. At some point, it sprouts through the surface. Similarly, people may become socially aware of a change only when it reaches a certain crucial point. Another important factor, however, is the direction of the change in relation to the standard dialect of the area. Changes above the level of social awareness tend to be those moving in the direction of the socially accepted norm, while changes from below the level of social awareness tend to be those moving away from it.

Meanwhile, the leaders of any change seem to be those in the mid ranks of any society, 'the curvilinear hypothesis'.

We have now looked at how changes spread from person to person. Let us now summarize some important realizations. First, changes are not comparable to meteorites falling from the sky. They usually originate from elements already in the language which get borrowed and exaggerated.

Second, there is a grain of truth in the popular notion that changes are catching, like a disease. In other respects, however, the disease metaphor breaks down. People do not want to catch a disease. They do, however, want to talk like those they admire and wish to imitate, even if they are not always aware of it. A change occurs when one group consciously or subconsciously takes another as its model, and copies features from its speech. The situation is somewhat like that described in Robert Browning's poem 'The lost leader':

> We that had loved him so, followed him, honoured him,
> Lived in his mild and magnificent eye,
> Learned his great language, caught his clear accents,
> Made him our pattern to live and to die!

Third, conscious changes are usually in the direction of speech forms with overt prestige. These often originate with the upper-working-class or lower-middle-class speakers, particularly women from these classes. Meanwhile, subconscious changes tend to be movements away from overt prestige forms, and often begin with working-class men, whose speech and habits are associated with toughness and virility, and so have covert prestige.

Fourth, changes move from group to group possibly via people who come casually into contact. In conversation, they are likely to 'accommodate' their speech to each other in minor ways, and then eventually pick up some of each other's accent, and so carry it across when speaking to their friends.

The spread of language change, then, is essentially a social phenomenon, which reflects the social situation. Changes do not occur unless they have some type of prestige. They are markers of group membership, and people outside the group want, consciously or subconsciously, to belong. However, as we shall see in later chapters, it would be a mistake to assume that social factors alone are all we need to know about.

5 Conflicting loyalties
Opposing social pressures

At the still point of the turning world. Neither flesh nor fleshless;
Neither from nor towards; at the still point, there the dance is . . .
T. S. Eliot, *Four quartets*

Introduction

This chapter explores conflicting social pressures, cases in which
different dialect features collide and briefly cause an uneasy calm,
in which neither appears to win out. In Norwich, England, an older
style *walkin', talkin'* with covert prestige used mainly by men contrasted with standard *walking, talking* usually in women's speech.
In Belfast, Ireland, two vowels were moving in different directions,
again with men and women tugging against one another. A third
linguistic battle of the sexes was between a non-standard -*s*, as in *you
knows*, versus the standard form *you know* in the speech of teenagers
in Reading, England. A somewhat different linguistic battle was
found in Detroit, USA, where teenage Jocks (followers of a conventional lifestyle) contrasted with Burnouts (non-conventional
breakaways). A struggle between norms was that of new immigrants trying to adapt their Canadian speech patterns to a British
yardstick. Vocabulary adaptation was relatively easy, but pronunciation adjustment depended on the age of the adopter, with the
younger ones being more successful. Overall, linguistic conflicts are
an important indicator of social attitudes: in each case, a linguistic
struggle reflected a social situation.

In general, people do not pay much attention to the behaviour of
others, unless it is dramatically different from the norm. A person can continue doing something marginally odd for a long time
without attracting attention. However, once people notice the odd-
ity, they tend to over-react. This phenomenon occurs with eating habits, cleanliness or personal mannerisms. People either do

not notice anything odd, or, if they do, they place the individual concerned into a category of deviant behaviour which probably exaggerates the situation considerably: 'Felicity drinks like a fish'; 'Marcia's house is like a pigsty'; 'Cuthbert's continually scratching himself'.

The same thing happens with language. People either do not notice a minor deviation from the norm, or they over-react to it, and make comments such as 'Egbert always drops his aitches', even though Egbert may only drop a few of them. Consider the case of words which end in *t* in British English, such as *what*, *hot*. A large number of people alter *t* to a glottal stop when it occurs before another word, as in *wha(t) stupidity, ho(t) water bottle*, but they usually do not realize they are doing so, nor do they notice other people doing so. Others, however, also change *t* at the end of a sentence, as in *Wha(t)? It's ho(t)*. This is usually noticed, and often censured. We frequently hear parents upbraiding their children with comments such as 'Don'(t) say "what" in tha(t) sloppy way!', not realizing that their own speech shows a fluctuating *t* also. *T*-dropping, then, is a change against the standard norm which emerges into public view when it occurs in certain linguistic environments.

Similarly, in the city of Norwich the standard British English forms *walking* and *talking* alternated with forms ending in *n*: *walkin'*, *talkin'*. Labov noted that listeners reacted in one of two ways to these *walkin', talkin'* forms: 'Up to a certain point they do not perceive the speaker "dropping his *g*'s" at all; beyond a certain point, they perceive him as always doing so.'[1] At both times, there was likely in fact to have been fluctuation, but this fluctuation was not perceived by the listener.

Let us now consider what happens when a non-standard linguistic feature suddenly emerges into popular consciousness. This can happen either when a change below the level of conscious awareness becomes noticed, or when a dialect feature which has existed in the language for some time is perceived as clashing with a spreading standard feature. In both cases there will be conflict between the social forces which fostered the non-standard feature, and those promoting the accepted norm. At this point, one sometimes finds a period of apparent calm – the change superficially stops. On closer examination, however, we see that it is the artificial calm in the centre of the cyclone, a momentary balance of opposing social factors.

As in the Eliot quotation at the start of the chapter, 'at the still point, there the dance is'. Let us go on to examine this type of situation. We will look at the case mentioned above of *g*-dropping in Norwich.

Walkin' and talkin' in Norwich

> The man in the moon
> Came down too soon
> And asked his way to Norwich;
> He went by the south
> And burnt his mouth
> With supping cold plum porridge.[2]

If the man in the moon came down today, he probably wouldn't want to go to Norwich, a smallish city in East Anglia, situated a few miles from the east coast of England. The children's rhyme quoted above is perhaps a memory from the sixteenth and seventeenth centuries when Norwich briefly laid claim to being the second-largest city in England. Nowadays, however, it is small in comparison with big cities such as London or Birmingham, though it remains a centre of considerable cultural and commercial importance for the surrounding area. Communications with the rest of England used to be poor, and according to one facetious account it was 'cut off on three sides by the sea and the fourth by British Rail'.[3]

The relatively cut-off situation of Norwich suggested that it might be an interesting area in which to study language change. Standard British English, spreading from London, was likely to interact in interesting ways with local speech habits, which remain entrenched because of the traditional independence and relative isolation of the area. And so it proved.

Norwich speech was studied by Peter Trudgill, a one-time native of the city.[4] Using Labov-type methods, he interviewed a cross-section of the population, eliciting four speech styles: casual speech, formal speech, reading passages and reading word lists. He confirmed Labov's finding that, when there is both class and stylistic variation, a change was likely to be in progress. More interesting than the actual changes he charted, however, was one which seemed to be in the balance, held in abeyance by opposing forces, like a car driver with one foot pressed on the clutch and the other on the accelerator, so the car remains motionless halfway up a hill. Trudgill found a situation like this when he examined the final consonant in words such as *walking* and *running*. In Standard British English, the sound spelt *-ng* is a so-called 'velar nasal' [ŋ]. In Norwich, however, the pronunciation *walkin'*, *talkin'* was frequently heard, as if there was simply *n* [n] on the end. This is a remnant of an older style of speech. The ending *-in'* for *talkin'*, *walkin'* used to be considerably more common, and even in the 1930s was an acceptable pronunciation among large sections of speakers of Standard British English. Its widespread usage in the past is shown in rhymes and mis-spellings. For example, Shakespeare's *cushing*, *javeling* for 'cushion', 'javelin', which were never pronounced with *-ing*, indicate that he added *g* because he thought it ought to be there in the spelling. More vividly, consider Swift's couplet (dating from around 1700) in which *fitting* and *spit in* rhyme:

> His jordan [= chamber pot] stood in manner fitting
> Between his legs, to spew or spit in.[5]

The currently standard use of the *-ing* [iŋ] (with velar nasal) was perhaps due to the spread of a hypercorrect pronunciation in the first part of the nineteenth century, an imposed pattern like New York *r*. In Norwich, this pattern was never fully imposed, and local *-in'* remained. Later, however, the alternation between local *-in'* and Standard British *-ing* emerged into speakers' consciousness, resulting in a conflict of great interest to anyone concerned with the mechanisms of linguistic change. Trudgill noted an interplay not only between social classes, but also, as in the New York change, between the sexes.

At first, Trudgill's results did not look particularly surprising. He found that in all social classes, the more careful the speech, the more likely people were to say *walking* rather than *walkin'*. *Walkin'* was definitely a feature of casual, not careful, speech. He also found that the proportion of *walkin'*-type forms was higher in the lower socio-economic classes. Forms such as *walkin'*, *talkin'* appeared

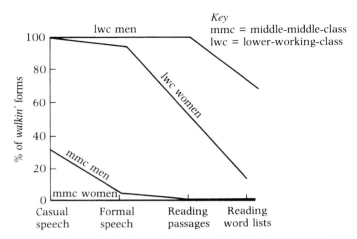

Figure 5.1   *Walkin'* and *talkin'* in Norwich (based on Trudgill, 1976)

100 per cent of the time in the casual speech of the lower working class, but only 28 per cent of the time in the casual speech of the middle middle class. This was entirely the result that one might have expected. But when he examined his results more carefully, he found an interesting phenomenon. The non-standard forms occurred considerably more often in men's speech than in women's in *all* social classes. This is illustrated in Figure 5.1,[6] which compares the percentage of *walkin'*-type forms in the speech of middle-middle-class and lower-working-class men and women.

Judging from these figures, there appeared to be a tug-of-war going on, with the men pulling one way, and the women the other. The men were pulling away from the overt prestige form, and the women were pulling towards it. This was further confirmed when Trudgill questioned people from both sexes about what they thought they were saying. He found that women thought they were using the standard form more often than they in fact were, whereas men tended to give the opposite response. They claimed to be using the *non*-standard form more often than they actually were! This reflected wishful thinking in both cases. The women wanted to think of themselves as speaking the standard prestige form, whereas the men wanted to think of themselves as speaking the 'rougher' speech of their fellow workers.

Trudgill suggested two related reasons for this phenomenon.[7] First, women are often more status-conscious than men, and are therefore more aware of the social significance of different speech forms. Secondly, male working-class speech tended to be associated with roughness and toughness, which were considered by many to be desirable masculine attributes, though not desirable feminine ones. Trudgill went on to suggest that conscious changes may well be initiated by women. Women were consciously striving to 'speak better', partly because of a certain social insecurity, partly because they were not aiming to sound 'tough'. They presumably encouraged their children to talk in a socially acceptable way, and so aided changes in the direction of the standard language. Subconscious changes, on the other hand, might well have been initiated by working-class men. Other men tended to admire their supposed masculinity and toughness and imitated them, often without realizing they were doing so. These suggestions are supported by the New York and Martha's Vineyard changes. In New York, *r*-insertion was led by lower-middle-class women. On Martha's Vineyard, the vowel change was initiated by a group of fishermen. In fact, this difference between the sexes appears to be a widespread phenomenon, at least in the Western world. It has been found in Switzerland, Paris, Detroit, Chicago and New York, and most people can provide anecdotal evidence to support it in other areas also. We all know couples like Edna and Eric, who were of working-class Liverpool stock, but who came south and moved into the fashionable 'stockbroker belt' on the outer fringes of London. Edna rapidly lost her working-class Liverpool accent, though Eric retained his for the rest of his life.

To return to *walkin'*, *talkin'*, it was not possible to predict a movement in any one direction, as there seemed to be a pull between the *walkin'* pronunciation, which had covert prestige, and the *walking* pronunciation with overt prestige. Overall, the tug-of-war provided a useful guide to social pressures within a community, and the progress or regression of a change reflected the state of the struggle.

Let us now consider another situation in which social pressures tugged against one another.

Wat grawss and bawd nacks in Belfast

'Now Ireland has her madness and her weather still,' said the English poet W. H. Auden, commenting on the widespread belief that it rains all the time in Ireland, and that the Irish are somewhat illogical. The reputation for illogicality could well have arisen out of English attempts to understand an Irish accent, with its wide range of possibilities.

After the rain in Belfast, you might get advised not to sit on the *wat grawss* [wat grɔːs] or on the *wet grass* [wet grɑːs]. The damp might give you a *bawd nack* [bɔːd nak] or a *bad neck* [bad nek]. Starting in the 1970s, the Milroys probed into this confusing situation, with the aid of their detailed network analyses of working-class communities in the inner city (Chapter 3).[8]

To an outsider, variation in pronunciation was not surprising, in view of the unusual social set-up in Belfast at that time. The inner-city communities were in some ways similar to one another. They were poor, and officially described as 'blighted'. Unemployment was high, premature death was above average, sickness and juvenile crime were widespread. In other ways, they were profoundly dissimilar. There was a deep-rooted division between Protestants and Catholics, two religious–ethnic groups who, at best, barely spoke to one another, and, at worst, were in open conflict. For a long time they were physically separated in some places by a brick-and-barbed-wire structure between them called (ironically) the Peace Line. In such a split city, differences in language might be expected.

Surprisingly, perhaps, the varying vowel sounds turned out not to reflect a straight clash between Protestant and Catholic, but a subtler tugging, primarily between men and women.

In the 1970s, two changes were under way in the vowels *a* and *e*, judging from *Provincialisms of Belfast*, a book published in 1860.[9] Compared with the mid nineteenth century, many more words spelt with *a* were pronounced as if they were spelt *aw* (*grawss* for older *grass*, *bawd* for *bad*). So *a*-sounds were moving further back in the mouth. On the other hand, a fairly pronounced 'Irishism' of the nineteenth century, the pronunciation of words such as *wren*, *desk*, as *ran*, *dask*, seemed to be on the decline. So *e*-sounds were moving further forward in the mouth. Two similar sounds, therefore, are apparently moving in different directions:

[e] ←			→ [ɔ:d]
wren	[a]	[ɑ]	bawd
desk	wran	bad	grawss
	dask	grass	

On investigation, a hidden cross-current was revealed, in which men were dragging *a*-sounds (*bad*, *grass*, *hand*) in one direction, and women were drawing *e*-sounds (*bed*, *best*) in another. This became clear when the speech of the Protestant community of Ballymacarrett in east Belfast was compared with that of the Roman Catholic community of the Clonard in west Belfast.[10]

Let us consider these conflicting undertows in more detail, starting with the *a*-question. The most 'backed' pronunciations of *a* (*bad* as *bawd* [bɔ:d], *grass* as *grawss*) occurred in the speech of men from Ballymacarrett. (*Backed* means 'with tongue pulled back in the mouth'.) On a score range of 0–4 (4 most backed), these men averaged 3.5 in casual speech:

	Men 40–55	Women 40–55	Men 18–25	Women 18–25
East Belfast	3.6	2.6	3.4	2.1
West Belfast	2.8	1.8	2.3	2.6

The Ballymacarrett men with this backed *a* have been called a 'labour aristocracy'. More of them were employed, and they were better off than the poorer Clonard community in west Belfast. Pronunciations such as *grawss* and *bawd* could therefore be regarded as a key feature of inner-city speech in Belfast. They marked the speakers as being highly integrated, core members of a relatively superior social network. The change therefore seemed to be radiating out from these inner-city men, especially as the extreme forms of the backed *a* were not apparently found in outer-city speech.

The Clonard (Catholic, west Belfast) had an overall lower score of backed pronunciations, suggesting that the people here were following, rather than leading, the change. But the details were somewhat puzzling. Young women (18–25) had a higher score than young men – even though women typically lag behind in pronunciations associated with working-class men. There were therefore two puzzling features. First, why were the Clonard young women ahead of their menfolk? Second, how did the backed *a* spread from Ballymacarrett to Clonard, when Protestants barely spoke to Catholics? In short, how did a change apparently initiated by east Belfast males move across to west Belfast females?

Social factors provided the answer. In the Clonard, unemployment was high among young males. The women, however, had jobs, mostly in the same rather poor city-centre store. This store was located on the interface between Protestants and Catholics, and was used by both. In all probability, the girls had picked up the usage from their customers. Shop assistants tend to match their speech to that of their customers, as was obvious in Labov's New York department-store survey. And further research has confirmed this tendency: an assistant in a travel agency in Wales was shown to vary the number of *h*s in her speech (*house* vs *'ouse*) in proportion to the number used by her clients: she herself produced on average twice as many when speaking to '*h*-pronouncers' as she did when talking to '*h*-droppers'.[11] This 'shop-assistant phenomenon' has important implications. First, it highlights the tendency for people chatting together to partially imitate one another. Each picks on aspects of the other's speech, and incorporates them into her own. This linguistic **accommodation** is the way alterations are picked up, according to some sociolinguists.[12] Second, the shop-assistant phenomenon suggests that changes move from one network to another via weak links.[13] When people simply talk to their old pals, they reinforce existing trends. But a change normally comes from outside. So it possibly crosses from one network to another via weak links, such as the one between customer and shop assistant. These girls, then, carried the backed *a* from their Ballymacarrett customers across to the Clonard network.

The *a*-question therefore seems to have been solved. To summarize, a change was under way in which *a* was moving progressively backwards in the mouth, so that extreme back pronunciations such as *bawd* and *grawss* were often heard. This change was most advanced among working-class Protestant males in east Belfast. From there, it was diffused to a Catholic community in west Belfast, probably via young women shop assistants, who had 'picked up' the accent of their customers.

But what about *e*? The movement from an 'Irish' [a] to a more 'standard' [e] pronunciation (*wat* to *wet* for 'wet') was another change. This shift was initiated by Ballymacarrett women, who had the lowest percentage of 'old' ([a]) pronunciations in words such as *wet, best*:

	Men 40–55	Women 40–55	Men 18–25	Women 18–25
East	100	68	100	56
West	97	81	84	73

The figures for some outer-city communities were somewhat like those of the inner-city working-class women, and many middle-class speakers had *e*-pronunciations with [e] everywhere. The change therefore appeared to be one towards more 'standard' speech, with overt prestige.

The Belfast case was therefore similar to the situation in Norwich, in that the men and women were pulling in different directions. But it was dissimilar, in that each sex was leading a different change, the men towards a non-standard *a*, the women towards a standard *e*. However, the Clonard young women showed that women may be ahead of men in a change towards a non-standard pronunciation, in certain social circumstances. They do not inevitably veer towards the standard. Furthermore, the Belfast changes were important in that they suggested a way in which changes might jump across from one network to another. The alterations started as temporary shifts in casual face-to-face conversation, when the participants accommodated their accent to that of the person they were talking to. Then this temporary shifting was partially incorporated into their normal speech, and used when chatting to their friends. In this way it was carried across to a new set of speakers.

All the changes discussed so far have been sound changes. Let us now look at a change in word endings – which was in certain respects like the Norwich and Belfast changes just considered, in that it again represented a conflict between opposing social pressures.

We knows how to talk in Reading

In Reading, a moderately big town some forty miles or so west of London, England, it is not uncommon to hear sentences such as:

I *knows* how to handle teddy boys.
You knows my sister, the one who's small.
They *calls* me all the names under the sun.

Jenny Cheshire, a linguist then at the University of Reading, studied the incidence of these non-standard verb forms in the speech of a number of adolescents in adventure playgrounds.[14]

These playgrounds were all seen as 'trouble spots' by the local residents because of the fights and fires that took place there, and the children concerned were in many cases 'tough' children who swore, fought, uttered obscenities and did not go to school regularly. In all, twenty-five children were studied: thirteen boys and twelve girls. Their ages ranged from nine to seventeen, though most were between eleven and fifteen. They were clustered into three groups of friends, two of boys and one of girls.

Superficially, the use of these non-standard verbs alternated randomly with the use of the conventional forms in the speech of these adolescents. Careful analysis, however, showed that there was a clear pattern in their distribution. In casual speech, the overall average of the non-standard forms was fairly high, around 55 per cent. In formal speech, when the children were recorded in the presence of their schoolteacher, the percentage dropped to less than half this total, around 25 per cent. The girls seemed more aware of the need to conform to standard English in a formal situation than the boys. There was relatively little difference between the sexes in the number of non-standard forms in casual speech, but in formal speech the girls' percentage of non-standard forms was much lower than the boys': the girls adjusted their speech more sharply in the direction of 'acceptable' English than the boys did. This is shown in the table below, which shows the percentage of non-standard forms in the casual and formal speech of the three groups studied:

	Casual (%)	Formal (%)
Boys (1)	54	27
(2)	66	35
Girls	49	13

We noticed in our discussion of sound change that women tend towards the standard 'prestige' pronunciation. The figures above suggest that this works for word endings also. Further light was shed on this phenomenon when Cheshire analysed the individual speech of each child – an analysis which showed, however, that sex was not the only relevant social factor. More crucial was the extent to which the individual concerned conformed to the demands of the local adolescent subculture which required a youngster to be 'tough'. The use of non-standard verb forms was closely correlated with 'toughness'.

Consider Noddy, the boy who used non-standard forms most often – around 81 per cent of the time. Noddy, the investigator discovered, was one of the 'central core' members of the first boys' group. He scored high on a 'toughness' index, in that he figured in stories about past fights, was reputed to be a good fighter, carried a weapon, took part in shoplifting or in setting fire to buildings, and did not lose his nerve when confronted by a policeman. In addition, Noddy scored high on an 'ambition to do a tough job' index. He wanted to be a slaughterer like his father rather than a teacher or someone who worked in an office or shop. Noddy, then, was seen as a 'tough' central member of his group, and enjoyed considerable social prestige among his contemporaries. The other two boys who had a high percentage of non-standard verb forms in their speech, Perry and Ricky, also had high status among their contemporaries, for the same reasons as Noddy.

Let us compare Noddy with Kevin, a boy who used non-standard forms only 14 per cent of the time. Kevin was not really part of the group at all. He was only around so much because he lived in the pub next door to the playground where the Noddy group met. He was often jeered at and excluded from group activities by the other boys, but seemed to have decided that the best way of getting along with them was to allow himself to be the butt of the group's jokes. His toughness rating was low, and he wanted to do a white-collar job.

Noddy's speech illustrated a finding true of both boys' groups, that the use of non-standard verb forms among the boys was closely correlated with toughness and 'core' membership of a group. What about the girls? The girls did not go in for toughness like the boys. Their interests were generally pop singers and boyfriends. They disliked school, often stayed away, and looked forward to the time when they could leave and, they hoped, get married and have children. Four girls however, Dawn, Margaret, Karen and Linda, stood out from the others in that they attended school regularly, did not swear or steal, and said that the other girls were 'rough' or common. These girls had a far lower percentage of non-standard verb forms in their casual speech, around 26 per cent compared with the 58 per cent which was the average for the rest of the girls.

The pattern of non-standard forms favoured by 'tough' boys, and standard forms used by 'goody-goody' girls strikes a familiar note. The pull between *I knows* and *I know* in Reading was surprisingly similar to the tug-of-war situations in Norwich and Belfast. In each case, the non-standard forms were preferred by males and had covert prestige, whereas the standard forms were favoured by females and had overt prestige.

Where did the Reading boys get forms such as *I knows* and *you knows* from? Did they make them up to be different? No one knows the answer for sure, but there is some evidence that these forms were not an innovation, but a relic from an earlier time when, in south-western dialects of English, there was an *-s* all the way through the present tense: *I knows, you knows, he knows, we knows, they knows.* This verbal paradigm gradually lost ground as Standard British English spread from London. So it is likely that the Reading adolescents were not innovators, but were maintaining an old tradition, and in so doing were delaying a change which may have been spreading towards Standard British English.

So far, the changes discussed have mostly revealed a battle of the sexes, with men pulling one way, and women the other. But this is not always the case, as will be discussed in the next section.

Jocks vs Burnouts

Jocks wanted to follow a conventional lifestyle. Burnouts tried to break away. This was the pattern among teenagers at Belten High, a school in the suburbs of Detroit, in the state of Michigan, USA, studied by Penelope Eckert.[15]

Jocks and Burnouts tried to be as dissimilar as they could: they listened to different music, consumed different substances, hung out in different places, and wore different clothes. Jocks had shirts in pastel colours, and the girls used pale cosmetics. Burnouts wore mostly dark colours, and the girls daubed on dark eye make-up.

Socially, it was important for these teenagers to belong to one group or another. The 'In-betweens' felt marginalized: 'And I was never a jock and I was never a burnout . . . And so that kind of made me feel like a slight outcast, you know. Somebody left in between the realms, you know.'[16]

The two groups appeared to be in part self-consciously creating their own image, which made them as similar to their friends as possible, and as different from those they disliked as could be. Linguistic style formed part of this general attitude, especially 'those aspects of style which are most easily controlled and most easily associated with parts of the social landscape'.[17] So each group adopted particular words, pronunciations, trendy expressions, and intonation patterns.

Take the sound in the first syllable of words such as *mother*, *butter* and *something*, sometimes known as the (uh) variable. This had a wide range of pronunciations. The one preferred by the Jocks was nearest to the standard [ʌ] heard (for example) in British English *hut*, *some*. The Burnouts had a non-standard vowel, somewhat like the sound in British English *put*, *foot* [ʊ]. In-betweens had a pronunciation between these two variants. Similar patterns applied to a range of other correlated vowel sounds: these also reflected the division between the conventional Jocks and the breakaway Burnouts. (Links between vowel changes will be discussed in Chapter 13.)

The most extreme variants were produced by a number of 'burned-out burnout girls'. Gloria and Eunice, for example, were trendsetters. They prided themselves on having many friends, and they were both well liked and well known. Their language, dress and behaviour made them people to imitate. Gloria in particular was flamboyant and outgoing, and described herself as a flirt.

At Belten High, the girls dared to be different, and the boys conformed: 'The female lead in the use of these [linguistic] variables, then, stems from girls' greater inclination and/or freedom to engage in flamboyant stylizing. And the most conservative speakers will be those who are constrained, whether by male gender norms or by shyness to avoid a flamboyant style,' noted Eckert.[18]

The Jocks vs Burnouts study, therefore, revealed that attitude and lifestyle are important: a bold 'get-with-it' approach led a group of trendsetters to push a set of linked changes onwards faster, and these innovators were female.

Immigrant adaptation

Yet another type of social conflict is when new arrivals adapt to changed linguistic circumstances. The situation considered here is not one of learning a new language, but of acquiring some new vocabulary items, and an altered accent.

Six Canadian youngsters from two families moved to southern England in the 1980s.[19] Vocabulary replacement happened faster than pronunciation alterations. For example, *phone box* (instead of *phone booth*), *pushchair* (for *stroller*), *dustbin* (for *garbage can*), *bonnet* (for *hood*) were fairly speedy replacements. Phonological innovations started as variant pronunciations, and seemed to occur via lexical diffusion, creeping from one word to another. Speakers modified their pronunciations of particular words, with the result that some words were affected before others. The elimination of old rules happened faster than the acquisition of new ones: [d] was eliminated inside the word *tomato* fairly swiftly, but the vowel in words such as *bath, class* took longer to reach their British norm. Many more similar studies are needed to be sure that these findings are reliable. But this type of work provides interesting pointers towards future research possibilities.

The topic is by no means straightforward: 'Linguistic diffusion is far more complex than previous work might suggest . . . The diversity of patterns . . . simply reflect the variety of demographic processes at work in a complex society and the complex motives people have for using the variety of language that they use.'[20] This is clearly an important topic for future investigation.

6 Catching on and taking off
How sound changes spread through a language

Large streams from little fountains flow,
Tall oaks from little acorns grow.

David Everett, 'Lines written for a school declamation'

Introduction

This chapter considers the linguistic progress of a sound change, where it starts, and how it makes its way through the language. Frequently used words often (but not inevitably) get affected early. But these words need also to be linguistically susceptible. Typically, the change follows an S-curve (slow-quick-quick-slow) pattern. It starts slowly, then speeds up; eventually it gradually fades away. But as the change happens, individual speakers tend to vary in their treatment of words: on one day, a speaker may use the new form, on another day the old. Neatness may happen in the long run, but not in the course of the change.

Language change spreads in two ways: outwardly through a community, and inwardly through a language. Let us now consider this inner linguistic burrowing. Like a seed, any change is likely to have small beginnings. But if it puts down firm roots, it can develop into a massive growth which affects the whole landscape. This spreading process is the topic of this and the next chapter. This chapter will deal with sound change, and the following with syntactic change.

Just as a seed is likely to enter the ground where the soil is soft, such as a crack between paving stones, so a sound change is likely to creep into a language at a vulnerable point. In the words of Edward Sapir, a sound change is a 'consummated drift that sets in at a psychologically exposed point and worms its way through a gamut of psychologically analogous forms'.[1] We need to know what is meant by 'a psychologically exposed point', and how it 'worms its way through'.

Until relatively recently, this was a question neglected by the majority of linguists, who did not realize that anything needed explaining. It was widely assumed that a sound change affected all the relevant words in a dialect simultaneously. This belief dated back to the so-called Neogrammarians, a group of scholars centred on Leipzig around 1870. In the words of two of the most famous, 'All sound changes, as mechanical processes, take place according to laws with no exceptions'[2] – implying that sound changes were controlled, as it were, by a master switch which altered the sound in question to the same extent in all the words concerned, automatically and simultaneously. This strange assumption was based on the belief that sound changes were purely a matter of physiology, beyond the conscious awareness of the speaker. 'The regularity in the transmission of sounds results from changes in the articulatory system and not the articulation of an isolated word,' said one famous French linguist at the end of the nineteenth century.[3]

Yet when linguists started actually looking at changes instead of simply theorizing about them, they discovered that this supposed mechanical simultaneity was hard to find. At the most, it occurred in only some types of change,[4] or at the beginning of a change.[5] But in many cases, perhaps the majority, a change affected different words at different times – as was clear from even a cursory glance at New York's fluctuating *r*.

Which words were affected in the case of the New York *r*? Was there some consistent pattern? When Labov examined this question, he noticed that some words tended to get affected before others, but even those most affected did not receive the 'new' pronunciation every time. Speakers used different forms of the same word on different days, and, on more than one occasion, different forms of the same word in a single sentence. For example, on one day a New Yorker read the sentence 'He darted out about four feet before a car, and he got hit hard', inserting an *r* into *darted, car* and *hard*. The next time she read it, some days later, she missed out the *r* in *hard*.[6] Similarly, a Martha's Vineyard fisherman used the word *knife* twice within the same sentence, once with a local vowel, and once with a fairly standard one.[7]

It would, however, be a mistake to think that the situation was one of pure chaos. In the start and progress of a change, certain consistent factors are beginning to emerge. We can, with some degree of confidence, build up a profile of a 'typical' change. This is what we shall do in the current chapter.

Getting a foothold

Trying to find out where a change started is like trying to locate the epicentre of an earthquake some years after the event. Our best chance of discovering some general facts about how changes begin, therefore, is to look at changes in progress. We can note which words have been affected, and try to find the reason.

There is a growing body of evidence that frequently used words quite often get affected early – an observation first made in the nineteenth century. As examples, let us look at two changes in English which have started with such words, but have not yet progressed to infrequently used ones. These changes are happening independently in certain varieties of British, American and Australian English.

Consider the words *adultery, century, cursory, delivery, desultory, elementary, every, factory, nursery, slavery*. If possible, write them down on a piece of paper and ask several friends to read them out loud. Better still, get people to read sentences which include the words. For example: *A cursory glance at the newspapers suggests that adultery is on the increase in this century. If you think slavery has been abolished, go and look at the factory at the end of our road. Every mother will tell you that nursery schools are a mixed blessing.* Make a careful note of how the crucial words are pronounced, and see if your results agree with those of a linguist who carried out an investigation of this type.[8]

The investigator noted that, according to the dictionary, all words which are spelt with *-ary, -ery, -ory* or *-ury* are pronounced somewhat as if they rhymed with *furry*. The vowel preceding *r* is a so-called schwa, a short indeterminate sound written phonetically as [ə], and sometimes represented orthographically as *er* (British English) or *uh* (American English). In practice, the schwa was not always pronounced. It was usually omitted in common words such as *ev(e)ry*, *fact(o)ry*, *nurs(e)ry*, which were pronounced as if they were spelt *evry*, *factry*, *nursry* with two syllables only. In slightly less common words, such as *delivery*, there was fluctuation. Some people inserted a schwa, others omitted it. A schwa was retained in the least common words, such as *desultory, cursory*.

A similar thing is happening in another set of words, those with an unstressed first syllable.[9] Say the names of the months through to yourself, at normal conversational speed. The last four, *September*, *October*, *November*, *December*, all have an unstressed first syllable. If an unstressed first syllable is followed by a single consonant, it is common for the vowel in this syllable to be reduced to schwa, as in *November*, *December*. But if the unstressed vowel is followed by two consonants, as in *September*, *October*, the full original vowel normally remains. This has been the situation for some time. Recently, however, schwa has started to creep into the first syllable of common words when two consonants follow. In conversation, the words *mistake*, *astronomy*, *mosquito* and *despair* quite often have schwa in their first syllable, whereas less common words with a similar structure, such as *mistook*, *esquire* and *muscology* (the study of mosses), retain a fuller vowel. This phenomenon can also be observed intermittently in the conversation of people talking about places, objects and activities which they refer to often. For instance, Australians reduce the first vowel in the word *Australia*, while the rest of the world tends to use the full vowel. New Yorkers reduce the first vowel in *Manhattan*, and professional trombonists do the same with the first vowel in *trombone*.

To take another example, read the following sentences aloud:

Bill's gone to play football
Daisy followed the footpath
The door was opened by a footman
The coach was attacked by a footpad.

If you live in England, then instead of *t* [t] in the very common word *football*, you probably produced a glottal stop [ʔ], a change currently working through Standard British English. But the *t* is likely to have become more distinct in *footpath* and *footman*, and be most noticeable in the fairly rare word *footpad*.

The effect of frequency is possibly detectable in a change happening in certain Dravidian languages, a group of languages spoken mainly in southern India and Sri Lanka.[10] This particular change is progressing exceptionally slowly. It has been going on now for around two millennia, and is apparently still in progress. In it, *r* in the middle of words is gradually making its way to the front. For example, **ūz-* 'to plough' became ūr- then rū-. Because the change is moving so slowly, it has been possible to discover from past records which words were affected first. They turn out to be words fundamental to the culture, such as those for 'two', 'moon', 'month', 'burn', 'open', 'enter', which are also presumably relatively frequent ones.

But frequency or importance in a culture are not the only factors to be taken into consideration. Words can only be in the forefront of a change if they are linguistically susceptible to that particular change. In every change, there are likely to be factors which are outside the conscious control of the speakers. This is illustrated at its simplest by the loss of schwa in words such as *fam(i)ly, ev(e)ry*. The words in the vanguard of this particular change are not only frequent ones, but also those in which the resulting new sequence of consonants is easy to pronounce. The change has not affected common words such as *burglary* or *forgery*, where the resulting new sequence would be the unusual and difficult-to-pronounce combinations [glr] and [dʒr].

A less obvious example of linguistic susceptibility occurred in the Martha's Vineyard changes, where words beginning with a vowel tended to be the most affected, so that *I* was more susceptible than *my*, and *out* more than *trout*. Similarly, words ending in *t* tended to be more involved than those ending in *d* or *n*, so *right* and *night* were more affected than *side* and *tide*, and *out* and *trout* more than *down* and *round*.[11]

The Belfast changes provided further examples of concealed linguistic factors.[12] Take the change in which 'Irish' [a] is moving towards standard [e], so that *bed*, once pronounced *bad* [bad], is now moving towards its British English pronunciation of *bed* [bed]. Some words were hanging behind in this change, and intermittently resisting the general movement towards [e]. The dawdling words almost always had a voiceless stop following the vowel, as in *jat* [dʒat] for 'jet', *nack* [nak] for 'neck'. (A voiceless stop is a sound such as [p], [t] or [k], in which the vocal cords do not vibrate, and there is a complete stoppage of air.)

A change is therefore most likely to 'get its foot in the door' in places where frequency of usage is combined with linguistic susceptibility. However, although such words *may* be in the vanguard of a change, they are not invariably so. They may, in other circumstances, retard or even be left out of changes, as in the case of the verb *to be*, which is irregular and archaic in form in many of the world's languages. In short, 'frequent words can do exceptional things'.[13]

Once a change has got a firm foothold in certain words, it will probably catch on and spread to others. Let us now look at this process of 'catching on'.

Catching on

A change therefore gets started in a few common words, or a group of words important to a particular subculture. It is then likely to start moving through the vocabulary. This is a messy business, with different words affected at different times. Amidst general fluctuation, change spreads gradually across the lexicon (vocabulary) of the language, one or two words at a time. This word-by-word progress is known as **lexical diffusion**.[14]

A Welsh change is instructive.[15] Words beginning with *chw*- such as *chwaer* 'sister', *chwannen* 'flea', were at one time pronounced with a soft *khw*-like sound [xw] at the beginning ([x] symbolizes the sound at the end of Scottish *loch*, which in these Welsh words was combined with [w] as in *wet*). Then this initial consonant began to disappear, first in South Wales, then in Central Wales, and finally in the north. When the progress of this change was examined, an interesting phenomenon emerged. Even when the initial sequence *chw*- was followed by the same vowel, different words lost their initial consonant at different times. Take the three words *chwarae* 'to play', *chwannen* 'flea', and *chwaer* 'sister' in Figure 6.1. One of these three words was likely to lose its initial consonant without there being any alteration in the other two at

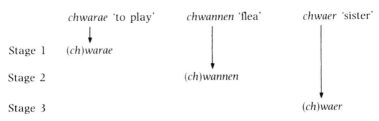

Figure 6.1   Consonant loss in three Welsh words

first. Then the change was likely to affect one of the remaining two, then all three.

Lexical diffusion can also be seen in a slow-moving change that is creeping through English, affecting the stress pattern of certain nouns with two syllables.[16] Read out loud the sentence, 'He hid the treasure in a recess in the wall,' and ask other people to do so too. Where did you and your informants place the stress on the word *recess*? According to the 1982 edition of the *Concise Oxford Dictionary*, it should be accented on the last syllable, *recéss*. But many people in England and almost everybody in America now place the stress on the first syllable, *récess*. The history of this ongoing change goes back five centuries or so. In the early sixteenth century, there were a number of two-syllable words which could be either a verb or a noun. All of these were stressed on the second syllable. The stress shift began, apparently, in the second half of the sixteenth century. By 1570, according to a dictionary published at the time, the stress on three nouns, *outlaw, rebel* and *record*, had moved to the first syllable, giving pairs such as *récord*, noun, as in 'We keep a *récord* of Fergus's cute little sayings', and *recórd*, verb, as in 'We recórd Fergus's cute little sayings'. Twelve years later, in 1582, another five items had been added. There were 24 by 1660, 35 by 1700, 70 by 1800, and 150 by 1934, according to one count. This gradual climb through the vocabulary is illustrated in Figure 6.2. In spite of the seemingly large number of words affected, such as *áddict, áffix, cónvict* and *défect*, there are still around 1,000 which the change has not yet reached, such as *mistáke, dislíke, repórt*. One that is wavering at the current time is *address*, as in *What's your **address?*** Some people, particularly Americans, say *áddress*, others still prefer

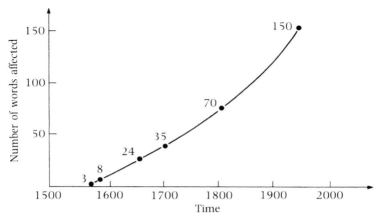

Figure 6.2   Stress shift in nouns such as *convict*

addréss. Since the change seems to be working its way through the language, it is likely that *áddress* will become the standard form, and that other words, as yet unaffected, will begin to waver.

Taking off: S-curves

Can we say anything more about the way a change diffuses? One obvious question involves the rate of diffusion. Does a change proceed through a language at a steady pace, like a tortoise climbing up a hill? Or does it leap forward by fits and starts? Or is there any other discernible pattern? Research suggests that a typical change fits into a slow-quick-quick-slow pattern.

In the majority of cases, an innovation starts slowly, affecting relatively few words. When a certain number have been affected, the innovation gathers momentum. There comes a sudden take-off point when a great number of words are affected in a relatively short time span. Then, when the bulk of the change has been completed, the momentum appears to slacken, or even peter out, leaving a handful of words which lag behind the others. These might eventually change, or they might not. A change appears to clear up this residue very slowly, if at all, like someone who has swept a floor

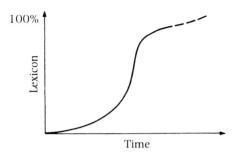

Figure 6.3   S-curve progression of sound change (based on Chen, 1972)

with mighty effort, but just cannot be bothered to clear away the last few cobwebs.

When plotted on a graph, this slow-quick-quick-slow progression shows a characteristic S-curve.[17] As many linguists now agree, 'the time course of the propagation of a language change typically follows an S-curve'.[18] This is shown in Figure 6.3. This is now a generally accepted pattern: 'The S-curve has ... been observed in diffusion of all kinds ... and is now established as a kind of template of change.'[19] At first, when diffusion is slow, the line on the graph runs almost parallel to the horizontal time axis. At a certain critical point, it climbs sharply, then again it flattens out.

An example of a change which is now complete, and so shows a characteristic S-curve, is found in spoken French in words such as *an* 'year', *en* 'in', *fin* 'end', *bon* 'good', *brun* 'brown'.[20] Over several centuries, the final [n] was lost, and the preceding vowel was nasalized (pronounced with the air expelled partially through the nose). This is illustrated in Figure 6.4. As can be seen, this change started relatively slowly in the tenth and eleventh centuries. It speeded up in the twelfth and thirteenth, then slowed down again in the fourteenth.

Overlapping S-curves

The slow-quick-quick-slow pattern of an S-curve is found in a large number of changes. A closer look at each S-curve, however,

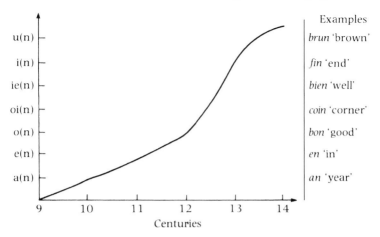

Figure 6.4   Change in French words ending in *-n*

suggests that many S-curves are themselves composed of smaller S-curves. Each little S-curve covers one particular linguistic environment. Take the loss of final *n* in French, an S-curve which stretched over five centuries or so. It seems likely that each separate vowel had a smaller S-curve within the big S-curve. So the loss of *n* after *a*, as in *an* 'year', itself occurred as a little S-curve. The change spread to a few examples of *-an*, then to the majority, then finally rounded up the few remaining stragglers. After this it proceeded to *-en*, following the same procedure. However, the stragglers in *-an* overlapped with the earliest *-en* changes, so in effect we have a series of overlapping S-curves, as in Figure 6.5. The French changes happened several centuries ago, but sometimes current S-curve changes can be found.

A series of overlapping S-curves actually in progress was found in the Shuang-Feng dialect of Chinese.[21] In this dialect, a change is altering voiced stops at the beginning of words into voiceless ones. (A voiced stop is one whose production involves the vibration of the vocal cords as in [b], [d], [g], as opposed to voiceless stops such as [p], [t], [k], in which the vocal cords do not vibrate.) Chinese, unlike English, distinguishes between words not only via

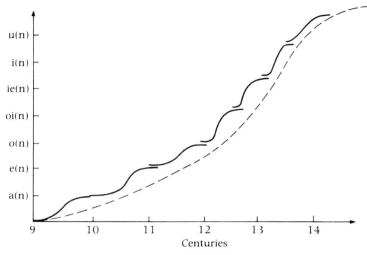

Figure 6.5   Overlapping S-curves (French words ending in *-n*)

contrasts between the actual sounds pronounced, but also via the tone or pitch of the voice. This particular change moved from tone to tone, starting with tone IV, in a series of overlapping S-curves. The situation (as documented in 1972) is shown below:

Tone	Number of words	Voiced (unchanged)	Voiceless (changed)	(%)
IV	88	4	84	95.45
III	140	120	20	14.29
II	100	90	10	10
I	288	286	2	0.7

These figures can be interpreted as follows: a change was in progress altering voiced stops at the beginning of words into voiceless ones. This change reached tone IV words first. Here 95.45 per cent of possible words already had the new pronunciation, so the change was almost complete for this tone. The change had started on tone III, and with 14.29 per cent of words affected, had perhaps reached take-off point. Tone II was following relatively closely behind tone III. Tone I was virtually unaffected, with only two altered words.

The tendency of a change to spread from one linguistic environment to another is sometimes referred to by linguists as rule generalization, a name which is self-explanatory, since a linguistic rule becomes **generalized** to an ever wider range of environments. Rule generalization can sometimes be deceptive, since later generations may misinterpret a series of overlapping events as one single sweeping catastrophe. Some people, for example, assume that in French there was a sudden and sweeping loss of final *n*, when in fact there was a series of overlapping events which occurred over the course of centuries.

In recent years, a controversy has arisen as to whether all changes fit this S-curve pattern. Were the Neogrammarians totally wrong in their belief that sound changes are simultaneous 'mechanical processes', or only partly mistaken? Mostly, they were wrong because they looked at the end result of a change, which provided a spurious picture of neatness and tidiness.

But a few changes *may* take place simultaneously due to phonetic processes which are caused by the nature of the sounds themselves (to be discussed in Chapter 11). In the Southern United States, if someone asks you for a *pin*, what do they want? Most probably a *pen*, a writing implement. A nasal consonant [m], [n] or [ŋ] sometimes causes the vowel [e] to move towards [i], as in the pronunciation of the words *employ*, *enough*, *England* – and a change of this type may affect several words simultaneously. So the Neogrammarian claims may be right in certain circumstances.[22]

Summarizing the spread

Let us now summarize how a sound change spreads within a language. Any change tends to start in a small way, affecting a few words. At first, there is fluctuation between the new forms and the old, within the same speaker, and sometimes within the same style of speech. Gradually the new forms oust the old. When the innovation has spread to a certain number of words, the change appears to take off, and spreads rapidly in a relatively short time span.

After a period of momentum, it is likely to slacken off, and the residue is cleared slowly, if at all. The slow beginning, rapid acceleration, then slow final stages can be diagrammed as an S-curve, which represents the profile of a typical change. Yet changes do not, on the whole, happen in isolated bursts. One original change is likely to expand and spread to progressively more linguistic environments in a series of related changes (rule generalization), though a series of related changes might appear to future generations as one single, massive change, especially if written records are sparse.

The spread of a sound change from one word to another has led to a further insight, on the links between sound change and other types of change. The Neogrammarians thought that sound change was a disruptive factor, tugging apart the patterns of language. It was the task of analogy – reasoning from parallel cases – to smooth out the chaos left by sound change, they assumed, as when *cows* formed parallel to *cow* replaced earlier *kine* (to be discussed further in Chapter 12).

But most sound changes are themselves a kind of analogy, as words copy each other's sound patterns. 'Genuine instances of "lexical diffusion" . . . are *all* the result of analogical change . . . "It walks like analogy, it talks like analogy,"' as Paul Kiparsky expressed it.[23]

An uninterrupted sound change is likely to be 'regular' in that it will eventually spread to all, or most, of the relevant words. Regularity, however, does not mean simultaneity, since different words are affected at different times. Nor does it mean a regular rate of attrition. A change affects a few words first, then a vast number in quick succession, then the final few. The process is not unlike that of leaves falling off a tree. A few are blown off in August, but the vast majority whirl down in September and October, while a few stubborn remnants cling till November or even December.

But the image of leaves falling off trees may oversimplify the situation: it implies that a change happens in definite steps, leaf by leaf, as the wind blows. Yet in many cases, the old form co-exists alongside the new, as discussed in Chapters 4–5. So a different image is required, as will be outlined below.

From tadpoles to cuckoos to multiple births

A tadpole-to-frog view of sound change[24] prevailed in the nineteenth century, and also in the first half of the twentieth. A linguistic tadpole gradually changed into a frog, it was assumed, in a slow and undetectable process. But this has proved unrealistic.

A young cuckoo model then took over. A new variant arises alongside the old. For a time, they co-exist, with both versions in use. Then the new typically ousts the old. It behaves like a young cuckoo who at first lives alongside the other nestlings. Then, as it gets bigger, it pushes an existing inhabitant out of the nest.

But even the young cuckoo picture may be oversimple. Often, several forms compete in a multiple-births scenario, somewhat as if a whole nestful of chicks fought against one another, each trying to outdo the others. In linguistic terms, 'we may best understand the basic mechanism of diachronic change in terms of a kind of competition between, or selection from among, a pool of variants'.[25] It may take decades, or even centuries, for one variant to achieve supremacy.

This chapter has looked at sound change. The next chapter will look at how syntactic change occurs – change in the form and order of words – and consider to what extent it is similar, or dissimilar to sound change.

7 Caught in the web
How syntactic changes work through a language

> With as little a web as this will I ensnare as great a fly.
> William Shakespeare, *Othello*

Introduction

Syntactic change typically creeps into a language via optional stylistic variants. Particular lexical items provide a toehold. The change tends to become widely used via ambiguous structures. One or some of these get increasingly preferred, and in the long run the dispreferred options fade away through disuse. Mostly, speakers are unaware that such changes are taking place. Overall, all changes, whether phonetic/phonological, morphological, or syntactic, take place gradually, and also spread gradually. There is always fluctuation between the old and the new. Then the changes tend to move onward and outward, becoming the norm among one group of speakers before moving on to the next.

To a superficial observer, alterations in syntax attack without warning. Like a hidden spider's web, they lie in wait and stealthily catch on to pieces of language, which are suddenly entrapped in inescapable silken threads.

Syntactic change – change in the form and order of words – is therefore sometimes described as 'an elusive process as compared to sound change'.[1] Its apparently puzzling nature is partly due to its variety. Word endings can be modified. Chaucer's line *And smale foweles maken melodye*[2] shows that English has changed several of them in the last 600 years. The behaviour of verbs can alter. Middle English *I kan a noble tale*[3] 'I know a fine story' reveals that *can* was once a main verb. And word order may switch. The proverb *Whoever loved that loved not at first sight?*[4] indicates that English negatives could once be placed after main verbs. These are just a random sample of syntactic changes which have occurred in English in the last half-millennium or so.

It's hard to chart syntactic change. If a schoolboy says *I didn't bash Pete, I never bashed Pete*, are the two different negative structures interchangeable, signalling that a change may be in progress? Or is the second statement emphatic, meaning: 'I really and truly didn't bash Pete'? It's almost impossible to tell.[5]

But one thing is certain. All syntactic change involves variation. As in the case of sound change, the old and the new co-exist. As we have already seen, the Reading teenagers (Chapter 5) sometimes added non-standard *-s* to verbs (*I sees, we knows*) and sometimes they didn't. Or take Indian English (as spoken in Delhi, India). This is slowly moving away from British English. Fluent speakers often produce sentences which sound odd to people in England; for example:

> Your friend went home yesterday, isn't it?
> We have a party tonight – why don't you come and enjoy?
> I am understanding the lesson now.

Surveys of these constructions among Indians showed that not all of them accepted these supposed 'Indianisms' as 'good English'.[6] A number of Indians from South Delhi, a smart, Westernized section of the city, were asked to judge how acceptable they found various constructions claimed to be typical of Indian English. In almost all cases, the responses were mixed. For example, the use of *enjoy* with nothing after it was judged to be perfectly all right in all situations by about one-third of the respondents, but two-thirds said it was all right in casual, but not in formal, speech. This shows the stylistic and social variation typical of changes in progress.

Fluctuation between the old and the new is characteristic of changes in the past as well as the present. Shakespeare's characters vary between using questions in which the main verb and the pronoun switch places, as in 'Talk'st thou to me of ifs?',[7] and those in which *do* is inserted, as is normal today: 'Dost thou call me fool, boy?'[8] – and similar variation is found in other records of past speech.[9]

All change, therefore, involves variation. The reverse is not necessarily true. Variation can exist without change. Stylistic variation (such as *The octopus which/that I caught*) can persist for decades, or even centuries, without necessarily involving a change. However, variation creates a situation in which change can easily occur. Let us consider how this might happen.

Varying the options

All of these pens don't work
Evidence that it is not so has come recently
Three all-India ski champions told this reporter that even Kashmir had not had enough snow for skiing.

These sentences of Indian English tend to get mixed reactions from non-Indians. In the case of the first sentence, speakers of British English would definitely prefer *None of these pens work*. But in the others, the situation is not so straightforward. They're a bit peculiar to British ears, but they're not really wrong. On closer examination, it turns out that Indians and British people have virtually the same range of negative constructions. Their preferences differ, however, showing one of the mechanisms by which dialects drift further apart.

Fifty fluent speakers of Indian English, and fifty British university students were asked to turn a number of sentences into their opposites, in as many ways as they could.[10] For example:

I think I'm capable of working all night.

produced one quite extraordinary sentence from one student:

I deny that I'm incapable of not working all night.

but mostly elicited predictable responses such as:

I think I'm not capable of working all night
I think I'm incapable of working all night
I don't think I'm capable of working all night.

Surprisingly, perhaps, the Indians and the English provided almost equal numbers of possible opposites, and they used the same constructions for doing this. However, differences showed up in preferred constructions. Those taking part had all been asked to list their answers in order of preference. The Indians preferred to have an overt negative near the verb it negated, as in:

I think I'm not capable of working all night
We decided that Ahmed was not telling the truth.

The English avoided overt negatives in this position, preferring sentences such as:

I don't think I'm capable of working all night
We decided that Ahmed was lying.

There are various possible reasons for this result. Hindi, the language spoken by most of the Indians, tends to have overt negatives next to the verb, for a start. But the interest lies in what this experiment revealed about syntactic change in general. It showed that change occurs when the balance gets tipped towards one or the other of existing options.

To take another example, French has two ways of saying a sentence such as 'Lulu is at home'. You could either say: *Lulu est à la maison* (Lulu is at the house), or, more idiomatically, *Lulu est chez elle* (Lulu is at-home-belonging her). In Canadian French, in the area around Ontario where contact with English is highest, the first option is gaining ground, probably because of its greater similarity to the English version.[11]

To take a further example,[12] English today can use verbal nouns in two ways:

the writing of this book was a difficult job
writing this book was a difficult job

But in preceding centuries, further options were available, which are now no longer permitted:

*the writing this book was a difficult job
*writing of this book was a difficult job

This is shown by the following sentences:

The writing the verbs . . . on this slate will be a very useful exercise (1829)
She is fallen to *eating of chalk*. (1712)

In present-day English, however, the last two constructions are no longer possible, and four options have been whittled down to two.

The varying of options is therefore an important mechanism of syntactic change, as it is with sound change. However, the cases discussed so far are ones in which options already exist in the language. Let us now consider how variants might creep in in the first place.

Creeping in

Syntactic variants often infiltrate the language in an almost underhand way, sneaking in unseen like a disease which can get a hold on a person before it is diagnosed. Or, to use a more positive metaphor, they creep in like a deep friendship which grows unnoticed. On closer investigation, they nearly always steal in at a single, vulnerable point in the language, at a place where it is possible to reinterpret the structure in a new way, as the following examples show.

A change is creeping in almost unnoticed in Brazilian Portuguese, gradually destroying the distinction between singular and plural verb endings.[13] At one time, there was a clear difference between singular *come* 'eats' and plural *comem* 'eat'. Then in fast speech, a number of speakers began to omit the final *m* in this type of verb. At first, the vowel had a nasal twang to it, then this disappeared, leaving the singular and plural identical. So it's possible to hear sentences such as:

Eles come banana com mel
'They eat bananas with honey.'

with *come* instead of *comem*. So a distinction that was hard to hear in fast speech simply disappeared. This led to a general feeling that there was no need to make a difference between singular and plural verbs. The change is now creeping onward to other types of verbs – ones in which singular and plural forms are less alike than the *come/comem* type – but it is leaving till last verbs which are quite different, as with *é/são* 'is/are'. The author of the study noted: 'The change thus sets in at the zero point of surface differentiation between the old and the new systems, and so spreads to other points along the path of least surface differentiation.'[14]

A similar sneaky manoeuvre was performed in Middle English by the English verb *can*.[15] To begin with, English *can* meant 'know', as in *Ne can ic eow* (not know I you) 'I don't know you', *I kan a noble tale* 'I know a fine story'. Before another verb, it meant 'know how to'. This 'know how to' meaning could easily be reinterpreted as 'be able to':

> The cat kan klimbe suthe well
> 'The cat knows how to / is able to climb pretty well.'

Ambiguous sentences of this type allowed the ability meaning to creep in and become established, and laid the groundwork for a gradual reanalysis of the verb as an auxiliary, a subsidiary verb which could not stand alone.

A similar reanalysis has taken place more recently, in Tok Pisin, a pidgin (restricted language) spoken in Papua New Guinea.[16] In Tok Pisin, *save* 'know' is found as a main verb in sentences such as:

> God i save olgeta samting
> (God PRT (= PARTICLE) know everything something)
> 'God knows everything.'

Like English *can*, Tok Pisin *save* developed a meaning of 'know how to', 'be skilled at', when it occurred before another verb. As in English, this was ambiguous, and was in this case reinterpreted as 'be in the habit of', 'be accustomed to', as in:

> Mi save kukim kaukau
> 'I know how to / am accustomed to cook yams.'

and in the following toothpaste advertisement:

> Planti switpela kaikai i save bagarapim tit bilong yu hariap
> (lots sweet food PRT know-how-to wreck teeth of you fast)
> 'Lots of sugary foods are skilled at / are accustomed to wreck your teeth fast.'

Once again, ambiguous sentences laid the basis for the gradual development of an auxiliary verb meaning 'be accustomed to, be in the habit of', found with its new meaning in:

Yu save smok?
'Do you smoke?'

This auxiliary *save* is now often shortened to *sa*, which distinguishes it from main verb *save* which still exists.

A further example of a change creeping in via ambiguous sentences occurred with English verbs such as *like* and *lack*. Originally, these verbs behaved somewhat differently from the way they do today, in that the person liking or lacking was usually an object of the verb, and the thing they liked or lacked was the subject. So we get sentences such as 'Something pleases me, something lacks me', as in the following Old English examples from around 1,000 years ago:[17]

Hu him se sige gelicade
(how to-him the victory pleased)
'How the victory pleased him!'

Ac Gode ne licode na heora geleafleast
(but to-God not pleased not-at-all their faithlessness)
'But their faithlessness did not please God at all.'

Numerous verbs once behaved in this way, but many of them dropped out of existence. Alongside these *like, lack* verbs there were many others which by Chaucer's time (the fourteenth century) were used identically to verbs today:

He knew the tavernes well in every toun
He loved chivalrie, trouthe and honour
He hadde a semely nose.[18]

Around this time, the *like, lack* verbs switched themselves around to behave like ordinary verbs. The change crept in in places where a *like*-type verb was bracketed with a normal verb:[19]

Arthur loked on the swerd and liked it passynge well
'Arthur looked at the sword and it pleased him enormously.'

Strictly speaking, this should be *him liked it* (to-him pleased it). But *him* was omitted. A similar example occurs in:

Lewed men leued hym well and liked his wordes
'Ignorant men loved him well, and his words pleased [them].'

Here, *them* has been omitted. In both these cases, the person being pleased has been left out, because it's obvious. But this minor omission shows how the switch-around of verbs is likely to sneak in, infiltrating itself at a 'zero point in surface differentiation'. These occasional examples let in variants, which later took over.

Syntactic change, therefore, like sound change, moves in as a variant in a single environment. It sneaks in, like a mouse through a very small hole in the floor, at a single point where there is a possibility of analysing the structure in more than one way.

To put it another way:

> speakers in the process of using – and thus of changing – their language often act as if they were in a fog, by which is meant not that they are befuddled but that they see clearly only immediately around them, so to speak, and only in a clouded manner farther afield. They thus generalize only 'locally' . . . and not globally over vast expanses of data, and they exercise their linguistic insights only through a small 'window of opportunity' over a necessarily small range of data.[20]

Let us now consider how syntactic change manages to get a firm toehold.

Clutching on to words

Changes in syntax clutch on to particular lexical items, even more noticeably than in sound change. This is perhaps what enables them to get a strong grip on the language.

Consider the Reading teenagers (Chapter 5).[21] They had a number of 'special' verbs, verbs which are either not used in Standard English, or are used with a different meaning. For example:

We fucking *chins* them with bottles. (*chin* 'hit on the chin')
We *bunks* it over here a lot. (*bunk* 'play truant')
We *kills* them. (*kill* 'beat in a fight')
I *legs it* up Blagdon Hill. (*leg it* 'run away')

The non-standard *-s* ending was attached to these verbs over 90 per cent of the time in all three groups of teenagers studied, whereas the non-standard *-s* was added to other verbs only around 50 per cent of the time.

A change is catching on to groups of words in Tok Pisin (Papua New Guinea) as it develops plural forms.[22] There are two primary ways of marking plurals. The main one is by placing *ol* in front of a noun, as in *ol man* 'men' vs *man* 'man'. A subsidiary method is by adding English *-s*, as in *frens* 'friends'. Sometimes both are found, as in *ol frens*. At the moment, plural marking is variable, but it is not random. *Ol* seems to have started out by becoming attached to the names of people and places: *ol Tolai* 'the Tolai', *ol Hailans* 'the Highlanders', *ol Jerusalem* 'the inhabitants of Jerusalem', *king bilong ol Juda* 'king of the Jews' (the last two being translations from the New Testament). It has since spread to all humans: *ol man* 'men', *ol meri* 'women', *ol pikinini* 'children'. But it is variable with inanimate things, so 'leaves' could be either *lips* or *ol lip*, 'stones' could be *stons* or *ol ston*. Meanwhile, the English *-s* is found on a variety of words, but particularly often on words relating to time and date, such as *minits* 'minutes', *auas* 'hours', *wiks* 'weeks'.

In French, a two-part negative may be in the process of getting simpler.[23] French forms its negatives by putting *ne* in front of the verb and *pas* afterwards, producing pairs such as *Je sais* 'I know' vs *Je ne sais pas* 'I do not know'. The first section *ne* of this two-part negative is increasingly being left out in everyday casual speech. It is left out particularly often in a few common phrases:

Je sais pas, (also) je pas
'I don't know'

C'est pas
'It isn't'

Il faut pas
'One shouldn't'.

A further case occurs in the Spanish of some Mexican-Americans living in Los Angeles.[24] Standard Spanish has two words meaning 'is', *es* for permanent properties (*El edificio es redondo* 'The building is round'), and *está* for temporary ones (*La taza está vacía* 'The cup is empty'). However, the word *está* is taking over, moving onwards in a semi-orderly fashion, in that some types of words are affected before others. It is now used quite often in descriptions of size and age (*Está muy alta la muchacha* 'She's very tall, that girl') but is still fairly rare when it describes things that are sweet or hot, or anything else perceived by taste, smell or hearing.

All these examples suggest that people get acclimatized to a change by hearing it repeatedly attached to a few prominent lexical items. These provide the toehold needed for it to be carried further. However, hooking on to a few lexical items is insufficient to guarantee that a change will definitely take off – even though it's likely. As with sound change, there are hidden linguistic factors which can either push forward or hold back a change. Each of the changes mentioned above had some of these hidden factors, which were beyond the speakers' control.

In Reading,[25] for example, the adolescents invariably used standard forms such as *I know, I believe, I think*, in certain types of complex sentence (sentences which contain more than one verb). If, in a sentence with a main verb and a subordinate verb, the subordinate verb had an ending *-s*, then the teenagers always omitted the *-s* from the first main verb, as in:

> I *believe* that there is, you know, life after death.
> You *know* if anything breaks on that pushchair . . .

This phenomenon occurred even in the speech of Noddy, who used non-standard verb forms most of the time.

In the Tok Pisin plurals,[26] English *-s* was intermittently added to quite a lot of nouns describing humans: *frens* 'friends', *sistas* 'sisters', *bratas* 'brothers'. But there were no examples of *pikininis or *meris. This subconscious avoidance seemed to be partly due to a dislike of adding *-s* to words ending in *-i*, and partly due to a dislike of adding it to words which were not similar to English ones.

In the change in the French negative,[27] *ne* was never omitted at the beginning of a sentence, so commands always kept the full negative, as in:

> Ne touchez pas!
> 'Don't touch!'

These examples therefore show that changes get a foothold by hooking on to particular items. Then unseen linguistic factors can either push forward or retard a change. People are usually unaware of these hidden factors, and so have no control over them.

Syntactic snowballs

Syntactic changes therefore have a number of similarities with sound change. They involve variation. They get a foothold in a particular environment, often associated with particular lexical items. In some cases at least, they follow the typical S-curve slow-quick-quick-slow pattern associated with sound change. They start out slowly, then, like a snowball bounding down a hill under its own impetus, they suddenly gather up numerous other environments. Then they slow down.

This snowball-like progress is evident in the history of English modal verbs, such as *can, may, shall, must, will*.[28] Today, they behave rather differently from ordinary verbs, as can be seen from the chart below, which indicates some of the major differences between a modal such as *must* and an ordinary verb such as *wash*. (An asterisk signifies an impossible sentence.) Originally, none of these differences existed. Modals could occur with direct objects, as in *Yet can I musick too* 'Yet I can make music too', after *to*, as in *to may*, and with an *-ing* suffix, as in *maeyinge*. Meanwhile, ordinary verbs could undergo inversion and be followed by the negative *not*, as shown by a number of lines of Shakespeare: 'Thinkst thou I'd make a life of jealousy?'[29] 'You go not, till I set you up a glass . . . '[30]

	Modal	Ordinary verb
Direct object	*Alice musted the cat	Alice washed the cat
to + verb	*To must the cat was stupid	To wash the cat was stupid
Verb + *-ing*	*Musting the cat was stupid	Washing the cat was stupid
Inversion	Must Alice try again?	*Washes Alice again?
Modal + *not*	Alice must not try again	*Alice washes not again

The separation of modals from other verbs happened gradually. First, they stopped taking direct objects. Then in the sixteenth century came a bunch of changes. They no longer occurred with *-ing* or after *to*, they were no longer found with *have*, and they were limited to one per sentence. In the seventeenth century, ordinary verbs stopped undergoing inversion, and no longer preceded the negative *not*. However, as with other changes, there are still a few remnants which never got swept away. Occasional instances are preserved in proverbial or biblical phrases: 'He who knows not and knows that he knows not, can be taught.'[31] In brief, we seem to have a syntactic S-curve, with the steep part of the curve occurring in the sixteenth century.

Another change which seems to be following an S-curve pattern in present-day English involves the so-called 'progressive'.[32] This construction consists of part of the verb *to be* followed by a verb ending in *-ing*, as in *Tom is having a bath*, or *Felix is drinking whisky*. It is called the 'progressive' because it is, or was, mainly used to indicate that an action was currently in progress, as in the examples above, which suggest that Tom is actually in the process of having a bath, and Felix is halfway through a glass of whisky.

The construction started slowly. Occasional progressive forms are found in the English of 1,000 years ago, in the heroic epic *Beowulf*, and in King Alfred's translations from Latin. It occurs from time to time in Shakespeare. For example, at one point Antony says, 'I am dying, Egypt, dying',[33] though a little earlier he had said, 'I come, my queen',[34] when it would sound more natural to us to say, 'I'm coming.' Since then, there has been a gradual increase in the use of the progressive. It is now the normal form for an ongoing action. Anyone who said 'What do you read, my lord?', as Polonius did to Hamlet,[35] instead of 'What are you reading?' would be considered very odd. In addition, the progressive has now spread beyond its original use of indicating an action in progress. Increasingly, we hear people saying things like *Tom is having a bath as soon as Arabella is out of the bathroom*, or *Felix is tired of whisky, he's drinking gin these days*, when at the time of the conversation, Tom is possibly washing his car, and Felix is cleaning his teeth.

Furthermore, there used to be a set of verbs expressing mental states which were never normally used with the progressive, even when they indicated an action in progress, as in:

Ursula loves God (not *Ursula is loving God)
Angela knows my brother (not *Angela is knowing my brother)
I understand French (not *I am understanding French).

Nowadays, however, one hears an increasing number of sentences in which mental-state verbs are found with the progressive:

> Billy is kissing Petronella, and *is loving* it.
> Charles *is understanding* French a lot better since he's been to France.
> The matron does not know all she should *be knowing* about this affair.[36]
> We're certainly hoping they'll *be wanting* to do it again.[37]

A related change is the sudden expansion of *going to*, to express the future. This construction occurred occasionally in Shakespeare, usually when someone was literally on his way to do something, as in 'I am going to visit the prisoner,'[38] meaning 'I am on my way to visit the prisoner.' In Dickens' novel *Oliver Twist*, written in the mid nineteenth century, it occurs twenty-four times and accounts for 4 per cent of expressions of future time. In Salinger's *Catcher in the rye*, written in the mid twentieth century, it occurs seventy-five times, accounting for around 30 per cent of expressions of future time.[39] This is a construction whose progress is likely to be interesting for some time to come.

Syntactic change typically takes place more slowly than sound change, and smooth S-curves are hard to find. This has raised the question of whether they truly exist in syntactic change.[40] However, researchers have not yet teased out the particular vocabulary items involved. These need to be identified before any firm conclusions can be reached.

Gradual implementation, gradual spread

We have now looked both at the spread of a change from person to person, and at its implementation within the language. In theory, this could have happened in one of four different ways:

1   sudden implementation, sudden spread;
2   sudden implementation, gradual spread;
3   gradual implementation, sudden spread;
4   gradual implementation, gradual spread.

As we have seen, only the last possibility, gradual implementation and gradual spread, represents the true state of affairs. Changes catch on gradually, both within a language and when moving from person to person. At first, there is fluctuation between the new and the old. Then, the new form takes over, ousting the old. Changes move outward and onward in an ordered way. Within the language, they typically saturate one linguistic environment at a time. Within the community, they become the norm among one particular group of speakers before moving on to the next.

Although we have now analysed *how* changes spread, we have not yet considered in any depth *why* they occur. In the following chapters, we shall look at the whole question of causation in more depth.

But before we discuss causes in general, we need to consider reductions and abbreviations, which have escalated in recent years, partly due to the growth of text messaging.

8 The wheels of language
Reductions and abbreviations

> Abbreviations are the wheels of language, the wings of
> Mercury. And though we might be dragged along
> without them, it would be with much difficulty, very
> heavily and tediously . . . Words have been called
> *winged* . . . but compared with the speed of thought, they
> have not the smallest claim to that title . . . What wonder,
> then, that the invention of all ages should have been . . . to
> add such wings to their conversation as might enable it, if
> possible, to keep pace in some measure with their minds.
>
> John Horne Tooke, *The diversions of Purley* (1786)[1]

Introduction

This chapter discusses reductions and abbreviations, known in
more modern terms as grammaticalization and text messaging.
The former used to be described as a previously autonomous word
becoming an affix, as in *spoon-full* → *spoonful*. But this is oversimple. Grammaticalization covers the whole of language, taking
in semantic attrition, grammatical reduction, and phonetic reduction, as well as some idioms. Meanwhile, phonetic cropping has long
been in use for a few well-known sequences, such as *PTO* 'please
turn over', *RIP* 'rest in peace'. Recently such abbreviations have
escalated in number, due to the use of text messaging in emails and
on mobile phones.

Words, like cliffs, erode over time. Latin *mea domina* 'my lady'
changed to French *ma dame*. French *ma dame* became *madam*.
Madam has become *ma'am*, and even *'m*, as in *Yes'm*.[2] Words with
lexical content empty out, then get attached to others. The word
full as in 'a basket *full* of apples' has became a compound, as in 'a
spoonful of sugar', and also an affix, as in *hopeful*.[3] Similar examples
can be found in almost every sentence.

This pruning-down process is known as grammaticalization.
John Horne Tooke, the eighteenth-century writer whose ideas on

the 'wheels of language' are quoted at the top of this chapter, has sometimes been called 'the father of grammaticalization studies'.[4] Unusually for his time, he had a positive attitude towards language pruning, viewing it as a way of speeding up speech so as to keep up with the pace of thought. Most early writers referred to linguistic compression negatively, as some kind of slippage, or wearing out.

Yet the true father of grammaticalization was undoubtedly the French linguist Antoine Meillet, who coined the term (French *grammaticalisation*). He defined it (perhaps oversimply) as 'the attribution of a grammatical character to a previously autonomous word'.[5] Meillet realized the importance of grammaticalization, and, insightfully for 1912, claimed it caused more radical change than analogy (reasoning from parallel cases): 'Whereas analogy may renew forms in detail, usually leaving the overall plan of the system untouched, the "grammaticalization" of certain words creates new forms and introduces categories which had no linguistic expression. It changes the system as a whole.'[6]

Recent work on the topic has once again viewed grammaticalization in a positive light, as a natural process which linguists are beginning to recognize as important and all-pervasive: 'Grammaticalization . . . is in fact probably the source of the majority of grammatical changes that languages undergo,' it was claimed in the year 2000.[7]

Meillet's much-quoted definition of grammaticalization as a word which loses its independence probably led to a belief that the process is simpler than it actually is. The grammaticalization process changes a word semantically, grammatically and phonetically:

1 Semantic reduction or 'desemanticization', also referred to as 'bleaching', 'weakening of meaning'.
2 Grammatical reduction or 'decategorialization', also spoken of as 'loss of word status'.
3 Phonetic reduction, loss of phonetic substance.

All of these are seen in the *madam* and *spoonful* examples given earlier. Linguists still argue about the extent to which the different changes are simultaneous, or, if not, the order in which they occur.

Layer upon layer

Grammaticalization is not a simple slide from one usage to another. The various stages overlap, sometimes for centuries. This has been called layering:[8] 'New layers are continually emerging . . . the older layers may remain to coexist with and interact with the newer layers.'[9]

Take present-day English *let's*.[10] A longstanding imperative (command) usage exists in which *let* means 'allow', as in: 'Let my people go.' Alongside, a construction introduced by *let us* or *let's* is found, used to urge and encourage, as in '*Let us* pray', '*Let's* go for a picnic.' It is sometimes known as an **adhortative**, and means something like: 'I urge you and me to . . . ' But in colloquial English, *let's* needs only to refer to a single person, as in:

> Let's give you a hand 'I'll give you a hand'
> Let's you go first, then if we have any money left I'll go 'You go first . . . '
> Let's eat our liver now, Betty (to a child) 'Eat up your liver.'

In these examples, *let's*, perhaps now better spelled *lets*, is used as a simple exhortation, and is no longer thought of as a verb plus a pronoun. This new usage has come in alongside the pre-existing older ones.

Or consider the Modern Greek future morpheme *tha*, one of the original constructions used by Meillet as an example:[11]

> *tha* élthoume stis eptá
> FUTURE we-come at seven
> 'We'll come at seven.'

Tha is a blending of *thélo: na* 'I want that'. But *thélo:* and *na* both still exist independently, as in:

> *thélo: na* te:lepho:ní:so:
> 'I want to make a phone call.'

Language, then, builds up layer after layer of usage. It behaves like an enthusiastic gardener who keeps taking cuttings from existing plants in order to propagate new ones, but who keeps all the specimens, both old and new, side by side in the greenhouse. Occasionally old plants die, but only after a longish period during which they survived alongside the newer cuttings.

Predictable chains

'Language moves down time in a current of its own making. It has a drift . . . The linguistic drift has direction.'[12] This much-discussed comment was made by the linguist Edward Sapir in 1921. Possibly, he was talking about the predictable grooves of change which we are beginning to be able to forecast.

The overlapping stages of grammaticalization form chains.[13] The word chain refers to a graded continuum, sometimes called a cline.[14] This was in origin a biological term, defined as 'a gradation of differences of form'.[15] But these clines or chains are not random. Clines are unidirectional for the most part. Just as streams always flow downhill, not uphill, so language squeezes words together; it does not normally pull them apart. Occasional exceptions are found,[16] but they represent a minority of cases: 'Although it can be violated in the presence of alternative cognitive principles, the unidirectionality principle turns out to be statistically significant and can serve as a basis of both linguistic evolution and language structure.'[17] 'Grammaticalization, i.e. the change by which lexical categories become functional categories, is overwhelmingly irreversible'[18] – though arguments continue about why this should be so.

Similar clines recur around the world. Full verbs become auxiliaries, and then verb endings.[19] And the type of full verb affected can be predicted. Verbs of volition, those meaning 'want', 'wish', 'desire', typically become future markers. Take Old English *willan* 'to want'. In Middle English this became a subsidiary or auxiliary verb, signifying intention, as in:

I *wyl* nauther grete nor grone[20] (fourteenth century)
'I will neither cry nor groan.'

Modern English *will*, sometimes shortened to *'ll*, often expresses a simple future, as in:

Ask Paul, he'*ll* go.

A parallel progression is found in the Swahili verb *-taka* 'want', 'wish'.[21] This still means 'want', 'wish' when it is found as a main verb. But it has two additional 'layers'. The form *-taka* also occurs with the meaning 'to be about to', a so-called proximative:

mvua i-na-*taka* ku-nyesha
rain it-*PRESENT-want* to-rain
'It is *about to* rain.'

In another usage, *-taka* has been reduced and converted into the future tense marker *-ta-*:

mvua i-*ta*-nyesha kesho
rain it-*FUTURE*-rain tomorrow
'It *will* rain tomorrow.'

Similarly, words for 'know' follow predictable patterns (Chapter 7): the English word *can* changed from a full verb meaning 'know', like German *können* 'know', to an auxiliary 'be able', and Tok Pisin *save* 'know' has acquired a meaning 'be accustomed to'. Further examples of verb grammaticalization will be discussed later in this book.

Numerous other recurring clines are found. Demonstrative pronouns such as *that* become complementizers, as has happened in both English and German:

I think *that* Peter is coming
Ich glaube *dass* Peter kommt.

Traces of earlier stages are found in Old English, where *that* probably originated as a demonstrative pronoun, followed by an explanation,[22] as (in modern English translation):

That was their custom: they the dead froze
He *that* said: Abraham was a holy man.

Various recurring clines, then, are gradually being documented,[23] in which words slowly move out of their original word class, then into a different category entirely.

Recurrent chains not only reveal pathways along which languages are likely to develop, but can also play a role in language reconstruction: knowledge of which forms and meanings typically emerge out of earlier ones can help linguists to 'wind back' evolved states to previous earlier ones.

Crunching up words

Diachronically, languages could be regarded as 'gigantic expression-compacting machines'.[24] But this word-crunching habit does not just affect single words. Numerous examples of grammaticalization stretch over more than one, as with *let's* (p. 116), or the negative *not* from Old English *ná wiht* 'not a thing',[25] where *ná* is the simple negator, and *wiht* an emphatic element meaning 'thing', 'creature'.

Or consider *be going to*, which has become *gonna* in several spoken English dialects. Similarly, *want to* has become *wanna*:

> *I'm going to* see Pete > *I'm gonna* see Pete
> *I want to* go home > *I wanna* go home.

And although no conventional spelling is yet recognized, a clump of other similar formations are regularly used in spoken speech:

> *I gotta* go home < *I've got to* go home
> *I hafta* go home < *I have to* go home
> *I oughta* go home < *I ought to* go home.[26]

As these examples show, Meillet's widely quoted definition of grammaticalization, which talked about the demotion of words to affixes (p. 115), is clearly too narrow. Quite often, adjacent words become 'habitual and hence routinized'.[27]

Others have suggested that the compacting process starts even earlier than syntax, with discourse. (Discourse is a stretch of spoken or written language longer than a sentence.)

> Loose, paratactic 'pragmatic' discourse structures develop – over time – into tight, 'grammaticalized' syntactic structures . . . we are dealing here with cyclic *waves* . . . : Discourse → Syntax → Morphology → Morphophonemics → Zero.[28]

This brings a much wider range of constructions under the increasingly umbrella term **grammaticalization**, as will be discussed below.

Petrified phrases

Grammaticalization extends like a blanket across a whole range of constructions. It encompasses not just chopped down words, but also petrified phrases, as with **discourse markers**, the words and phrases which link one section of speech or writing to another.

Take the English phrase *instead of*.[29] In Old English, *stede* meant 'place', as in *to thaem stede* 'to that place' (*c.* 880), a usage still found in the word *homestead*. Then *stede* was used in a phrase meaning 'in the place of ', referring to one person substituting for another:

Matthias . . . waes gecoren on Judan stede (*c.* 1000)
'Matthias was chosen in Judas' place.'

This substitution was extended to abstract actions, as in Chaucer's *Canterbury tales*:

Therfore *in stede of* wepynge and preyeres
Men moote yeve silver to the povre freres (*c.* 1388)
'Therefore instead of weeping and prayers, people should give silver to the poor priests.'

At a later stage, *in stede* joined up to become *instead*.

Or consider the word *indeed*.[30] At first, *deed* was a simple noun, as it also still is in modern English:

in thohut, in speeche and in dede (*c.* 1300)
'in thought, in speech, and in deed'

Next, it came to be an adverb attached towards the front of its clause, where it highlighted an unexpected fact:

they [the teacher] sometyme purposely suffring [allowing] the more noble children to vainquysshe . . . though *in dede* the inferiour children have more lernyng. (1531)

In the next century, it coalesced into a single word, and became a full discourse marker. As with *instead*, the movement was from manner adverb, to sentence adverb, to discourse marker.

Or take the phrase *at least*.[31] In its earliest use, dating from the thirteenth century, *at least* is attached to a numeral, as in this fourteenth-century example:

> dayes foure, or thre dayes atte leeste (*c.* 1395)
> 'four days, or at least three'

This usage contains the seeds of further developments. Notably, *at least* refers to other parts of the sentence, a usage which became increasingly common:

> putte the chylde in to the water, or *at the leest* caste water on the chylde. (1528)

Other examples show not only a syntactic link, but also a meaning alteration:

> Thoughe he be nat your frende yet sythe he cometh to you, *at the leest* you ought to welcome him. (*c.* 1530)

The sentence above shows a development from the original factual meaning of *at least* to a so-called epistemic meaning, that is, one which expresses the speaker's assessment of the situation – a type of meaning change which recurs in grammaticalization.[32]

Peaches and cream

Typically, a grammaticalization change involves both form and meaning, as in the examples so far. But are form and meaning inevitably linked, or could they evolve separately? Are they like carriages which must follow trains or horses, or like peaches and cream, which could be consumed separately?

No *necessary* relationship exists between the two processes, it turns out. They are interleaved, rather than linked.[33]

Take the word *have* as in 'I *have* to write a letter' with its sense of obligation, which developed out of an earlier 'I have a letter to write' construction. The meaning change began earlier than the grammatical one. Even in Old English, instances of *have* occur which are certainly not cases of genuine possession:

And her *beoth* swythe genihtsume weolacas . . . Hit *hafath* eac, this land, sealtseathas . . . (Bede)

And here *are* very abundant whelks . . . it *has* also, this land, salt-springs . . .

This situation lasted for hundreds of years: 'It is difficult, therefore, to see any *necessary* relationship between the semantic and syntactic developments in this particular process of grammaticalisation.'[34]

Various other cases of independent semantic and syntactic weakening are emerging, in numerous languages.[35] Grammaticalization therefore covers a wide range, far more than the demotion of a word to an affix.

But it is not the only linguistic process which involves squeezing together: abbreviations are crowding into everyday life. We are all used to numerous, mundane examples of 'cropping': NB 'nota bene', PTO 'please turn over', RIP 'rest in peace'. But these have recently been supplemented by many more, as will be discussed below.

Text messaging (txting)

'wd u b wilin 2 hlp me?' ran an email I received from a university student. This probably seems fairly modern, yet language play and abbreviations go back centuries. So does the use of rebuses, with a *rebus* defined as 'a representation of words or syllables by means of objects or by symbols whose names resemble the intended words or syllables in sound'.[36]

Even our own alphabet came about by means of a 'rebus principle'. For example, an Egyptian hieroglyph with a wavy line meant 'water'. This became Semitic *mem*, the forerunner of the Greek letter μ/M (mu) which became our own m/M. Or, to give modern examples, a picture of an eye could either represent an eye or (rebus) 'I', or a picture of the sun could refer to either the sun or (rebus) 'son', or the word *to* could be written as (rebus) 2, as in the text messaging example at the beginning of this section.

Further rebus examples can be found in the nineteenth century. In 1860, an inventive American writer, Charles Carroll Bombaugh, published a collection of what he called 'emblematic poetry'. This included various types of typographical substitution. For example, 'Essay to Miss Catherine Jay' contains lines that look like text messaging:

'I 1 der if you got that 1 I wrote 2 U B 4' [I wonder if you got that one I wrote to you before];

'Now fare U well, dear KTJ, I trust that U R true – When this U C, then you can say, an S A I O U.'[37]

KTJ would have been quite happy with modern texting, which contains sequences such as *b4* 'before', *cul8r* 'see you later', *gr8* 'great', *l8* 'late', *2day* 'today', *2u* 'to you', where numbers in particular abound as in 2 'to', 4 'for', 8 '-ate'.[38]

Texting is undoubtedly very popular, especially for what were once called 'short text messages' (SMS) delivered by mobile phones. In the year 2000, on 14 February (St Valentine's Day), the message 'I LUV YU' reportedly outnumbered the total sum of Valentine cards sent by ordinary 'snail mail'.[39]

Such texting has been the source of a lively debate over the past few years. As with anything new, complaints have poured in from both sides of the Atlantic:

The English language as we once knew it is out the window, and replacing it is this hip and cool slang induced language, obsessed with taking the vowels out of words and spelling fonetikally.[40]

This was an American complaint, and it ties in with an English moan about texters being vandals (Chapter 1, p. 6).

Yet it's hard to see what the problem is. Language speakers and writers have always been inventive, and texting is just one further example of human creativity. As David Crystal has expressed it: 'it . . . is the latest manifestation of the human ability to be linguistically creative . . . In texting, we are seeing, in a small way, language in evolution.'[41]

And anybody who still has any doubts about the value and creativity of texting should maybe consider carefully the text poem which won a competition for text poetry in a national newspaper:

> I left my picture on the ground
> so that somday if th sun was jst right

> & the rain didn't wash me awa u might c me
> out of the corner of yr I & pic me up.[42]

Netspeak

Netspeak is a neat way of referring to 'Internet language', a term popularized by David Crystal.[43] Text messaging (which was discussed in the last section) is probably the most widely used type of netspeak. But we need to ask whether netspeak, or in particular emails, is affecting our language today.

Emails are of course written. But style-wise, they are midway between spoken and written communication. Although they are written, people interact as if they are having a face-to-face conversation, often starting with the greeting *Hi*, followed by a Christian name, and finishing with an ending such as *Bye*. But are they affecting our language? Yes, but only in minor ways.

First, they are accelerating a trend which has been going on for some time, a preference for informality and an avoidance of anything pompous. Just as we dress more informally these days, so we tend to talk to almost everybody as if they were friends rather than intimidating strangers. This also links in with an emphasis on youth culture.

Second, emails are helping to spread a number of newish, but widely used words,[44] such as *spam* (1994) 'to flood the Internet with tedious or inane postings, especially sending the same message or advertisement to large numbers of newsgroups', *surf* (1993) 'to move from site to site on the Internet', *blog* (1999) 'a shortening of *weblog* (1997) . . . an Internet website containing an eclectic . . . assortment of items of interest to its author', *podcasting* (2004), 'the making available of a digital recording of a radio broadcast or similar item on the Internet for downloading to a personal audio player or a computer'. Of course, other Internet vocabulary is found. The word *flame* 'talk aggressively' has been around in a general sense since the 1960s, but is now found most often in Internet guidance manuals, with the instruction 'Don't flame', though flaming seems to be associated more with Internet chatrooms than with email.[45] It may be that flaming was an early symptom of a medium that had not yet established itself, when its users were uncertain about how to behave.[46]

Nobody is sure how Internet communication will develop in the future. But most people think it is here to stay, alongside older communication methods which may be declining. As one researcher expressed it:

> Perhaps, like teenagers, we are going through an experimental phase that we will outgrow. Perhaps more normative (and contemplative) writing will return to fashion, in turn reshaping our notion of what email messages should look like. My own guess is that even if such a linguistic about-face does take place, it will not happen any time soon. For now, too many people are enjoying their linguistic recess.[47]

Crystal has summarized the whole situation well: 'The human linguistic faculty seems to be in good shape . . . The arrival of Netspeak is showing us *homo loquens* at his best.'[48]

9 Spinning away
Change of meaning

> Words can have no single fixed meaning. Like wayward
> electrons, they can spin away from their initial orbit and
> enter a wider magnetic field. No one owns them or has a
> proprietary right to dictate how they will be used.
>
> David Lehman, *Signs of the times* (1991)

Introduction

This chapter deals with word meaning. Fears about meaning slippage were common in the nineteenth century. In the mid twentieth century structural linguists suggested that words were assembled like a patchwork quilt, each patch having its place in the overall pattern. But this turned out to be a mirage. Prototype theory was a key model of language change in the 1970s, when it was realized that humans do not rank all members of a category equally: they regard some exemplars of both nouns and verbs as better (more prototypical) than others. In fact, multiple meanings (polysemy) are the norm, and different meanings co-exist for most words, sometimes for centuries.

'When *I* use a word . . . it means just what I choose it to mean – neither more nor less.' This comment by Humpty Dumpty in Lewis Carroll's *Through the looking-glass* (1872)[1] confirmed to nineteenth-century readers that Humpty Dumpty lived in a strange, back-to-front world: at that time, most people were convinced that words had a 'proper' meaning which needed to be preserved.

Fears about meaning slippage recur throughout history. In the fifth century BC, the Greek historian Thucydides linked changes in meaning with a decline in moral values, caused by the dispiriting effect of war, a time when: 'The ordinary accepted meaning of words in their relation to things changed as men thought fit.'[2]

These anxieties reached their height in the nineteenth century. Slipped words 'bear the slime on them of the serpent's trail',[3] according to Richard Chenevix Trench, the influential nineteenth-century figure who later became Archbishop of Dublin. Meaning change was a falling away from the original standard which God had imposed, he assumed. He deplored those from whom words 'received their deflection and were warped from their original rectitude'.[4] In his thunderous pronouncements, he linked meaning change with general demoralization:

> This tendency of words to lose the sharp rigidly defined outline of meaning which they once possessed, to become of wide, vague, loose application instead of fixed, definite, and precise, to mean almost anything, and so really to mean nothing, is . . . one of those tendencies, and among the most fatally effectual, which are at work for the final ruin of a language, and, I do not fear to add, for the demoralization of those that speak it.[5]

These worries have persisted into the twentieth century. Semantic change is a crucial part of brainwashing in George Orwell's novel *Nineteen eighty-four*: its 'labyrinthine world of doublethink'[6] promoted the slogans 'WAR IS PEACE, FREEDOM IS SLAVERY, IGNORANCE IS STRENGTH'.[7] And some writers on language have even provided disapproving labels, such as 'weakening', 'verbicide', 'distortion', for selected types of meaning change: 'The problem with verbicide is that words no longer die: having been drained of their vitality . . . they become zombies.'[8] *Phenomenal*, *flirtation* and *democratic* were listed among the zombified words.

Partly because of this negative attitude, and partly because of the difficulty of knowing how to handle it, meaning change has long been the poor relation within historical linguistics. As a recent textbook noted, 'In the majority of cases semantic change is . . . fuzzy, self-contradictory, and difficult to predict . . . This is the reason that . . . just about all linguistic theories . . . concentrate on the structural aspects of language.'[9]

This chapter will outline traditional approaches to the topic, and show where they fail. Then it will show how recent work has begun to shed light on the processes involved.

Left in the dark

> The study where we invite the reader to follow us is of such a new kind that it has not even yet been given a name . . . the laws governing changes in meaning, the choice of new expressions, the birth and death of idioms, have been left in the dark . . .[10]

This somewhat exaggerated claim was made in 1883, by Michel Bréal in a landmark article.[11] He was not in fact the first to look at changing meanings. Intermittent work on the topic is found from the 1820s onward, but it tended to be ignored by mainstream scholars, who concentrated on linguistic reconstruction and sound change (Chapter 2). Bréal gave the name semantics to this new 'science of meaning', a term which has remained, though which now includes far more than meaning change alone.

Bréal's optimistic hope of finding general 'laws' was never realized. A more practical aim was pursued by others, that of providing a comprehensive classification scheme for meaning changes. This turned out to be as difficult as counting snowflakes.

Early work – and even some relatively recent work – typically listed various types of meaning change, and exemplified them. A plethora of labels are found, such as expansion, restriction, pejoration, amelioration, acceleration, retardation, association, differentiation.[12] The word *boy*, for instance, showed amelioration, from 'fettered person' to 'male servant' to 'male child'. *Knave* illustrated the opposite, pejoration, moving from 'male child' to 'male servant' to 'rascal'.

Or take the word *clothes*, once the plural of *cloth*. This has extended its range to cover garments made from wool and other fabrics. The word *costume* has taken the opposite route, one of restriction. In the eighteenth century it referred to the custom or fashion of a particular period, and then became the mode of dress appropriate to a particular time or place. It eventually moved to meaning simply 'garments', 'outfit'.[13]

Yet if words can slip-slide in all directions, displaying amelioration or pejoration, extending or restricting their meanings, then such classifications are unhelpful: it's a bit like trying to chart the directions in which an ice skater can glide, and ending up by saying 'Every which way.'

But while some semanticists continued unsuccessfully to list types of change, others explored causes of meaning change.

Counting causes

Changes of meaning can be brought about by an infinite multiplicity of causes . . . but no matter how fine a mesh of distinctions one may devise, there will always be some cases which will slip through it.[14]

This pessimistic statement was made by Stephen Ullmann in 1962. It summarized the view of many, that meaning change was an impossible topic to handle.

Perhaps the most widely quoted, relatively restricted enumeration of causes was proposed by the French linguist Antoine Meillet in the first decade of the nineteenth century. Words, he suggested, could alter their meaning for linguistic, historical or social reasons.[15]

As a linguistic change, French *pas* 'step' was originally used to strengthen the negative *ne*, and then itself became regarded as a negative, as in *je ne sais pas / je sais pas* 'I do not know' (Chapter 7). A historical change is exhibited by the word *pen*, originally from Latin *penna* 'feather': a change from quill pens to other types of writing implement has led to a meaning change. A recent example of a social change is the word *hack* 'cut', 'chop', which has been re-applied to breaking into computer systems.

These three causes are sometimes supplemented by psychological reasons, such as taboo (from a Polynesian word meaning 'forbidden'). Words may be avoided for religious reasons, as when the word *L'Autre* 'the other one' is found in French for addressing the devil. Or their use may be restricted by delicacy: euphemisms abound for words meaning 'die', 'be killed', such as *pass away, kick the bucket, push up the daisies, turn up one's toes*.[16]

But traditional lists of causes reduce semantic change to the level of stamp collecting, an assembly of colourful bits and pieces. They wrongly give the impression that words exist in isolation from one another.

Patchwork quilts?

Words are not isolated fragments. Any word is held in place by a mesh of surrounding words. This insight was due above all to structural linguistics, which dominated linguistic thinking for much of the first half of the twentieth century. The lexicon, like the other layers of language, was viewed as a mosaic of interlocking units. Words were presumed to cover the human world like patches on a patchwork quilt.[17]

If one item in the mosaic changed its meaning, a chain reaction was presumed to occur among its neighbours. In Late Latin, for example, the word *femur* 'thigh' dropped out of use, possibly because of its similarity to the word *femus* (earlier *fimus*) 'dung'.[18] Latin *coxa*, originally 'hip', took its place, as shown by its descendants, French *cuisse*, Italian *coscia* 'thigh'. The resulting gap in the pattern led to the adoption of an old Germanic word, presumed **anca*, for 'haunch', 'hindquarters', as the new term for 'hip', as in French *hanche*, Italian *anca*:

```
STAGE 1              hip → thigh
STAGE 2 haunch → hip
```

This switch around was aided by the general confusion which often surrounds neighbouring body parts.

But the switchovers and replacements in chains are rarely neat and tidy. And the links often seem strange. The English word *wrath* was replaced by *anger*. Yet *anger* is derived from an Old Norse word *angr* 'grief'.[19] Meanwhile, the word *grief* or *gref* 'feeling of sorrow' originally meant 'suffering' or 'hardship'. Word meanings do not lock together in a neat and tidy jigsaw: cultural biases affect the picture. The patchwork quilt idea turned out to be a mirage. Words are not tidily stitched together in the way early researchers hoped. They behave more like jam and cream on top of scones: heaped up double in some parts, but with bare patches left in others.

Above all, different meanings of the same word overlap, as outlined in the last chapter. They may co-exist for centuries, then, eventually, some of the meanings drop away.

Cuckoos and multiple meanings

Word meanings, then, do not suddenly push each other out of the way. In the simplest situation, a young cuckoo scenario is found, with the new meaning joining the old, and co-existing for a time (Chapter 8). Eventually, the intruder may heave the old occupant out of the nest. Take the word *tabby*.[20] This once referred to a cloth *attābī* made in an area of Baghdad named after Prince Attāb who lived there. It came into English via French, and denoted a sort of rich silk taffeta: 'This day ... put on ... my false tabby waistcoat with gold lace,' noted Samuel Pepys in his diary for 13 October 1661. But since such cloth was usually striped, the word was also applied to brindled cats. Then the 'striped cat' meaning gradually took over, and the fabric sense faded away.

The young cuckoo idea for word meaning is not entirely new. Co-existence followed by replacement was recognized as a possibility by the German Hermann Paul at the end of the nineteenth century. In 1880, he pointed out that words had both 'normal meaning' (*usuelle Bedeutung*) and 'occasional meaning' (*okkasionelle Bedeutung*), and that the occasional meaning may become the usual one.[21] But Paul's insight was mostly forgotten, until recently.

As we now know, multiple births – several new meanings – may arise, and may co-exist semi-permanently, often with no loss of the original meaning. Take the word *hand*. This still means 'the extremity of the arm', but it also means 'applause', as in 'Give her a good hand'; 'aid' as in 'Lend me a hand'; 'skill which requires practice' as in 'I must keep my hand in'; 'a set of cards in a card game' as in 'he was dealt a good hand', and so on and so on. And some of these extended usages have become further extended, as in 'Life dealt him a good hand.'[22]

Co-existence is therefore the key, as with sound change. Polysemy – the birth of multiple meanings – is the norm. New meanings, sometimes several of them, creep in alongside the existing ones, and may last for centuries, as a glance at any page of the *Oxford English Dictionary* can confirm.

The number of meanings acquired by a word differs from word class to word class. The *Collins English Dictionary* lists almost 45,000 different nouns, but fewer than 15,000 verbs.[23] Yet this difference between nouns and verbs is partly compensated for by the polysemy count: verbs are more polysemous than nouns. Verbs have an average of 2.11 senses, but nouns 1.74.[24] Let us now consider how these new meanings arise.

Natural fuzziness

'Language develops by the felicitous misapplication of words,' commented two writers at the beginning of the last century,[25] as they tried to explain how different meanings arise. But 'misapplication' is the wrong word. Words are by nature incurably fuzzy. They are like an uncooked pie crust which can be rolled to fit different shapes of dish.

A word is likely to have a central meaning, which can be pulled and stretched round the edges. In the long run, this can give rise to various overlapping senses, and even homonyms, as with *pig*, the pink farmyard animal, and *pig*, a lump of iron ore theoretically shaped like a pig. 'Henry is a *pig*' shows that the word can be extended even to cases where only some pig characteristics are found, in this case, its greed.

A way of handling all this fuzziness was proposed in the mid 1970s by a psychologist, Eleanor Rosch.[26] Humans do not rank all members of a category equally, she pointed out. Take birds. English speakers judge some to be very good examples, and others less so. Robins and blackbirds are very good birds, which she labelled prototypes. Canaries and doves are less good, owls and ducks are bad birds, and a penguin is a very bad bird indeed. People analyse the characteristics of the best bird, the prototype, and allow anything which sufficiently resembles it to belong to the category 'bird'. This explains how humans deal with oddities: why ostriches, emus and one-legged albino blackbirds can be accepted as birds.

This general model works both for categories, as with *bird*, and for individual category members. So you could have a 'good' blackbird or a 'less good' blackbird: a female blackbird tends to be a shade of brown.

Extreme non-prototypical usages tend to be known as metaphors. Native speakers may indicate that this is so by providing clues, often the use of an intensifier, as: 'Henry's *a genuine night owl*,' 'Pamela is *a real nightingale*,' 'Toby's *an absolute ostrich* when it comes to facing facts.' But eventually, if the usage becomes fully conventional, the intensifier can be dropped, as with 'Henry's a *pig*,' 'Fenella's a *bitch*.'

Verbs also can be handled in this way. Take the word *climb*.[27] Prototypical *climb* involves both upward movement and effortful movement of limbs, as in:

> Paul *climbed* a lamppost.

Provided one of these characteristics is present, *climb* can still be used, as in:

> The plane *climbed* into the sky (upward movement)
> Derek *climbed* into his clothes (effortful use of limbs)

No clear divide exists between 'ordinary' and 'metaphorical' usage, as these examples show. A metaphor is a word, or group of words, used in a non-prototypical way.[28] In many cases, it is impossible to decide whether a word is a temporary metaphor, a conventional metaphor, or a permanently changed meaning. These overlap, as in:

> The price of petrol *climbed* daily
> With courage, you can *climb* life's mountains.

Or consider the word *fall*. Prototypical *fall* involves an inadvertent downward movement, as in:

> Sheila *fell* down the stairs
> Paul *fell* from the tree.

Downward movement is more important than inadvertency, as in:

> Pamela *fell* into his arms.

where the falling was presumably intentional. (To *fall up the stairs*, incidentally, probably means falling down while attempting to go up.)

But inadvertent falling has given rise to a host of new applications: *prices fell*, *her face fell*, *Jerusalem fell*, *he fell asleep* and so on. All of these different extensions co-exist with the original usage, which still remains.

The layering process and polysemy

Linguistic forms might be envisaged as employees of the state. They are hired, promoted, later put on half-pay, and finally retired. Forms grow pale (*verblassen*), and their colours bleach (*verbleichen*). They may even die, and become mummified, lingering on as preserved corpses. This was the view of the German Georg von der Gabelentz in 1891.[29]

But this pessimistic view is now outmoded. The 'growing pale' and 'bleaching' is an illusion. More realistically, words multiply, like ever-splitting amoebas. New meanings creep in alongside the older ones. Typically, a word develops several layers of meaning: 'Meanings expand their range through the development of various polysemies . . . these polysemies may be regarded as quite fine-grained. It is only collectively that they may seem like weakening of meaning.'[30]

Some types of words are particularly prone to split into layers, such as words for catastrophic events. Take the word *disaster*. Judging from dictionaries, its main meaning is: 'a sudden event such as an accident or natural catastrophe that causes great damage or loss of life',[31] as in:

the Hillsborough football *disaster* which killed 95 people

But alongside this serious incident usage are numerous trivial ones, such as:

To get a panama hat wet is to court *disaster*. The hat becomes limp and shapeless.

According to one count, over 45 per cent of examples involved serious loss of life, almost 20 per cent described events of moderate seriousness, such as an oil spill, and trivia accounted for the remainder.[32] These could be classified and counted because the circumstances were clarified in the surrounding words. Partly they were explicitly specified, and partly covert conventions operate, which are understood by native English speakers. For example, the naming of a geographical location is the main clue that a serious incident involving multiple deaths has occurred, as: *the Clapham disaster, the Hillsborough disaster*. For lesser events, the type of problem is usually specified, as in: *ecological disaster, electrical disaster*. And a fuller explanation often accompanied trivial events:

> There have been many *disasters* along the road. Yorkshire puddings you could sole your shoes with . . . and last Christmas a chocolate log disintegrated, the proud little Santa on top sinking without trace in a sea of chocolate gunge.

But how did the new, trivial usages arise? As with other types of change, new usages creep in by attaching themselves to particular contexts. Cookery attracted the word *disaster*:

> Stefanie likes cooking. I don't, not since my *disaster* with the soup
> The gravy's a *disaster*. It's got too much fat in it.

Sport also pulled in *disasters*.

> The last wicket fell . . . So it was another blackwash, another *disaster* for England
>
> Poor old Tommy had a *disaster*. He three-putted from three feet and made a double-bogey at the very first hole.

But given all this layering, how can serious and trivial usages of a polysemous word be distinguished, when both frequently co-occur? Further subtle clues exist, picked up by native speakers, often without them realizing it. Minor events frequently had an intensifier attached, such as *absolute, complete, total*:

> The next morning was an *absolute disaster*. Loretta's hopes of a conciliatory chat with Bridget over breakfast were dashed.

Similarly, the phrases *disaster strikes/struck* often related to trivial events:

> With four minutes of the first half left, disaster struck for City . . . as they suddenly found themselves 4–1 down.

Disaster, then, gives some indication as to how words 'layer' in meaning. New meanings slip into particular topic areas, and these topics themselves provide the word with a partially new sense identity. Collocational clues – information from the words on either side – supplement these topic clues. In this way, multiple layers can build up, with minimal chance of misunderstanding.

Almost half of the so-called *disasters* were potential ones, rather than actual, as in:

> the old Christmas tree lights . . . *could be* the cause of an *electrical disaster*.

The hypothetical nature of the disasters was shown by the linguistic expressions used with them, such as *avert*, *avoid*, *foretell*, *predict*, also by modal expressions such as *can be*, *could be*. These potential disasters were presumably invoked by speakers and writers in an attempt to dramatize their utterances. Such usages partially explain why the word *disaster* has become so widespread, and susceptible to layering.

Universal laws?

> There are universal laws of thought which are reflected in the laws of change and meaning . . . even if the science of meaning has not yet made much advance towards discovering them.[33]

This comment was made by Otto Jespersen in 1925, and is still true today. Linguists have not yet discovered firm 'universal laws'. But they are beginning to comprehend some of the mechanisms behind meaning change, and to specify some of the directions it is likely to take – and even to suggest how meanings were generalized at the origin of language.[34]

Humans begin with the human body, and move outward to other parts of the physical world:

the *foot* of the mountain
the *ribs* of the ship
the *head* of the organization.

They also move inward, using everyday external bodily behaviour to describe internal events:

I *see* what Helen means
Peter *held on* to his point of view
Let's *go over* that plan again.

Humans also generalize from space to time:

from tree *to* tree → *from* day *to* day
in the wood → *in* the morning

and so on.

Language therefore reflects the interaction of humans with the environment around. To continue, body parts are often expressed in terms of spatial concepts: 'Sexual organs, for example, can be called "the thing in front" or "the bottom thing", . . . in some Swahili dialects . . . the expression *mbeleni* "in front" came to become a regularly used term for "genital organs".'[35] And many more examples of similar world-to-language transfers can be found.[36]

This chapter then has shown how early attempts to catalogue meaning change were mostly discouraging. In recent years, however, insights as to how it happens are leading to a greater understanding not only of how language works today, but also of how it possibly began.

Part 3
Causation

10 The reason why
Sociolinguistic causes of change

> Phaedrus . . . had noticed again and again . . . that what
> might seem to be the hardest part of scientific work,
> thinking of the hypotheses, was invariably the
> easiest . . . As he was testing hypothesis number one by
> experimental method a flood of other hypotheses would
> come to mind . . . At first he found it amusing. He coined a
> law intended to have the humour of a Parkinson's law
> that 'The number of rational hypotheses that can explain
> any given phenomenon is infinite.' It pleased him never to
> run out of hypotheses . . . It was only months after he had
> coined the law that he began to have some doubts about
> the benefits of it . . . If the purpose of scientific method is to
> select from among a multitude of hypotheses, and if the
> number of hypotheses grows faster than experimental
> method can handle, then it is clear that all hypotheses
> can never be tested.
>
> Robert Pirsig, *Zen and the art of motorcycle maintenance*

Introduction

This is the first of four chapters on the causes of language change.
This chapter begins by discounting the oldish idea that changes are
purely random. It then discusses the infiltration of foreign elements and borrowing, and, finally, explores the notion of linguistic
'need'.

For centuries, people have speculated about the causes of language
change. The problem is not one of thinking up possible causes, but
of deciding which to take seriously. In the quotation at the top of
the chapter, Phaedrus, a scientist, is overwhelmed by the number
of possible theories which come to mind in his work on physics.
A similar problem faces linguists. As one noted: 'Linguists are a
marvellously clever bunch of scholars; there is really *no limit* to the

imaginative, elegant, and intellectually satisfying hypotheses they can dream up to account for observed linguistic behaviour.'[1]

In the past, language change has been attributed to a bewildering variety of factors ranging over almost every aspect of human life, physical, social, mental and environmental. At one time, for example, there was a suggestion that consonant changes begin in mountain regions due to the intensity of expiration at high altitudes. 'The connection with geographical or climatic conditions is clear,' asserted one scholar, 'because nobody will deny that residence in the mountains, especially in the high mountains, stimulates the lungs.'[2] Luckily this theory is easily disprovable, since Danish, spoken in the flat country of Denmark, seems to be independently undergoing a set of extensive consonant changes – unless we attribute the Danish development to the increasing number of Danes who go to Switzerland or Norway for their summer holidays each year, as one linguist ironically suggested.[3]

Even when we have eliminated the 'lunatic fringe' theories, we are left with an enormous number of possible causes to take into consideration. Part of the problem is that there are several different causative factors at work, not only in language as a whole, but also in any one change. Like a road accident, a language change may have multiple causes. A car crash is only rarely caused by one overriding factor, such as a sudden steering failure, or the driver falling asleep. More often there is a combination of factors, all of which contribute to the overall disaster. Similarly, language change is likely to be due to a combination of factors.

In view of the confusion and controversies surrounding causes of language change, it is not surprising that some reputable linguists have regarded the whole field as a disaster area, and opted out altogether: 'The causes of sound change are unknown,' said Bloomfield in 1933.[4] 'Many linguists, probably an easy majority, have long since given up enquiring into the why of phonological change,' said Robert King in 1969.[5] 'The explanation of the cause of language change is far beyond the reach of any theory ever advanced,' said yet another around the same time.[6]

This pessimism is unwarranted. Even if we cannot consider all possible causes, we can at least look at a range of causes that have been put forward over the years, and assess their relative value. We can begin by dividing proposed causes of change into two broad categories. On the one hand, there are external sociolinguistic factors – that is, social factors outside the language system. On the other hand, there are internal psycholinguistic ones – that is, linguistic and psychological factors which reside in the structure of the language and the minds of the speakers.

In this chapter, we shall deal with three proposed sociolinguistic causes: fashion, foreign influence and social need. Then in the following chapters we shall deal with some psycholinguistic ones.

Fashion and random fluctuation

An extreme view held by a minority of linguists is that language change is an entirely random and fortuitous affair, and that fashions in language are as unpredictable as fashions in clothes:

> There is no more reason for language to change than there is for automobiles to add fins one year and remove them the next, for jackets to have three buttons one year and two the next . . . the 'causes' of sound change without language contact lie in the general tendency of human cultural products to undergo 'non-functional' stylistic change

argued an American linguist, Paul Postal, in 1968.[7]

Another similar view is that random fluctuations occur subconsciously, as sounds gradually drift from their original pronunciation. A theory that speakers accidentally 'miss the target' was prevalent in the 1950s, popularized by an American, Charles Hockett. Hockett suggested that when we utter a speech sound, we are aiming at a certain ideal target. But since words are usually comprehensible even if every sound is not perfectly articulated, speakers often get quite careless, and do not trouble too much about hitting the 'bull's-eye' each time. As he expressed it:

> When a person speaks, he aims his articulatory motions more or less accurately at one after another of a set of bull's-eyes . . . charity on the part of hearers leads the speaker to be quite sloppy in his aim most of the time. The shots intended for initial [t] will be aimed in the general direction of that bull's-eye, but will fall all about it – many quite close, some in the immediate vicinity, a few quite far away.[8]

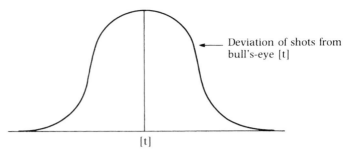

Figure 10.1   Hockett's theory of random deviation (based on Hockett, 1958)

The actual shots, he suggests, will cluster round a single point at which there will be a 'frequency maximum' (see Figure 10.1).[9] As time passes, and quite a lot of shots miss the target, people hear numerous near misses. Eventually they begin to think the bull's-eye is in a different place:

> It is just this sort of slow drifting about of expectation distributions, shared by people who are in constant communication, that we mean to subsume the term 'sound change' . . . The drift might well not be in any determinate direction: the maxima might wander a bit further apart, then come closer again, and so on. Nevertheless, the drift thus shown would constitute sound change.[10]

How are we to assess these theories? Certainly, fashion and social influence cannot be ignored, as we saw in the case of New York *r*. It is also clear that a person's speech can gradually alter over the years in the direction of those around, as is shown by British people who pick up an American accent in a very short time. Nevertheless, there are three reasons why fashion and 'wandering targets' cannot be regarded as major causes of language change.

First, if sounds wandered around randomly in the way Postal and Hockett suggest, language would soon end up in chaos. Their theories suggest that sounds are like a room full of blindfold or drunken men randomly weaving and wandering around, and occasionally crashing into one another. Instead, language remains a well-organized patterned whole, and never disintegrates into the confusion implied by random fluctuation theories.

A second argument against random fluctuation is that similar changes tend to recur in quite unconnected languages. This cannot be chance. If language were purely governed by fashion, we would not expect so many different, far-flung languages to hit on the same whims of fashion in pronunciation over the centuries.

Thirdly, there seem to be hidden and inbuilt constraints concerning which elements can change in a language. There are often identifiable 'weak spots' in a language structure where change will be likely to strike, as well as stable elements which are likely to resist change.

For these reasons, the majority of linguists regard fashion changes simply as a triggering factor, something which may set off a tendency whose deeper causes lie hidden beneath the surface.

Foreign bodies

According to some people, the majority of changes are due to the chance infiltration of foreign elements. Perhaps the most widespread version of this view is the so-called substratum theory – the suggestion that when immigrants come to a new area, or when an indigenous population learns the language of newly arrived conquerors, they learn their adopted language imperfectly. They hand on these slight imperfections to their children and to other people in their social circle, and eventually alter the language. Consider four lines from Joel Chandler Harris's 'Uncle Remus' (1880):

> Oh, whar shill we go we'en de great day comes,
> Wid de blowin' er de trumpits en de bangin' er de drums?
> How many po' sinners'll be kotched out late
> En find no latch ter de golden gate?

This is an attempt, accompanied by a certain amount of poetic licence, to represent the pronunciation of an American speaker of Black English. According to one theory, this variety of English arose when speakers of a West African language such as Mandingo or Ewe were brought over to America as slaves. When these Africans learned English, they carried over features of their original language into their adopted one.

In this type of situation the adopted language does not always move in the direction of the substratum language. Sometimes immigrants attempt to *over*correct what they feel to be a faulty accent, resulting not only in a movement away from the substratum language, but also in a change in the adopted language. Labov found an interesting example of this phenomenon in New York.[11] He noticed a tendency among lower-class New Yorkers to pronounce a word such as *door* as if it were really *doer* [dʊə] (rhyming with *sewer*). At first he was puzzled by this finding. When he looked more closely, he found that this pronunciation was related to ethnic groupings. He discovered that it was most prominent in the speech of youngish lower-class people of Jewish and Italian extraction, and suggested that this may be a case of children reacting against their parents. He pointed out that the Jewish immigrants who came to New York at the beginning of the twentieth century spoke Yiddish. Yiddish speakers would normally find it difficult to hear differences between English vowels when these distinctions did not exist in Yiddish. They would therefore tend to ask for a *cop of coffee*, making the vowel in *cup* the same as the first vowel in *coffee*. Italian immigrants would have a similar problem. The second generation of immigrants, however, would be aware and perhaps ashamed of the foreign-sounding speech of their parents. They therefore made an exaggerated difference between the vowels confused by their parents, so making a word such as *coffee* sound like *cooefee* [kʊəfi] and *door* sound like *doer* [dʊə].

Another situation in which the infiltration of foreign elements commonly causes change is when different languages come into contact, which often happens along national borders. Inhabitants of such regions are frequently bilingual or have a working knowledge of the other language(s) in the area, in addition to their native language. In this situation, the languages tend to influence one another in various ways. The longer the contact, the deeper the influence.

A number of strange and interesting cases of language mixture have been reported in the literature. One of the most bizarre occurred in southern India, in the village of Kupwar, which is situated roughly 200 miles southeast of Bombay.[12] Here, two dissimilar language families, Indo-European and Dravidian, came into contact. In this village of approximately 3,000 inhabitants, three languages were in common use: Kannada, which is a member of the Dravidian language family, and Urdu and Marathi, which are Indo-European languages. These languages have probably been in contact for more than six centuries, since many of the inhabitants are traditionally bilingual or trilingual. The Kupwar situation was strange in that, due to social pressures, borrowing of vocabulary was rare. This was unusual, because vocabulary items normally spread easily. The inhabitants seem to have felt the need to maintain their ethnic identity by keeping separate words for things in different languages. Meanwhile, the syntax of all three languages had crept closer and closer together, so that the Urdu, Marathi and Kannada spoken in Kupwar became fairly different from the standard form of these languages, with Urdu in particular having changed. The translation of the sentence 'I cut some greens and brought them' would normally be very different in the three languages concerned, both in word order and vocabulary. In the Kupwar versions, however, the syntax was surprisingly similar, with each translation having the same number of words in the same order, so that each language said, as it were, 'Leaves a few having cut taking I came'. It is unusual for the syntax of adjacent languages to affect one another to the same extent as the Kupwar example, though it illustrates the fact that with enough time and enough contact there is no limit to the extent to which languages can affect one another.

Ma'a, a language spoken in Tanzania (east Africa), provided another extreme contact situation.[13] Ma'a is usually classified as Cushitic, a language family loosely related to Ancient Egyptian and Arabic, whose thirty-five or so languages are spoken in northeast and east Africa. Two or three hundred years ago, a group of Ma'a speakers moved southwards. Some of the migrants adopted local languages from the Bantu family. But Ma'a speakers, a proud, reserved people, anxious to preserve their own customs, tried to retain their own native tongue. However, partly through contact with their Bantu neighbours, and partly through continued connections with their own kinfolk who had switched to Bantu languages, Ma'a became increasingly 'bantuized'. It retained a lot of its own vocabulary, but in many ways it became more like a Bantu language than a Cushitic one. For example, Bantu languages and Ma'a have objects following their verbs (*Lions eat meat*), but Cushitic languages have the reverse order (*Lions meat eat*). The Bantu languages and Ma'a have prefixes (attachments to the front of words) to show distinctions such as singular and plural. Cushitic languages mainly have suffixes (word endings). The result is a language which is neither truly Bantu, nor truly Cushitic. According to some, it is a rare but genuine example of a 'mixed language'.

So-called linguistic areas provide a further example of the way in which languages can influence one another over the course of centuries. These are areas in which some striking linguistic feature has spread over a wide range of geographically adjacent languages, which otherwise have little in common. In southeast Asia, Chinese, Vietnamese and Thai are all tone languages.[14] In Africa, Bush-Hottentot languages and the neighbouring unrelated Bantu languages contain a set of rare sounds known as clicks, which involve clicking noises somewhat like the *tut-tut* of disapproval, and *gee-up* sound made to horses.[15] In India, Hindi and other Indo-European languages share with the Dravidian language family certain unusual consonants known as retroflex sounds, in which the tongue is curled backwards to the roof of the mouth.[16] It seems unlikely that these uncommon features arose coincidentally in the languages concerned, and most linguists assume that they spread from their neighbours due to cultural contact.

The Balkans are another well-studied linguistic area.[17] Modern Greek, Albanian, Romanian and Bulgarian are all Indo-European languages, but from different branches. Yet they show unexpected syntactic similarities. For example, they all say the equivalent of *Give me that I drink* for 'Give me something to drink.' The similarities probably spread when Byzantine culture was a unifying force in the region. Meso-America, the link between North and South America, may be another linguistic area.[18] Here, a variety of languages have a surprising amount in common, such as the expression of possession by the equivalent of *his-dog the man* 'the man's dog'.

The infiltration of external foreign elements can therefore be extensive. It is not, however, chaotic, as the next section shows.

Substratum vs borrowing

In theory, importers of foreign elements can be divided into two types: imperfect learners, and pickers-up of useful bits. This distinction enables us (some of the time) to separate out substratum influence from borrowing, since these typically affect a language in different ways.[19] When people learn a new language, they unintentionally impose some of their old sound patterns and, to a lesser extent, syntax. But they leave the vocabulary mostly unchanged. However, when people pick up foreign bits and pieces as useful additions to their existing language, they take over mainly vocabulary:

Substratum influence		Borrowing
***	Sounds	*
***	Syntax	*
*	Vocabulary	***

These two sometimes fit together, like two sides of a coin. Supposedly, both things happened with Yiddish–English bilinguals in the United States.[20] Their English, the language they learned later, was affected by their native Yiddish accent and syntax. Their Yiddish, the language they use at home, has taken over numerous English vocabulary items, but has otherwise remained relatively unaffected. The same is true of some Indian immigrants in England. Their English is influenced by their native language as far as sounds and syntax are concerned, while their home language, such as Punjabi, is incorporating English loan words.

In practice, it's not always possible to separate out the two types of contact, especially long after the event. In addition, children who grow up bilingual can totally blur the substratum–borrowing distinction. In general, substratum influence varies, depending on the languages involved. Borrowing, however, seems to have a number of general characteristics. Let us consider these.

Borrowing on permanent loan

'Borrowing' is a somewhat misleading word since it implies that the element in question is taken from the donor language for a limited amount of time and then returned, which is by no means the case. The item is actually copied, rather than borrowed in the strict sense of the term.

There are four important characteristics of borrowing. First, detachable elements are the most easily and commonly taken over – that is, elements which are easily detached from the donor language and which will not affect the structure of the borrowing language. An obvious example of this is the ease with which items of vocabulary make their way from language to language, particularly if the words have some type of prestige. In England, for example, French food was once regarded as sophisticated and elegant, so even quite ordinary restaurants include on their menu items such as *coq au vin, consommé, gâteau, sorbet*. There seems to be no limit to the number of these detachable items which can be incorporated. It is, however, rare to borrow 'basic' vocabulary – words that are frequent and common, such as numbers. Some people have claimed it is impossible, but this is an overstatement. It has been found in northern Australia, where there are a number of small, loosely knit tribes who have intermarried extensively.[21]

A second characteristic is that adopted items tend to be changed to fit in with the structure of the borrower's language, though the borrower is only occasionally aware of the distortion imposed. English restaurant owners may well not notice how much they distort the French food words, though deformation is more obvious in the much-quoted case of the British sailors who referred to the warships *Bellerophon* and *Iphigenia* as the *Billy Ruffian* and the *Niffy Jane*. The way in which foreign items are adapted to the structure of the borrowing language becomes clearer when we look at English words which have been taken over by other languages. In Russia, for example, people wear *dzhempers* 'jumpers' and *sviters* 'sweaters', and listen to *dzhaz* 'jazz'. A *sportsmen* 'sportsman' has a plural *sportsmeny*, and a feminine form *sportsmenka* 'sportswoman', which in turn has a plural form *sportsmenki*. Similarly *biznismen* is clearly in origin our word *businessman*, and it has a plural *biznismeny*.[22]

Swahili has some even stranger adaptations of English words: *kiplefiti* 'traffic island' is from *keep left*. Swahili words which begin with *ki-* in the singular normally begin with *vi-* in the plural; we therefore find a plural *viplefiti* 'traffic islands'. Moreover, since a number of Swahili words have a plural prefix *ma-*, we find the English word *mudguard* adopted as a plural *madigadi* 'mudguards' with a corresponding singular form *digadi* 'mudguard'![23]

A third characteristic is that a language tends to select for borrowing those aspects of the donor language which superficially correspond fairly closely to aspects already in its own. Where France adjoins Germany we find that French has adopted certain German syntactic constructions. For example, French normally places adjectives after its nouns, as in *un visage blanc*, literally 'a face white'. On the Franco-German borders, however, French has taken over the German order of adjective plus noun: *un blanc visage* 'a white face'.[24] This particular borrowing has probably caught on because French already has a small number of adjectives which come before the noun, as in *le petit garçon* 'the small boy', *la jolie femme* 'the pretty woman'.

A final characteristic has been called the 'minimal adjustment' tendency – the borrowing language makes only very small adjustments to the structure of its language at any one time. In a case where one language appears to have massively affected another, we discover on closer examination that the changes have come about in a series of minute steps, each of them involving a very small alteration only, in accordance with the maxim 'There are no leaps in nature.'[25] Greek speakers living in Turkey have imported so many Turkish features that they now speak a language in which 'the body has remained Greek, but the soul has become Turkish'.[26] But this has been done over the centuries, one feature at a time, by a series of minimal adjustments. One Turkish feature prepares the language for the next, in a steady progression.

The 'no leaps' principle can be illustrated by looking at a substantial change in Guyanan Creole. Guyanan Creole is in fact based on English, but in the course of years it has moved very far away from it, so much so that many people regard it as a different language altogether. Recently, due to social pressures, more and more elements of Standard English are being borrowed into the Creole with the result that in some areas, and in the speech of some speakers, the Creole has reverted to something very like Standard English. The verb *to be* represents a typical example. Whereas English has one verb with different forms, *am*, *is*, *are*, *was*, *were*, Guyanan Creole uses different verbs depending on the construction, as in the following sentences:

	Guyanan Creole	**English**
1	Mi wiiri.	I am tired.
2	Abi a lil bai.	We were little boys.
3	Abi de til maanin.	We were (there) till morning.

In the first sentence, the Creole version does not use a verb 'to be', and the word *wiiri* should probably be regarded as a verb, 'beweary'. In the second, the Creole version uses the verb form *a*, which is the normal word for the verb 'to be' when it occurs before a noun. In the third, we find Creole *de*, the normal form before an adverbial phrase such as 'till morning'.

The first stage in the move away from the Creole seems to have been a realization that the forms *a* and *de* do not occur in Standard English, combined with a realization that English does not distinguish between three environments in its use of the verb 'to be'. Initially, therefore, Creole speakers simply dropped the forms *a*, *de*, and omitted the verb 'to be' entirely, except when this totally destroyed intelligibility. The next stage consisted of learning two of the English verb forms, *iz* for the present, and *woz* for the past, and using them in all circumstances, as in *yuuz a kyaapinta, nu?* 'you're a carpenter, aren't you?' The final stage consisted of learning the correct English forms and where to insert them.[27] This progression is illustrated in Figure 10.2 – though the situation was undoubtedly much messier than the diagram would suggest. As in all cases of language change, there was fluctuation initially, with the new gradually winning out over the old.

In short, we note that foreign elements do not infiltrate another language haphazardly. Individual words are taken over easily and frequently, since incorporating them does not involve any structural alteration in the borrowing language. When less detachable elements are taken over, they tend to be ones which already exist in embryo in the language in question, or which can be accepted

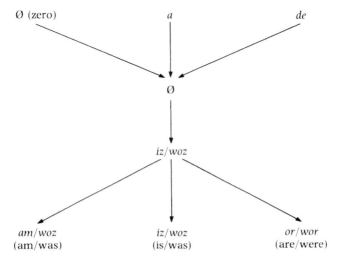

Figure 10.2   Development of Guyanan Creole towards Standard English

into the language with only minimal adjustment to the existing structure. Once one feature has been brought in, it prepares the language for the next, and so on.

Overall, then, borrowing does not suddenly disrupt the basic structure of a language. Foreign elements make use of existing tendencies, and commonly accelerate changes which are already under way. We may perhaps liken the situation to a house with ill-fitting windows. If rain beats against the windows, it does not normally break the window or pass through solid panes of glass. It simply infiltrates the cracks which are already there. If the rain caused extensive dry rot, we could perhaps say that in a superficial sense the rain 'caused' the building to change structurally. But a deeper and more revealing analysis would ask how and why the rain was able to get in the window in the first place.

Need and function

A third view on sociolinguistic causes of language change involves the notion of need. Language alters as the needs of its users alter, it is claimed, a viewpoint that is sometimes referred to as a functional view of language change.

Need is certainly relevant at the level of vocabulary. Unneeded words drop out: items of clothing which are no longer worn such as *doublet* or *kirtle* are now rarely mentioned outside a theatrical setting. New words are coined as they are required. In every decade, neologisms abound, and some settle permanently in the language. Recent arrivals are *netizen* a 'net citizen', a keen user of the Internet. *Twocking* 'taking without the owner's consent' is car theft.[28] *Chugger* 'a charity mugger' is someone collecting for a charity who refuses to take 'no' for an answer.[29] These words all became widely used in recent years. Names of people and objects are switched if the old ones seem inadequate. The word *blind* rarely occurs in official documents, and tends to be replaced by the 'politically correct' phrase *visually challenged*, which is supposedly less offensive to those who can't see. A British medical journal moaned that patients were now referred to as *clients* or *service users*.[30] Similarly, in an American novel, garbage at the Board of City Planning in New York was not called garbage: it was called 'non-productive ex-consumer materials'[31] – a new name which we may imagine was probably coined in order to attract employees to an otherwise unattractive-sounding job. The introduction of slang terms can also be regarded as a response to a kind of need. When older words have become over-used and lose their impact, new vivid ones are introduced in their place. As one writer expressed it: 'Slang is language that takes off its coat, spits on its hands, and goes to work.'[32]

Sometimes, however, social needs can trigger a more widespread change than the simple addition of new vocabulary items. Let us look at some situations in which social factors have apparently led to more widespread disruption.

Consider sentences such as:

Henry downed a pint of beer
Melissa went to town and did a buy.[33]

English, we note, lacks a simple means of saying 'to do something in one fell swoop'. This may be why the word *down* can be converted into a verb to mean 'drink down in one gulp', and the word *buy* into a noun which, when combined with the verb *do*, means 'go on a single massive spending spree'. This type of fast-moving, thorough activity may represent a change in the pace of life, which is in turn reflected in the language, since we increasingly make use of **conversions** – the conversion of one part of speech into another. If this trend continues, the eventual result may be complete interchangeability of items such as nouns and verbs, which were once kept rigidly apart. However, while it is true that conversions are becoming more numerous, there is no evidence that social need initiated them in the first place. Usages such as *Drusilla garaged her car*, or *Bertie upped his score*, have been around in the language for a long time. In other words, social need has accelerated a tendency which has been in existence for a considerable number of years. It did not in itself instigate a change, but is merely carrying an ongoing one along a little faster.

A more complex, and perhaps more interesting, example of need fostering a syntactic change occurred in New York Black English.[34] Consider the sentence *It ain't no cat can't get in no coop*, spoken by Speedy, the leader of the Cobras, a gang of New York City adolescents, in a discussion about pigeon coops. What does he mean? is one's first reaction. Speedy, it appears, means 'No cat can get into any of the coops.' Has Speedy made a mistake, or does he really talk like that? is one's second reaction. We confirm that Speedy's sentence was intentional by noting a number of other similarly constructed sentences. For example, an old folk epic contains the line *There wasn't a son of a gun who this whore couldn't shun*, meaning 'This whore was so good, no man could shun her.' One's third reaction is to ask how such a seemingly strange construction came about in the first place. On examination, it seems to have arisen from a need for emphasis and vividness. Let us look at the stages by which such sentences developed.

We start out with a simple negative sentence such as *No cat can get in any coop*, which was at one time found in both Standard and Black American English. However, in order to make the negatives emphatic, and say as it were 'Not a single cat can get in any coop at all', Black English utilized a simple strategy of heaping up negatives, a device common in Chaucerian and Shakespearian English, and in many languages of the world. So we find emphatic negative sentences such as *No cat can't get in no coop*. In the course of time, the heaping up of negatives was no longer treated as an extra optional device used for emphasis, but became the standard obligatory way of coping with negation. Therefore a new method of expressing emphasis had to be found. This was to attach the phrase *it ain't* 'there isn't' to the front of the sentence. So we get *it ain't + no cat can't get in no coop*, giving Speedy's sentence: *It ain't no cat can't get in no coop*, parallel to a more standard 'There isn't a single cat that can get into any coop.'

Here, then, we have a state of affairs where a need for vividness and emphasis has led to the adoption of a new, optional stylistic device, in this case the heaping up of negatives. In the course of time, the optional device is used so often that it becomes the normal, obligatory form. So a newer, different device is brought in to cope with the need for emphasis – a process which could go on ad infinitum. Note, however, that although a new and superficially odd type of sentence has been introduced into the language, it came about by the utilization of two constructions already in the language: the heaping up of negatives, and the use of *it ain't* at the beginning of the sentence. So, once again, social need has made use of and accelerated already-existing tendencies.

The example just discussed arose out of a need for vividness or emphasis, a requirement which is probably universal. But other types of social need arise, which are also possibly universal. Let us consider two of these.

It pays to be polite

> This bill should be paid by return of post.
> Prompt payment would be appreciated.

These familiar-sounding messages reveal one apparently universal fact about human nature: humans are usually polite to one another, partly because polite behaviour gets better results than rudeness. Someone would be more likely to pay an outstanding bill when prompted by the sentences above, than by a blunt command:

> We order you to pay immediately.

Two observations can be made: first, humans all over the world are polite in similar ways. Second, politeness can affect the structure of the language.[35] Therefore, we find similar changes induced by politeness in different parts of the world. This is particularly noticeable in the pronoun system.[36]

Plural 'you' becoming singular polite 'you' is perhaps the most widespread 'politeness' change. Many languages have at least two forms of a pronoun meaning 'you', a singular and a plural. However, the plural form is widely felt to be more deferential. In numerous languages the plural 'you' has become the polite 'you', while the singular 'you' has become the familiar and intimate 'you', spoken to family, close friends and children. Its use to strangers is regarded as odd and offensive. In Germany, a woman fruit-seller was reportedly fined for addressing a police officer by the familiar *du* rather than the polite *Sie*. This deferential distancing is found not only in Europe – French, German, Italian, Spanish, Hungarian and Swedish are among the languages affected – but also further afield, in languages such as Quechua (South America) and Tamil (South India and Sri Lanka (Eelam)).

Other pronouns can be affected also. Tamil has carried 'plural for singular' politeness into other pronouns, so it has become normal to refer to people commanding respect, such as the prime minister, as 'they'. In Japanese, extreme, formalized politeness has affected the whole pronoun system. For example, the most formal word for 'I' *watakusi* originally meant 'slave' or 'servant'. Nor is this simply an Eastern phenomenon, because similar processes are reported to be taking place in Madagascar.

Another widespread politeness phenomenon may indirectly affect the pronoun system. This is the avoidance of pronouns, as in the English requests for payment at the beginning of this section. It is common to convey commands or requests in an indirect, suggestive way, with the word 'you' avoided. In the short run, this utilizes optional impersonal constructions which are available in most languages. In the longer run, their frequent use may overbalance the system, as apparently happened in the Celtic branch of Indo-European.

Politeness phenomena, then, are likely to accelerate tendencies already present, and may eventually cause imbalances which can disrupt the language in various ways.

Trickling across information

In ordinary conversations, people drip-feed information across to one another. Hearers just cannot absorb very much when messages are presented in compact chunks. This trickling across can affect the structure of the language, it is sometimes claimed. This is therefore another way in which social need may cause language change. Take the sentence

Alfred ate a goose.

This is a perfectly good English sentence, but is a fairly unlikely one, even in a family which included a greedy person called Alfred with a predilection for geese. Studies of actual speech have shown that it is not very common to have a sentence which contains the sequence subject – verb – object, with two 'full' nouns. Anyone who wanted to convey the fact that Alfred had eaten a goose would be likely to spread it out a bit:

Alfred slept all day today. When he woke up, he was so hungry, he ate a whole goose.

Full nouns are used sparingly, in order to drip the information across slowly. It is therefore more usual to find verbs with only either a full subject or a full object, not both, as in:

Alfred slept.
He ate a goose.

This preference for trickling messages across gradually via the above sentence patterns may be universal. It has, it is suggested, been a subsidiary cause of languages developing a type of structure which seems unusual to English speakers.[37] These are so-called 'ergative' languages, such as Sacapultec Maya, spoken in Guatemala. In these, the subject of an intransitive verb (a verb without an object, such as *sleep*) has the same syntactic form as the object of a transitive verb (verb with an object, such as *eat*). In other words, in the sentences *Alfred slept*, *He ate a goose*, *Alfred* and *goose* would probably have the same ending. But the pronoun *he*, the subject of a transitive verb, would have a different ending, showing *he* was the agent, the person who had done the eating:

ALFRED slept.

(He) ate a GOOSE.

Supposedly, this apparently odd way of doing things (by English standards) arose because people tend to associate together nouns which occur in noun–verb or verb–noun structures, and reserve a different ending for the first noun on the few occasions when full-noun – verb – full-noun all occur together.

This explanation for the development of ergative structures is still under discussion. However, even if it is wrong in its details, it shows that conversation structure and the requirements of hearers is another type of social need which could potentially affect the language.

Exploiting weaknesses

All the changes considered in this chapter were superficially caused by sociolinguistic factors – fashion, foreign influence, or social need. On closer examination, many turned out not to be 'real' causes, but simply accelerating agents which utilized and encouraged trends already existing in the language. When a gale blows down an elm tree, but leaves an oak standing, we do not believe that the gale alone caused the elm to fall. The gale merely advanced an event that would probably have occurred a few months or years later in any case. However, the gale dictated the direction in which the elm fell, which might in turn set off a further chain of events. If the elm fell against another tree, it might weaken this tree, and leave it vulnerable in another gale. Sociolinguistic causes of language change are similar to this gale. They exploit a weak point or potential imbalance in the system which might have been left unexploited. This exploitation may create further weak points in the system.

Since sociolinguistic causes are often superficial rather than deep causes of language change, let us now go on to consider what these deeper causes of change might be.

Note, incidentally, that a number of linguists might disagree with the judgment that sociolinguistic causes are 'superficial' and other types 'deep'. It might be more accurate, perhaps, to replace the terms 'superficial' and 'deep' with the words 'immediate' and 'long-term', which do not imply that one type is more important than the other. It is clear that no long-term cause can take effect without an immediate trigger. It is equally clear that sociolinguistic factors do not set off changes randomly. The language must be ready to move in that particular direction. In the next chapter, we will consider some of these directions.

11 Doing what comes naturally
Inherent causes of language change

> Thou wilt not with predestination round
> Enmesh me, and impute my Fall to Sin?
> > Edward Fitzgerald, *Rubaiyat of Omar Khayyam*

Introduction

This chapter deals with inbuilt causes of language change. Sounds are made with the human vocal tract, mainly the mouth, throat and lungs. These sounds are obviously restricted by the nature of the apparatus which produces them, and this causes some inevitable changes. The human mind also contains a number of natural tendencies, which also affect language. Once these tendencies creep in, they can also cause ensuing disruptions. This chapter will outline these inherent causes of change.

The causes of language change are double-layered. On the top layer, there are social triggers. These set off or accelerate deeper causes, hidden tendencies which may be lying dormant within the language. The gun of change has been loaded and cocked at an earlier stage. In this chapter, we shall discuss this notion of underlying tendencies. Many of them appear disruptive. We shall therefore examine, in particular, changes which arise seemingly out of the blue to disrupt the language system.

Ease of effort, in the sense of ease of articulation, is the proposed cause of disruption which springs most easily to one's mind. There is a deep-rooted belief among quite a number of people that, were it not for the need to be understood, all human speech would be reduced to a prolonged *uh*. Ease-of-effort theories have been around for a long time. They were particularly prevalent in the nineteenth century, when educated men tended to idealize the 'noble savage', whose apparent virtues seemed to contrast strongly with the vices and decadence of civilization. At that time, we find the linguist

Max Müller claiming that, owing to a laziness inherent in civilization, sophisticated people do not use the forceful articulatory movements required for primitive tongues.[1] In civilized languages, he maintained, speakers avoid difficult guttural sounds, and show a preference for relatively easy sounds produced fairly far forward in the mouth – a claim which turns out to be totally unsubstantiated, since there is no evidence that any language is 'more primitive' than any other, or that primitive cultures use more 'throaty' sounds than advanced cultures.

A more sophisticated view of changes which are castigated as laziness, however, is that they are tendencies which are inevitably built into language because of the anatomical, physiological and psychological make-up of human beings. As the quotation at the beginning of the chapter suggests, we may be dealing with predestination rather than sin. Let us go on to substantiate this viewpoint by outlining some developments which have happened repeatedly, and are happening currently in the languages of the world.

Dropping off consonants

Let us begin with what seems to be a typical case of sloppiness, the loss of consonants at the end of words.

Consider French *n*. Between the ninth and fourteenth centuries AD, spoken French gradually lost *n* at the end of words such as *an* 'year', *en* 'in', *bon* 'good', *bien* 'well', *coin* 'corner', *fin* 'end', *brun* 'brown', and nasalized the preceding vowel.[2] As noted earlier (Chapter 6), this change began with the words where *n* was preceded by [a], a vowel in which the tongue is held low and the mouth kept relatively wide open. It then moved to mid-vowels such as [e] and [o], and finally to vowels such as [i] and [u], in which the tongue is high and the mouth relatively closed. In other words, the lower the tongue, and the more open the mouth, the earlier this change occurred. Why?

In the twentieth century, phoneticians discovered quite a lot about how sounds are produced. At first, techniques were crude, and relied on chance mishaps. In one early case, a cancer patient, unluckily for him, but luckily for phoneticians, had a large portion of his cheek and nose removed: his tongue movements were exposed to view, and carefully filmed. But these days, phonetics has become a sophisticated topic, which has helped historical linguists, among others.[3] Modern techniques have provided new insights, and also confirmed some things that phoneticians had long suspected: when the sequence [an] is pronounced, the nasal cavity – the space behind the nose – cannot be totally closed off during the vowel [a]. The result is that the sequence [an] is always [ãn], with a slightly nasalized vowel. This means that there is an imbalance between [ãn] and the other sounds [en], [in], [on], [un]. There will be a tendency to do two things: first, to omit an unnecessary [n] after [ã] – since the vowel is now nasalized, the final nasal is redundant; secondly, to allow the nasalization to spread to other vowels, in order to preserve the symmetry of the sound system (something which will be discussed further in the next chapter). In other words, any language which possesses the sequence vowel + *n* has a potential weak spot in the language. Starting with *a* + *n* the vowels may become nasalized, and the final nasal is likely to be lost.[4] This is a very common change, and has occurred in the last millennium in Chinese, as well as French.

So far then we have seen that the human inability to close off the nasal cavity during the pronunciation of the sequence [an] causes a weak spot in language which could potentially be exploited. However, this is not the only reason why final nasals (nasals at the end of words) are weak. *All* consonants are weak at the end of a word if no vowel follows. They are weakly articulated, and difficult to perceive. Within the last millennium, the voiceless stops [p], [t], [k] have been lost at the end of words in French, Chinese and Maori, among other languages. In Chinese, they were at first replaced by a glottal stop – a stoppage of the airstream with no sound involved. Then this glottal stop was lost. Several dialects of British English – Cockney and Glaswegian, for example – now have glottal stops in place of final [t] and [k], and, less often, [p]. So English is possibly following the same track.

This development is not just 'sloppiness', but is due to the general and inevitable weakness of articulation of sounds at the end of words. Let us consider the physical facts behind this occurrence.

The consonants [p], [t], [k] are produced, like all stops, by totally obstructing the air flow at some point, in this case at the lips for [p], the teeth (or just behind the teeth) for [t], and the palate (roof of the mouth) for [k]. The actual articulation of a stop consists of three successive stages: first, the placing of the obstruction; secondly, the building up of compressed air behind the obstruction; and thirdly, an explosion as the obstruction is removed. These three stages can be detected if you try saying slowly and with emphasis: 'You *p*ig! You *t*oad! You *c*uckoo!' Now try saying 'Have a good slee*p*! Good nigh*t*! Good lu*ck*!' Even if you say these emphatically, you are likely to find that the explosion is considerably weaker when [p], [t], [k] occur at the end of a word. Anyone who habitually exploded stops occurring at the end of a word as strongly as those at the beginning would sound both pompous and theatrical. In fact, it is extremely difficult to explode them strongly without adding an extra vowel on the end: 'Good sleep-a', 'Good night-a', 'Good luck-a'. The difficulty of exploding final stops means that it is not uncommon for stops at the end of a word to be 'unreleased', that is, unexploded. In the phrase 'Good night!', for example, normal breathing is often resumed after the closure and compression stages, without any explosion occurring.

The weakness and gradual loss of final consonants is not only due to feeble articulation. It is compounded and accelerated by the fact that such sounds are difficult to hear, particularly when unexploded. Speakers of Cantonese, a Chinese dialect which has unreleased final stops, were tested on their ability to distinguish between them.[5] When words were read in lists, out of context, hearers made wrong decisions about almost half of them. They perceived 668 correctly, and 520 wrongly, out of a total of 1,188. Final nasals produced a marginally better result. Hearers were wrong about approximately one-third: they perceived 845 correctly, and 343 incorrectly, out of a total of 1,188.

When final stops have become virtually indistinguishable, the next stage is for them to become *really* indistinguishable. Most Chinese dialects simply replaced all three voiceless stops with a glottal stop (which, as noted earlier, is a stoppage of the outgoing breath with no sound involved). Eventually, the glottal stop itself tends to be omitted, resulting in the total loss of the original consonant.

Overall, then, it is normal for consonants to disappear at the ends of words over the ages. It has already happened in numerous languages over the centuries, and will undoubtedly happen in many more. It is as much of a crime for words gradually to lose their endings as it is for rivers gradually to erode river beds, or rain to wear away limestone. Let us now go on to consider some other natural, predictable developments.

Linking sounds together

Anyone learning a new language speaks slowly, haltingly, one word at a time, with each section of a word pronounced carefully and clearly. As the learner becomes more fluent, these separate words and sounds are linked together into a smoother style of speech. The jerkiness and unnaturalness of saying words one by one is used to great comic effect by Bernard Shaw in *Pygmalion*, when Eliza Doolittle self-consciously carries her pronunciation exercises into practice in front of a group of people: 'How – do – you – do?'

The linking together of sounds and words is carried out primarily in two ways. First, by assimilation, 'becoming similar': when two sounds are adjacent, one often moves partially or wholly in the direction of the other. Secondly, by omission: in a group of sounds clustered together, one sometimes gets left out. As an example of the first process, try saying the sentences *I want you to warn Peter* and *I want you to warm Peter* fairly fast. At normal conversational speed, there is unlikely to be any difference between the two. *Warn* is likely to have been influenced by the following *p* and become *warm* also. As an example of the second process, say the sentence *George banged the drum hard as he marched through the town*. At normal conversational speed, you are likely to have omitted the final sound in *banged, marched*, and said: *George bang(ed) the drum hard as he march(ed) through the town*. Even people who criticize others for 'swallowing their words' are likely to assimilate and omit sounds in the way described above, though they would probably deny it. As noted in Chapter 5, such phenomena tend to creep into the language unnoticed. Suddenly, there comes an arbitrary point at which people stop ignoring them, and start noticing and complaining.

When assimilations and omissions occur between words, they are usually only temporary: we normally pronounce *would you* as 'wood-joo' [wʊdʒu:], but the word *you* is in no danger of changing to *joo* in other contexts. However, when assimilation and omission occur within words instead of between them, the effect is likely to be longer-lasting – though the spelling can often prevent people from realizing that a change has occurred. Almost everyone, for example, pronounces the word *handbag* as *hambag*, with omission of the *d* in *hand*, and a change of the *n* to *m*, due to the influence of the following *b* (since *m* and *b* are both produced by closing the lips). However, few people will admit to this 'sloppy' pronunciation. Many, when challenged, are convinced that they say *handbag* – though the same people will usually admit to saying *hankerchief*, rather than *handkerchief*. If a change occurs in enough words, people grow to accept it, and eventually treat the spelling rather than the pronunciation as aberrant. For example, no one nowadays worries that we do not pronounce the *t* in words such as *whistle, thistle, castle, fasten, hasten*, even though one might expect people to want to keep *t* in *fasten* and *hasten* in order to retain their connection with *fast* and *haste*. But in this case, it is the spelling which people generally want to reform.

Assimilation and omission are found the world over, especially when two or more consonants meet. Furthermore, there is some evidence that an alternating consonant–vowel–consonant–vowel sequence is the most natural one for the human vocal organs, and a few linguists have tried to argue that all languages are subconsciously striving towards this natural state. This view is perhaps somewhat extreme, but it is certainly true that fluent speakers in every known language inevitably simplify consonant sequences, particularly if they are able to make themselves understood without pronouncing each sound in detail. As one phonetician expressed it, 'Language does what it has to do for efficiency and gets away with what it can.'[6]

This can seem like laziness only to a real pedant – the equivalent of someone who, when dealing with the written language, prints each letter of each word slowly and separately, and who is likely to spend all day meticulously writing and mailing one letter. A more realistic view might be that language is simply being efficient. The situation is in some ways analogous to that described in Shirley Conran's best-selling book *Superwoman* (1975). How, she asks, can a woman be super-efficient and get more things done in her life? The answer is: 'Try cutting out anything which isn't essential. The secret is *elimination* . . . Consider these timesavers . . . Don't dry dishes. Don't lay a tablecloth or use table napkins. Don't make beds, don't iron handkerchiefs. Don't iron pyjamas or nightclothes.' Language leaves out or glosses over inessential sounds in much the same way. Conran noted that 'Life is too short to stuff a mushroom.' One might also say that life is too short to put a *d* on the end of each *and*: whether we are talking about *bread an' butter, bread an' honey* or *strawberries an' cream* – the *d* is not required.

Other natural tendencies

One of the major discoveries of the twentieth century was the tremendous amount of variation that exists in speech sounds: the 'same' sound is measurably different when spoken by different speakers, in different words, at different speeds, and at different levels of loudness.[7]

But amidst all this variation, how do people manage to understand one another? They mentally **normalize** or **correct** the sounds they actually hear, to what they think they should have heard. 'I taught I taw a puddy tat' is easily 'translated' into 'I thought I saw a pussy cat', and the speaker is assumed to be a cartoon character, or maybe someone with a heavy cold.

Yet if speakers automatically filter out any distortions, how does language ever change? Speakers mentally correct what they hear, it turns out, only if they notice that something needs correcting. Sometimes, they simply get confused by sounds which seem alike to the ear, even though they may be produced quite differently. The sound [kw], for example, as in *queen*, has two components: a velar [k] made fairly far back in the mouth, and a labial [w] made with the lips. Typically, hearers notice that a stop (sound produced with a stoppage of breath) is involved, and also that the lips are used. They combine these two elements and produce a labial stop, [p] or [b], and this change is found in far-flung languages. Proto-Indo-European *ekwos 'horse', as in Latin *equus* and the word *equestrian*, became Classical Greek *hippos*, as in the word *hippopotamus*, literally 'river horse'. In Proto-Muskogean (an American-Indian language family), *kwihi became Choctaw *bihi* 'mulberry'. And examples of this change could be multiplied.[8]

In recent years phoneticians have built up a fairly extensive list of changes which happen repeatedly. Some are due to the difficulty of co-ordinating a number of articulatory movements perfectly, others to perceptual problems, and others to idiosyncratic effects which certain sounds have on others.

Compare, for example, the word *fambly*, meaning 'family', as in 'I don't recollect that John had a fambly', said by the Oklahoma-raised preacher in John Steinbeck's famous novel *The grapes of wrath* (1939), the English word *bramble*, and the Greek word *ambrosia* 'food of the gods'. At an earlier stage, each of these words lacked a *b*: *fam(i)ly, braem(e)l, amrotia*. They show that a sequence [ml] or [mr] is likely to change in the course of time into [mbl] and [mbr].[9] This is because it is exceptionally difficult to co-ordinate the articulatory movements involved in the pronunciation of [ml] and [mr]. The lips are closed during the articulation of [m], and the nasal cavity open. If, at the end of [m], the nasal cavity is closed before the lips are opened, by even a fraction of a second, the result will be an intrusive [b]. Similarly, [p] tends to creep in between [m] and [t]: many people pronounce *dreamt, warmth, something, hamster*, as if they were spelled *drempt, warmpth, somepthing, hampster*. [t] tends to creep in between [n] and [s], so words such as *fancy, tinsel, mincer, prince*, often sound something like *fantsy, tintsel, mintser, prints*. Ask someone to repeat a sentence such as *Would you recognize the footprints of Prince Charles?* and check if there is any difference between *prints* and *prince*. Your informant is unlikely to make any distinction.

A recurrent change which is sometimes attributed to difficulty of perception is that of 'dark' *l* to *u*. English *l*, when it occurs at the end of a word, or before a consonant, as in *pill, bottle, film, milk*, is pronounced with the back of the tongue raised, a so-called 'dark' or 'velar' *l* [ɫ]. Compare the 'ordinary' *l* in *lip* [lip] with the 'dark' *l* in *pill* [piɫ]. Dark *l* [ɫ] can sound similar to *u* [ʊ][10] – and some varieties of English now have words sounding like *bottu, fium, miuk*, in place of *bottle, film, milk*.

These are a mere sample of the phonetic tendencies which are present in all human languages, tendencies which are the inevitable result of a human's physical make-up.[11] Some of them occur invariably whenever certain sounds are produced, others put in an appearance only intermittently. Some of them can be guaranteed to cause change, others wait in the wings, as it were, biding their time until some chance circumstance allows them to sneak in and take hold. Clearly, different languages do not implement all possible tendencies at once, and different languages will be affected in different ways. Something which profoundly affects one language can leave another untouched. For example, it has recently been noted that, the world over, there is a natural tendency to pronounce vowels on a slightly higher pitch after voiceless consonants such as [p], [t], [k], than after voiced consonants such as [b], [d], [g].[12] This tendency became exaggerated in Chinese many centuries ago, and the exaggeration was followed by a loss of the distinction between voiced and voiceless consonants. The result is that Chinese is now a tone language – one which distinguishes between words by means of variations in pitch. This potential development has left European languages untouched.

It can be instructive to look at dialects of the same language, and see which tendencies are implemented, and which not. It often happens that change infiltrates at the same weak spots in several dialects, though each dialect will respond in a different way. For example, it is physically difficult to maintain a single voiceless stop such as [t] when it is surrounded by vowels: these stops have become voiced in American English, where *latter* and *ladder* can be indistinguishable from the point of view of the consonants in the middle. In British English, on the other hand, people sometimes simply cut off the airstream, rather than pronouncing [t] fully, resulting in a glottal stop, heard in the Cockney pronunciations of *bu'er* (*butter*), *le'er* (*letter*), and so on.

Once a change has entered a language, it can be accelerated, slowed down or even reversed by both social and linguistic factors. A Swedish change which started in the fourteenth century involves the loss of final [d] in words such as *ved* 'wood', *hund* 'dog' and *blad* 'leaf'. Yet a survey in Stockholm showed fewer instances of omitted [d] in the city nowadays than there were previously.[13] The change seems to be reversing itself, perhaps due to the spread of literacy, which has caused Swedes to take note of the written form of the word, which is spelt with *d*. Again, in some dialects of American English, it is common to omit the second of two consonants at the end of words such as *kept, crept, swept*, resulting in *kep', crep', swep'*. But if loss of the final consonant would result in confusion between the present and past forms of the verb, it is retained: so we find *stepped, heaped*, not **step', *heap'*.[14] In this case, therefore, a change has been halted in one particular part of the language only.

A similar example of a partial holding back of a natural tendency occurs in French, a language which has a large number of vowels. Four of these are nasal vowels: [ã] and [ɔ̃] as in *blanc* [blã] 'white' and *blond* [blɔ̃] 'fair'; and [ɛ̃] and [œ̃] as in *brin* [brɛ̃] 'shoot, blade' and *brun* [brœ̃] 'brown'. From the point of view of the hearer, these pairs contain vowels which are relatively difficult to distinguish (a fact known by all English learners of French!). The second pair, [ɛ̃] and [œ̃], seem, predictably, to be merging. But members of the first pair, [ã] and [ɔ̃], seem to be maintaining their identity with no hint of confusion.[15] Why? Perhaps because this pair distinguishes between numerous common words such as *temps* 'weather', *ton* 'tone', *lent* 'slow', *long* 'long'. The other pair distinguishes between relatively few. So once again, natural tendencies cannot be looked at alone, since their implementation is governed by additional social and linguistic factors.

Although slowing down or reversals of changes are possible, as the above examples show, change usually creeps on inexorably, hindered to some extent by literacy and other social factors, but not for long. 'You may drive out nature with a pitchfork, but she will always come back,' said the Latin poet Horace.[16] This could apply to sound change.

Natural developments in syntax

Just as we find parallel sound changes occurring in geographically and culturally separated languages, so we find parallel syntactic changes. Ancient Greek, for example, and certain Niger-Congo languages changed their basic word order in a set of remarkably similar stages. It is likely, therefore, that universal mental tendencies exist parallel to the physical ones which we have already discussed. Such tendencies are more difficult to confirm, since in our current state of knowledge we cannot relate them to the structure of the brain in the same way that we can relate phonetic tendencies to properties of the ear and vocal organs.

Let us consider two possible examples of the type of tendency we are discussing, both of which are present in the Greek and Niger-Congo word order changes mentioned above. The first of these is a preference for keeping the object and the main verb close together in a sentence.[17] This can be exemplified in a trivial way in English. We say sentences such as *Henry seduced Petronella in the woods on Saturday* with a preference for putting the verb *seduce* next to the object *Petronella* rather than **Henry seduced in the woods on Saturday Petronella*. If in English a construction involves an object being moved a considerable distance from the verb, there is a tendency to repeat the object a second time, even though people do not usually realize they are doing this,[18] as in: *Petronella is the kind of girl who when he had arrived in the woods with the primroses blooming and the birds singing Henry felt impelled to seduce (her)*. The final word *her* is put in by a lot of people in sentences of this type, though strictly speaking it is unnecessary, since the object of the word *seduce* is really the preceding *who*, which occurred near the beginning of the sentence. These examples could be paralleled in numerous languages. In Ancient Greek[19] and in Kru,[20] the most western of the Kwa sub-group of Niger-Congo languages, we find a similar phenomenon which contributed in the long run to a fairly dramatic alteration in language structure. There was a preference for changing sentences such as:

The sceptre which was studded with golden nails he threw down (Greek)
The rice which the child bought he did not eat (Kru)

into sentences which maintain object–verb closeness as:

The sceptre he threw down which was studded with golden nails
The rice he did not eat, which the child bought.

This change was one of a number which weakened a previously strong tendency for placing the main verb at the end of the sentence.

Another, overlapping tendency concerns sentences which have two objects which share a single verb, as in *Aloysius likes shrimps and oysters*, which is, in effect, *Aloysius likes shrimps and Aloysius likes oysters.* There is a tendency in language to omit unnecessary repetitions. Now consider the effect of this on a language which normally places its verbs at the end of a sentence. The 'full' form is *Aloysius shrimps likes and Aloysius oysters likes.* When we omit the repetition, we end up with *Aloysius shrimps likes and oysters* – a deviant sentence in the sense that it does not end with a main verb like the other sentences in the language. So, in ancient Greek and Kru, we find sentences such as *They were barley feeding on and oats* (Greek) and *He not fish buy and rice* (Kru) at a time when the 'canonical' sentence form required a verb at the end.

In the case of both ancient Greek and Kru, then, a natural tendency to maintain object–verb closeness, and a natural tendency to delete repetitions, were factors which helped to destroy the normal pattern of placing verbs at the end of sentences. Gradually, the verb became more mobile, and eventually it became standard to place it in the middle of sentences, between the subject and the object, as in English.

Shadowing the world

Languages inevitably shadow the world, and try to retain this shadowing, it is sometimes claimed. That is, they weakly copy certain external features, a phenomenon known as **iconicity**.[21] Iconicity applies to the relationship between linguistic items, not to individual items (where the link between sound and meaning is mostly arbitrary, Chapter 2). Consider the case of the plural. Most, perhaps all, languages distinguish between more than one, and one (*cows* vs *cow*). On balance, plurals are 'heavier' than singulars. The extra items are apparently compensated for by a longer word. This parallelism can be shown in a diagram, so giving rise to the pompous term 'diagrammatic iconicity' to describe the situation (Figure 11.1).

To take another example, verbs have various attachments, which elaborate on the events they describe. The type of action is often specified (such as repetitive vs single action), and so is location in time or 'tense' (such as past). A study of fifty languages suggested that any attachments which described the type of action were likely to be nearer the verb stem than those for tense.[22] In

Cow   Cows

Figure 11.1   'Diagrammatic iconicity' of singular and plural

Latin, for example, *it* added to a verb stem originally indicated repetition. So *palpito* meant 'to palpitate, throb or flicker', and *crepito*
meant 'to rattle or clatter'. The tense (e.g. past *-ba-*) came afterwards, as in *cor palpitabat* 'The heart was throbbing.' This fits in
with our intuitions about the world, that the type of action is more
closely connected to the verb than the time of occurrence.

Veni, vidi, vici. 'I came, I saw, I conquered.' These well-known
words, supposedly said by Julius Caesar, list events in the order
in which they happened. In some ways, this is common sense,
since many sentences would be incomprehensible if the order was
reversed:

Herbert ran into the road and fell under a bus

is understandable. But

He fell under a bus and ran into the road

is bizarre and puzzling. As these examples show, this is another way
in which language shadows the world. Iconicity is deeply built into
language, possibly to a greater extent than has been realized.

Metaphor is a further example of iconicity. Phrases such as:

the *head* of the organization
the *ribs* of the ship
the *neck* of the bottle

suggest how links between the world and language are initiated
(Chapter 9) and perpetually maintained.

The iconicity claim is therefore twofold. First, when languages
develop plurals, or verb morphology, or words for new objects,
their general behaviour follows natural preferences which shadow

behaviour in the real world. Second, the statistical likelihood that languages retain this shadowing is so high that it must affect the way languages develop. This type of exploration is still relatively new and controversial. But it appears to be a variety of natural change which cannot be ignored.

With all these disruptions it would not be surprising, perhaps, if a language gradually collapsed under the increasing strain. In fact, this does not happen. Language seems to have a remarkable tendency to restore its patterns and maintain its equilibrium. This is the topic of the next chapter.

12 Repairing the patterns
Therapeutic changes

> I consider that a man's brain originally is like a little
> empty attic and you have to stock it with such functions
> as you choose . . . It is a mistake to think that that little
> room has elastic walls and can distend to any extent.
>
> A. Conan Doyle, A study in scarlet (1888)

Introduction

This chapter outlines how human language maintains its patterns. Language has an inbuilt self-regulating capacity which restores and maintains a patterned equilibrium. The most obvious examples of patterns are in the sound system, where sounds are often organized in pairs. Word endings tend to neaten themselves up in the morphology. Syntax also tends to keep itself neat, though this is sometimes via misanalysis, when difficult-to-interpret patterns are smoothed away. Finally, it shows how language can invent uses, and patterned rules, for apparently useless bits and pieces.

Many people believe, like Sherlock Holmes, that the human brain has a finite capacity. Recent work on memory, however, suggests that such a view is mistaken. A healthy person's memory is indefinitely extendable provided that the information it contains is well organized, and not just a jumbled heap of random items.

Every language contains a finite number of patterns, as we have already pointed out. It is these patterns which enable humans to remember any language so apparently effortlessly. If the patterns were to break down, a person's brain would become overloaded with fragmented pieces of information. Efficient communication would become difficult, if not impossible.

As this chapter will show, language has a remarkable instinct for self-preservation. It contains inbuilt self-regulating devices which restore broken patterns and prevent disintegration. More accurately, of course, it is the speakers of the language who perform these adjustments in response to some innate need to structure the information they have to remember.

In a sense, language can be regarded as a garden, and its speakers as gardeners who keep the garden in a good state. How do they do this? There are at least three possible versions of this garden metaphor – a strong version, a medium version, and a weak version.

In the strong version, the gardeners tackle problems before they arise. They are so knowledgeable about potential problems that they are able to forestall them. They might, for example, put weedkiller on the grass before any weeds spring up and spoil the beauty of the lawn. In other words, they practise prophylaxis.

In the medium version, the gardeners nip problems in the bud, as it were. They wait until they occur, but then deal with them before they get out of hand like the Little Prince in Saint-Exupéry's fairy story,[1] who goes round his small planet every morning rooting out baobab trees when they are still seedlings, before they can do any real damage.

In the weak version of the garden metaphor, the gardener acts only when disaster has struck, when the garden is in danger of becoming a jungle, like the lazy man, mentioned by the Little Prince, who failed to root out three baobabs when they were still a manageable size, and faced a disaster on his planet.

Which of these versions is relevant for language? The strong, the medium, the weak, or all three? First of all, we can dismiss the strong version, in which the gardener avoids problems by planning for them in advance. As far as language goes, we have not found any evidence for prophylactic change. Language does not show any tendency to avoid potential problems. In fact, quite the opposite is true: it tends to invite them, as the last chapter showed. There is considerable evidence, however, for both the medium and the weak versions of therapeutic change. In some cases, relatively minor deviations are smoothed away before any real disruptions occur. At other times, language is obliged to make massive therapeutic changes in order to restore some semblance of order, either because small imbalances have been allowed to creep in and expand, or because previous problems have been dealt with in a short-sighted way, causing in the long run more trouble than might have been expected. In this chapter we will look at some examples of pattern neatening, cases in which the gardeners keep problems at bay by dealing with them at an early stage. In the next chapter, we will look at more dramatic therapy, cases in which early actions have been unsuccessful or have in turn caused further problems.

Neatening the sound patterns

A well-organized gardener tends to grow vegetables in neat rows. Language also seems to have a preference for neat, formal patterns, particularly in the realm of sounds.

As everybody is aware, sounds differ from language to language. Each language picks a different set of sounds from the sum total which it is possible to produce with the human vocal organs. However, the sounds picked will not be a random selection. They tend to be organized in predictable ways. For example, there is a strong tendency towards symmetry: both vowels and consonants are generally arranged in pairs (or occasionally triples).

One common type of pairing found among consonants is the matching of a so-called voiceless sound (one in which the vocal cords are vibrated late) with a voiced sound (one in which the vocal cords are vibrated early). So, in many languages [p] has a partner [b], [t] has a partner [d], [k] has a partner [g], and so on. Each of these pairs is pronounced mostly in the same way, apart from the voicing.

voiceless	p	t	k
voiced	b	d	g

Now consider English fricatives, consonants in which the air flowing from the lungs is partially impeded at some point, resulting in audible friction. In the eighteenth century, there were eight fricatives:

voiceless	[f] fish	[θ] thin	[s] song	[ʃ] ship	[h] hen
voiced	[v] van	[ð] then	[z] zebra		

At this time [f], [θ] and [s] all had voiced partners, whereas [ʃ] and [h] did not. This is a situation in which we might predict alteration, and one in which alteration did indeed occur – and is still occurring.

Pattern neatening began in the nineteenth century, when a partner was created for [ʃ]. This is the sound [ʒ] found in words such as *pleasure, genre, beige*. The new sound came from two different sources. First, a *y*-sound [j] crept into the pronunciation of words such as *pleasure* and *treasure*. These had originally been pronounced as if they ended in *-zer* as in *geezer*. When this *-zer* changed to *-zyer*, *zy* soon became [ʒ] in fast speech, then was adopted as the standard pronunciation. You can test the tendency of *zy* to become [ʒ] by saying rapidly several times: *Are these **your** books?* The second way in which [ʒ] crept into the language was via words borrowed from French, such as *beige, rouge, genre* and, later, *aubergine, garage* and others. If there had not been a 'gap' for the sound [ʒ], we would have expected the French words to be altered to fit in with existing English sounds, as usually happens with loan words.

Now that [ʃ] has a partner, what about [h], the only unpaired English sound? [h] shows no signs of acquiring a mate. Instead, it may be in the process of disappearing. It has already been lost in a number of British dialects, such as London Cockney, which has been *h*-less for a long time. Consider Uriah Heep's claim to humility in Charles Dickens' novel *David Copperfield*: 'I am well aware that I am the 'umblest person going. My mother is likewise a very 'umble person. We live in a numble abode.' Or look at items in the so-called Cockney Alphabet: *A for 'orses* 'hay for horses', *I for lootin'* 'high-faluting', *N for eggs* 'hen for eggs'. [h] would probably have been lost more widely were it not for the strong and somewhat illogical social pressure to retain it. Numerous nineteenth-century etiquette books condemned *h*-dropping as a mark of inferiority: 'Nothing so surely stamps a man as below the mark in intelligence, self-respect, and energy, as this unfortunate habit,' huffed Henry Alford, Dean of Canterbury, in 1864.[2] However, the fight to retain [h] may be a losing battle, since it is not only partnerless but also relatively weakly articulated and difficult to hear.

The English treatment of [ʒ] and [h], then, is an example of how language tends to neaten up patterns by aligning the consonants in pairs. The symmetry of vowel systems is perhaps even more dramatic. Broadly speaking, vowels are formed by moving the tongue around the mouth in such a way as never quite to touch anything else, such as the teeth or roof of the mouth, so that the air flowing from the lungs is relatively unimpeded. A major distinction is that between **front** vowels, in which the highest part of the tongue is relatively far forward, and **back** vowels in which it is relatively far back. In addition, **high** vowels are those in which the tongue is relatively high, and **low** vowels are those in which it is relatively low. If we take X-ray photographs of the tongue producing the vowels [a] roughly as in Standard British English *part*, [e] as in *pet*, [i] as in *pit*, [o] as in *pot* and [u] as in *boot*, we can then make a note of the highest point of the tongue as each vowel is made (see Figure 12.1). As can be seen, these points form a rough triangle.

Now an interesting thing about vowel systems is that front vowels tend to be paired with back vowels.

In a system with five vowels like the one shown in Figure 12.2, [i] will be paired with [u], and [e] with [o]. If one of a pair moves, the other is likely to follow a few years or decades later. For example, if [e] moves closer to [i], [o] will follow suit by moving closer to [u] (see Figure 12.3).

The situation is reminiscent of two young lovers who cannot quite let one another out of each other's sight, or perhaps a better image would be that of a detective shadowing a suspect. The suspect moves up the street, and so does the detective, though keeping to the other side of the road, so the two never actually collide. An example of this type of shadowing is seen in the Martha's Vineyard change (Chapter 4) – it is not chance that [ai] and [au] are moving around together. Once one of these diphthongs starts to move, then it is almost inevitable that the other will follow suit.

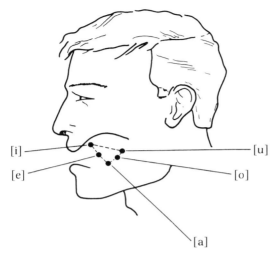

Figure 12.1   Sketch of tongue position in the vowels [i], [e], [a], [o], [u]

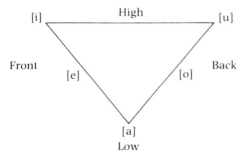

Figure 12.2   Vowel triangle

A more dramatic example of this phenomenon is seen in the early history of the Romance languages.[3] The various Romance languages each made different alterations in the vowels of Proto-Romance, the provincial Latin from which they were descended, yet each of them maintained parallelism between the front and back vowels. Compare, for example, Italian, in which both front and back vowels were lowered, with Sardinian, in which they were raised (see Figure 12.4 on p. 182).

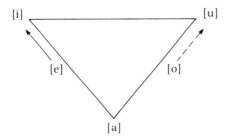

Figure 12.3   Vowel pairing

The shuttling around of sounds in company with one another is something to which speakers are usually totally oblivious. They are, however, generally more aware of pattern neatening when it involves words and word endings, which is often referred to under the catch-all term of **analogy**, as will be discussed below.

Tidying up dangling wires

The human mind often behaves like 'an electrician who is summoned to sort out a dangling wire and connects it up to the first other dangling wire that he or she finds', notes one linguist, commenting on the tendency of human beings to tidy up their language.[4]

This predilection for clearing away loose ends is evident in the treatment of English plurals. Earlier (Chapter 1), we mentioned a journalist who experienced a 'queasy distaste' whenever she heard the word *media* used as a singular noun. This plural tends to be treated as singular because it does not end in *-s* like most others. The reverse also happens, with singular nouns ending in *-s* treated as plural. The word *pea* was originally *pease*, as in the rhyme:

> Pease pudding hot, pease pudding cold
> Pease pudding in the pot nine days old.

It was gradually assumed that the form *pease* was plural, and a new singular *pea* came into being.

Although upsetting to individuals who do not want their language to change, these examples are part of a long-term tidying-up

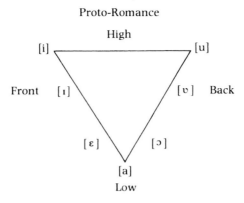

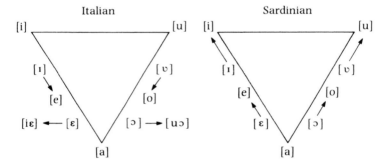

Figure 12.4   Vowel pairing in the Romance languages

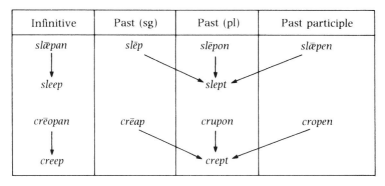

Figure 12.5   Changes in the verbs *sleep* and *creep*

process which has been affecting English plurals for centuries.[5] In Old English, there were a variety of different endings to express the concept of 'more than one': for example, *cwene* 'queens', *scipu* 'ships', *hundas* 'dogs', *suna* 'sons', *eagan* 'eyes'. Over the centuries these were gradually whittled down. First, they were narrowed down to a choice mainly between *-s* and *-n*. In Shakespeare's time we still find forms such as *eyen* 'eyes', *shooen* 'shoes', *housen* 'houses'. Now *-s* is the normal plural, apart from a few minor exceptions such as *men, sheep, oxen*. (It is slightly misleading to say that the normal plural is *-s*, since it is in fact [s] after voiceless sounds, [z] after voiced ones, and [ɪz] after affricates and sibilants, as in *cats, dogs, horses*.)

A similar tidying-up process is apparent in English verbs over the past millennium. Figure 12.5 shows the confusing alternations in the parts of the Old English verbs *slǣpan* 'sleep' and *crēopan* 'creep', beside their current replacements.

This type of neatening is often referred to under the general heading of **analogy** – the tendency of items that are similar in meaning to become similar in form. Children often iron out irregularities in language as they acquire it, and temporarily produce sentences such as *Toby comed today, We goed home, Polly catched it*. At one time, it seemed natural to linguists to assume that it was children who caused analogical neatening: 'If languages were learned perfectly by the children of each generation then languages would not change . . . The changes in languages are simply slight mistakes, which in the course of generations completely alter the character of the language,' asserted Henry Sweet in 1899.[6] This view rightly faded, though (somewhat surprisingly) enjoyed a temporary resurgence in the 1960s and 1970s: 'the ultimate source of dialect divergence – and of linguistic change in general – is the process of language acquisition', wrote Henning Andersen in 1978.[7] However, a few years later, a careful study showed that the 'children cause regularization' theory was false, since they soon acquired the normal forms from those around them.[8]

The term analogy is somewhat vague, and has been used as a general catch-term for a number of different phenomena: sound change may even be a type of analogy, as discussed in Chapter 6. It may be more useful to note two general principles behind the pattern neatenings:

1   There should be one form per unit of meaning. For example, the notion 'plural' or 'past' should each be expressed by a single ending, not a great number of them. This is sometimes known as the 'principle of isomorphism'.[9]

2   Alternation in the form of words should be systematic and easily detectable. For example, the rules which govern the formation of plurals and past tenses should be easy to work out by someone learning the language. A common way of expressing this is to say that language minimizes **opacity** in that it lessens confusing 'opaque' situations, and maximizes **transparency**, in that it moves towards constructions which are clear or 'transparent'.

In other words, language tends to eliminate pointless variety, and prefers constructions which are clear and straightforward. These principles work not only in the case of word endings, as in the examples of plurals and past tenses above, but also in more involved constructions. Let us examine some examples of these.

Smoothing out the syntax

People do not usually realize they are tidying up chunks of syntax. This is because the tidying up often happens by a process of misinterpretation. Speakers tend to misanalyse a construction which has become confusing or unclear in terms of a more familiar one with superficial similarities.

This happened with so-called impersonal verbs in English,[10] verbs which have an impersonal pronoun as their subject, of which we now find only sporadic examples, such as:

> *It is raining*
> *It seems* Matthew is ill.

Many more verbs once behaved in this way, as:

> *It chaunced him* that as he passed through Oxfoorde . . . (1568).

When these verbs were in frequent use, it was possible to put the object in front of the verb, in the place of the pronoun *it*, as:

> By fortune *hym happynd* to com to a fayre courtelage (*c.* 1470)
> 'By chance it happened that he came to a fair courtyard.'

> *Him chaunst* to meet upon the way a faithlesse Sarazin (*c.* 1590)
> 'It chanced that he met upon the way a faithless Sarazin.'

But soon after the year 1000, two changes became widespread, which in the long run affected impersonal verbs. First, endings were gradually lost off the end of nouns. Second, there was an increasing tendency to use subject–verb–object word order, which is standard today, even though it was not fixed until well after the first millennium. This meant that sentences such as:

> Achilles chaunced to slay Philles
> The kyng dremed a merveillous dreme.

were misinterpreted as simple subject–verb–object sentences. In fact, as was obvious when such sentences began with a pronoun – *Him chaunced to slay Philles*, *Him dremed a merveillous dreme* – *chaunced* and *dremed* and many others were really impersonal verbs. But, since these verbs were no longer in line with others in the language, speakers subconsciously misinterpreted them, and so neatened the syntactic patterns of language.

The development of French negatives illustrates the ideal of 'one form per unit of meaning', where a two-part negative is being reduced to one.[11] French *ne* (from Latin *non* 'not') was originally the only negative, and was placed in front of the verb. But quite early on, it became reinforced mainly by the word *pas* ('step') after the verb, which was added for emphasis: 'not a step' (somewhat like English *not at all*). Over the centuries, the emphatic negative became the normal one:

> Je ne sais pas
> 'I don't know.'

Eventually, the reinforcement *pas* came to be thought of as the main negative, and the preceding *ne* was regarded as less essential. This has led to the omission of *ne* in casual speech, particularly with some common lexical items (Chapter 7):

> Je sais pas, (or sometimes) je pas
> 'I do not know.'

French negatives are now therefore on their way back to the ideal of 'one form, one meaning', but with a new form taking up the negative function.

Changes which neaten up the syntax, therefore, seem to be further examples of the principles already discussed: the tendency to eliminate pointless variety, and a preference for constructions which are clear and straightforward. Exceptions, however, are not inevitably smoothed away. Sometimes, humans cope with dangling wires by inventing a new use for them, as will be discussed below.

Exaptation: making use of old junk

Many people must at some point have discovered some item of old junk in an attic, a leftover from the past that has no apparent use. Sometimes, it gets given away. But at other times, it is left around until, one day, a good idea comes: 'Ah! I'll use it as a door-stop,' or similar. Language behaves in much the same way. It often contains some useless thingummyjigs from the past. Sometimes, these relics just fade away. At other times, the human mind thinks up a use for them. Consider the following sentences:

> There don't be nothing in church now but sinners
> The cabbage bees the kind they have now.

The use of *be* in place of standard *am, is, are* is often associated with Black English in America. Most people assume it is a remnant of the English spoken on plantations by black speakers a century or so ago. Its exact origins are disputed. But two facts are clear: it is still around, and its use is variable.

There is a widespread belief that this is an old relic, used primarily in casual speech, which is fading away. However, a study of black speakers in Texas showed that far from dying out, it is on the increase among young Texan town-dwellers. A change is taking place in which the gradual decrease of *be* has been reversed, and its use is now accelerating.[12] How has this happened?

The young Texans (age 12–13), it turns out, had acquired the variable *be*, but not understood why it was variable. They had therefore given it a role in their speech, where it was used to describe habitual actions:

> He big, and he always *be* fighting
> You know Mary, I *be* messing with her ('she's my girlfriend').

A later study found that these schoolchildren may not have been the first to use *be* for habitual actions.[13] Some older inhabitants did, but the difference between generations was pronounced. None of the urban informants born before 1944 had *be + ing*, but all of those born after this date did so, as in the following sentences said by a grandmother born in 1945:

> I *be* doing those doctors (cleaning their offices)
> We *be* watching a cute little guy come in.

These Texans, therefore, show how a relic can be rationalized, and given a useful role.

This re-utilizing of old junk has been given a name, 'exaptation', which is already a standard term in evolution, but has only recently been incorporated into linguistics.[14]

Unattainable equilibrium

The examples discussed in this chapter show the strong tendency of language to maintain and neaten its patterns. So striking is this tendency that, a few years ago, a number of linguists believed that simplification was the most important motivating force behind language change – and a few people seriously wondered why languages never ended up maximally simple. It has become clear, however, that there are natural disruptive forces at work, as we discussed in the last chapter. In addition, attempts by the language to restore the equilibrium can in the long run sometimes lead to quite massive, unforeseen disruptive changes, which trigger one another off in a long sequence.

This type of chain reaction is the topic of the next chapter.

13 Pushing and pulling
Chain reaction changes

> 'I want a clean cup,' interrupted the Hatter: 'Let's all move one place on.'
>
> He moved on as he spoke, and the Dormouse followed him; the March Hare moved into the Dormouse's place, and Alice rather unwillingly took the place of the March Hare. The Hatter was the only one who got any advantage from the change: and Alice was a good deal worse off, as the March Hare had just upset the milk-jug into his plate.
>
> Lewis Carroll, Alice in Wonderland (1865)

Introduction

Language changes rarely happen in isolation, and sometimes sequences of linked changes occur in a kind of chain, especially sound changes. But the relationship between the changes is often disputed. Are the sounds pushing or pulling one another? This chapter discusses the controversy. It also briefly mentions the unsolved question of whether such changes affect the syntax also.

Sometimes changes affect languages in a relatively minor way. Natural tendencies, exaggerated by social factors, cause disruptions, then the language restores the equilibrium again. The situation is reminiscent of day-to-day house cleaning or simple weeding in a garden, when minor problems are quickly eradicated.

At other times, however, the problem is not so easily remedied. An apparent therapeutic change can trigger off a set of wholesale shifts in which the various linguistic elements appear to play a game of musical chairs, shifting into each other's places like the participants at the tea party in Lewis Carroll's book *Alice in Wonderland*. Sound shifts are better studied than syntactic shifts. In this chapter, therefore, we shall begin by looking at sound shifts. Afterwards, we shall discuss a possible syntactic shift.

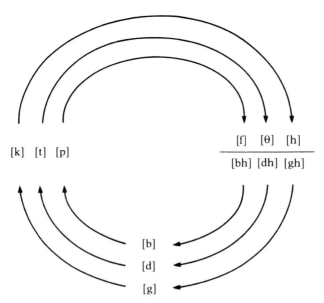

Figure 13.1   Grimm's Law

Shifting sounds

This section outlines two well-known examples of chain shifts involving sounds, one of consonants, the other of vowels.

The first example concerns the set of sound changes known as Grimm's Law.[1] These were described (but not discovered) by Jacob Grimm in his *Deutsche Grammatik*, published in the early nineteenth century. These far-reaching consonant changes occurred at some unknown date in the Germanic branch of the Indo-European languages, which includes English. They split the Germanic branch off from the other languages, and were certainly complete before our first written records of this branch of Indo-European.

In Grimm's Law, an original Proto-Indo-European [bh] [dh] [gh] became [b] [d] [g]; [b] [d] [g] became [p] [t] [k]; and [p] [t] [k] became [f] [θ] [h] (see Figures 13.1 and 13.2).

The proposed Proto-Indo-European sounds are the standard reconstructions of the language we assume to have existed around

Indo-European		became	English	
[bh]	[bhero:] 'I carry'	⟶	[b]	*bear*
[dh]	[dedhe:mi] 'I place'	⟶	[d]	*do*
[gh]	[ghans] 'goose'	⟶	[g]	*goose*
[b]	No sure examples	⟶	[pʔ]	
[d]	[dekm] 'ten'	⟶	[t]	*ten*
[g]	[genos] 'tribe'	⟶	[k]	*kin*
[p]	[pater] 'father'	⟶	[f]	*father*
[t]	[treyes] 'three'	⟶	[θ]	*three*
[k]	[kornu] 'horn'	⟶	[h]	*horn*

Figure 13.2   Grimm's Law: examples

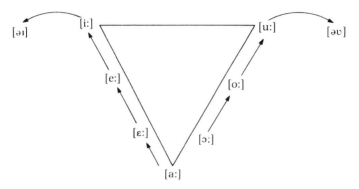

Figure 13.3   The Great Vowel Shift

4,000 BC, the ancestor of a number of European and Indian languages, as discussed in Chapter 2. Note that even if the newish, controversial 'glottalic' reconstruction of Proto-Indo-European turns out to be correct (Chapter 2), there was still a chain shift.

A second well-known musical-chair movement is one which occurred in the English long vowels. It started around the fifteenth century, and is generally known as the Great Vowel Shift (see Figures 13.3 and 13.4).[2] In this, all the long vowels changed

Great Vowel Shift						
Middle English		became	Early Modern English		became	Modern English	

	Middle English	became		Early Modern English	became		Modern English
[aː]	[naːmə] 'name'	⟶	[ɛː]	[nɛːm]	⟶	[eɪ]	[neɪm]
[ɛː]	[mɛːt] 'meat'	⟶	[eː]	[meːt]	⟶	[iː]	[miːt]
[eː]	[meːt] 'meet'	⟶	[iː]	[miːt]	⟶	[iː]	[miːt]
[iː]	[riːd] 'ride'	⟶	[əi]	[rəid]	⟶	[ai]	[raid]
[ɔː]	[bɔːt] 'boat'	⟶	[oː]	[boːt]	⟶	[oʊ/əʊ]	[boʊt/bəʊt]
[oː]	[boːt] 'boot'	⟶	[uː]	[buːt]	⟶	[uː]	[buːt]

Figure 13.4   The Great Vowel Shift: examples

places – though there is still considerable controversy as to which vowel started this general shift.

These dramatic shifts totally altered the appearance of the languages concerned within the course of perhaps a couple of centuries. How and why did they occur?

Push chains or drag chains?

The biggest problem, with any chain shift, is finding out where it started. After the event, how could we tell who started the shift? Essentially, we need to know the answer to one simple question. Were most of the sounds dragged, or were they pushed? Or could they have been both dragged and pushed? The terms **drag chain** and **push chain** (**chaîne de traction** and **chaîne de propulsion**) are the picturesque terms coined by André Martinet, a famous French linguist, who in 1955 wrote a book, *Economie des changements phonétiques*,[3] which attempted to account for these types of shift. According to him, in a drag chain one sound moves from its original place, and leaves a gap which an existing sound rushes to fill, whose place is in turn filled by another, and so on. In a push chain, the reverse happens. One sound invades the territory of another, and the original owner moves away before the two sounds merge into one. The evicted sound in turn evicts another, and so on (see Figure 13.5).

The question as to whether we are dealing with a drag chain or a push chain, or even both together, may seem trivial at first sight.

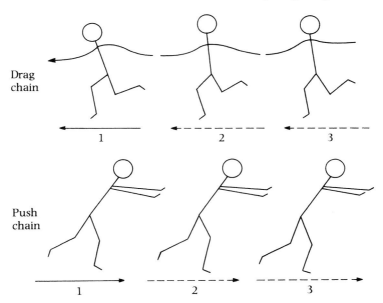

Figure 13.5   Drag and push chains

But since these chains have a more dramatic effect on the language structure than any other kind of change, it is of considerable importance to discover how they work. In recent years, there has been some doubt as to whether both types of chain really exist. Most linguists are happy with the notion that one sound can fill a gap left by another, but they are less happy with the notion that one can actually push another out of its rightful place. Unfortunately, we cannot solve this problem by looking at the shifts mentioned above – Grimm's Law and the Great English Vowel Shift. As we noted, Grimm's Law was already complete long before our first written records of the Germanic branch of Indo-European, and, as far as the Great Vowel Shift is concerned, there seems to have been so much fluctuation and variation in the vowel system from around 1500 onwards, that the exact chronological order of the changes is disputed. Let us therefore examine some better-documented musical-chair shifts in order to see if both types of chain are in fact possible.

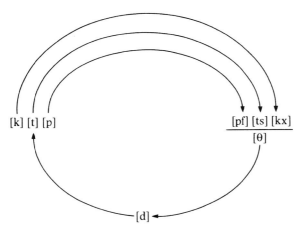

Figure 13.6   High German or Second Consonant Shift

This may shed light on Grimm's Law and the Great English Vowel Shift.

Sure examples of drag chains are relatively easy to find. A notable example occurs in German around AD 500, in the so-called High German or Second Consonant Shift (Figure 13.6).[4] This is called the second shift because Grimm's Law, outlined in the previous section, is generally known as the first shift. It was not nearly as sweeping as the earlier shift, however, and appears to have petered out before completing itself. Essentially [θ] became [d], [d] became [t], and [p] [t] [k] became [pf] [ts] [kx] (see Figure 13.6).

The chronology of this change has been relatively well established: [p] [t] [k] were the first to change, around AD 500. [d] changed in the seventh century, filling the empty space left by [t]. Some time after, [θ] moved into the space left by [d]. So we have a clear example of a drag chain, with sounds apparently being dragged into filling gaps in the system. English, incidentally, did not undergo this second shift, so the English translation of the examples in Figure 13.7 shows the unshifted sounds.

The shift described above is a particularly clear example of a consonantal drag chain, though numerous others exist, from a wide variety of languages, including one in Chinese which performed a

Second Consonant Shift			Modern German			English
[p]	⟶	[pf]	[pf]/[f]	[pfefə]	*Pfeffer*	'pepper'
[t]	⟶	[ts]	[ts]/[s]	[tsuŋə]	*Zunge*	'tongue'
[k]	⟶	[kx]	[kx]/[x]	[brexən]	*brechen*	'break'
[d]	⟶	[t]	[t]	[tu:n]	*tun*	'do'
[θ]	⟶	[d]	[d]	[drai]	*drei*	'three'

Figure 13.7   High German or Second Consonant Shift: examples

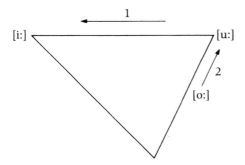

Figure 13.8   Drag chain in Yiddish dialect of northern Poland

complete circle, in the sense that each of three varieties of *s* changed into another, while the overall inventory of sounds remained the same.[5]

Drag chains involving vowels are also fairly easy to find. A change which has been relatively firmly dated is one in the Yiddish dialects of northern Poland (Figure 13.8).[6] Here, [u:] changed to [i:], followed by [o:] to [u:].

Let us now go on to consider push chains. Examples of these are harder to find, and some people have denied their existence altogether on the grounds that if [e] became [i], it could not then push [i] out of the way, because it would already *be* [i].[7] In other words, sounds could merge together, it was claimed, but not push one another out of the way. But this objection only holds if sounds

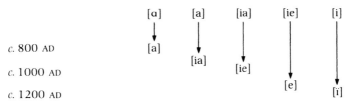

Figure 13.9   Chronology of the Great Vowel Shift of Late Middle Chinese

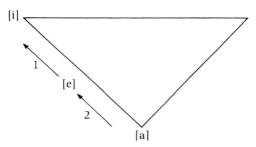

Figure 13.10   Combined push and drag chain

change in sudden leaps. Since there is now plenty of evidence that vowels move gradually, it is possible for [e] to move partially towards [i], and for [i] to move away a little in response. It is less easy to see how consonants could behave in this way, and there is not (to my knowledge) a convincing example of a push chain involving consonants. However, a good case has been put forward for a push chain involving vowels in the so-called Great Vowel Shift of Late Middle Chinese, which began in the eighth century AD.[8] The basic chronology is shown in Figure 13.9.

We may conclude, then, that drag chains and push chains both exist, though drag chains appear to be commoner than push chains. This raises the possibility of whether both types can be combined into one chain shift. Could a chain shift perhaps start in the *middle*, so that it dragged some sounds and pushed others, as in Figure 13.10? Could [e] in Figure 13.10 be the villain of the piece and *both* push [i] *and* drag [a]? The answer is unclear, though it is possible that the answer is 'yes', since if Chaucer's rhymes are genuine rhymes, and not near misses, there is some evidence that he sometimes made [e:] rhyme with [i:]. If this spelling reflects the genuine pronunciation, then his work contains the earliest hints of the English Great Vowel Shift, indicating that it perhaps began in the *middle* of the chain – and some work on the topic supports this suggestion.[9]

The situation over push and drag chains may soon be clearer. Two new English vowel shifts are taking place at the current time, one in Great Britain, the other in the USA. These will be outlined below. They indicate that drag chains and push chains can indeed be mixed. They also show that language retains its ability to maintain its equilibrium even in the modern world, where speakers come into contact with a confusing mix of different pronunciations.

Estuary English vowels

The current British shift is a feature of so-called 'Estuary English', the area around the Thames Estuary.[10] The Estuary English accent is somewhere between the pronunciation thought of as the educated standard, and a London Cockney one:[11] traditionally, a Cockney is someone born within earshot of the church bells of Bow, an area in East London. Recently, Estuary English has begun to spread far beyond its original homeland.

Superficially, the most noticeable feature of Estuary English is possibly the extensive use of a glottal stop in place of [t], as in 'Be'y 'ad a bi' of bi'er bu'er' for 'Betty had a bit of bitter butter.' Yet the vowel changes may cause more problems for outsiders, since each vowel appears to be moving into the slot originally occupied by a neighbour. These changes are taking place in British diphthongs, or 'gliding vowels', sounds in which one vowel slides seamlessly into another.

Consider the following words:

mean [miin]	*moon* [muun][12]
main [mein]	*moan* [moun]
mine [main]	*mound* [maund]

On a vowel triangle, the first part of each diphthong would be placed as in Figure 13.11 in a conventional (older) pronunciation

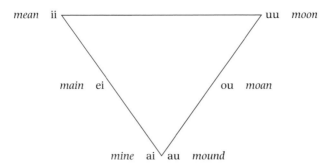

Figure 13.11   English diphthongs: conventional (older) pronunciation

(slightly simplified). But listen to a schoolboy or schoolgirl pronouncing these words today. The phrases in the first column (below) would probably sound somewhat like those in the second:

Don't be *mean* → Don't be *main* [mein]
The *main* road → The *mine* [main] road
It's *mine*   → It's *moyne* [moin]
See the *moon* → See the *moan* [moun]
Don't *moan*   → Don't *moun* [maun]
A little *mound* → A little *meund* [meund]

The slip-sliding vowels can be represented in a (simplified) diagram as in Figure 13.12.[13]

No wonder, perhaps, that the older generation has trouble comprehending the younger, even though this shift has now spread far beyond teenagers. 'The prime minister descended into estuary English in an attempt to reach out to the masses,' complained a newspaper article. 'Should our leaders be "dumbing down" in this estuarine way?'[14]

American Northern Cities Shift

Y'hadda wear *sacks*, not sandals.

The speaker, Jackie, meant 'socks', not 'sacks'.[15] She was a young woman who agreed to take part in experiments which explored the

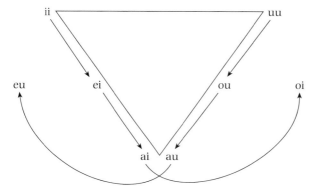

Figure 13.12   Estuary English vowels

Figure 13.13   Cities in the American Northern Cities Shift

so-called Northern Cities Shift, a series of changes taking place in the USA in all major northern cities from the White Mountains in Vermont westward: Rochester, Syracuse, Buffalo, Cleveland, Detroit and Chicago (Figure 13.13).

The American Northern Cities Shift is arguably 'the most complex chain shift yet recorded within one subsystem',[16] according to William Labov who has studied it in depth. It is also unusual in that it involves short, rather than long, vowels, since 'in the past millennium most of the rotations have affected the long vowels; the short vowels have remained relatively stable'.[17]

The Northern Cities Shift is essentially an urban phenomenon: the larger the city, the more advanced the change.[18] *Socks* pronounced *sacks* may be the alteration of which non-Americans are most aware, but it may not have been the earliest. The first may have been a move of the vowel in *sacks*, upwards towards the vowel in *six*. A number of 'slips of the ear', speech mishearings, have been noted, such as *Ian* heard as 'Ann', *cinnamon cake* as 'salmon cake', *singles* as 'sandals'. These mistakes were all made by people who knew about the change, and were trying to make sense of the words they heard around them: they were all assuming that the alteration had already taken place in the speech of those they were talking to.

These two linked changes, – [a] → [i], then [o] → [a], may have been the earliest changes in a drag chain:

$$a \rightarrow i \quad Ann \rightarrow inn \text{ (Ian)}$$
$$o \rightarrow a \quad socks \rightarrow sacks$$

Some other links in the shift may be a push chain, with *Bess* sounding like 'bus', and the vowel in *bus* moving backward to sound like *boss*:

$$e \rightarrow \wedge \quad Bess \rightarrow bus$$
$$\wedge \rightarrow o \quad bus \rightarrow boss$$

According to William Labov, the Northern Cities Shift has already described a complete circle, comprised partly of drag, partly of push, chains. But it has not yet fully affected all speakers. It will be interesting to see if the circle becomes more general in the course of the twenty-first century.

Typological harmony

So far, we have confined our discussion of pushing and pulling movements to sounds. What about syntax?

Larger constructions seem to be more stable and less promiscuous in that they do not leap into each other's chairs with such apparent alacrity as sounds. However, our knowledge of syntactic change is still sketchy, and there may be more covert leapings, pushings and draggings than we are aware of. Certainly there is some evidence for the existence of a certain type of drag chain in syntax. This involves the notion of **typological harmony**.[19]

As we noted in Chapter 2, it is possible – with some reservations – to divide the languages of the world into a number of different types. Each language type has certain constructions which are typically associated with it. Just as an animal with wings is likely to have claws also, so certain constructions are frequently found associated together in languages. An OV language (one in which the object normally precedes the verb, such as Japanese, Turkish or Hindi) tends to differ in certain predictable ways from a VO language (a language in which the object usually follows the verb, such as English). For example, English has prepositions while OV languages often have post-positions. So *with care* might be *care with* in an OV language. English places its auxiliaries in front of its main verbs, OV languages mostly do the reverse: so *Archibald must wash* would be *Archibald wash must* in an OV language. And so on. Over the centuries languages tend to alter their basic type. English, together with French, Greek and a variety of other languages, has changed from an OV to a VO language. Mandarin Chinese may be moving in the reverse direction, from a VO language to an OV one. When a typological shift takes place, it is not just a shift of verbs and objects, but also of all the other constructions associated with that type.

However, in spite of considerable work on the subject, there is no overall agreement as to why this harmony is necessary. One view is that it is related to certain comprehension problems which are likely to arise if the constructions are not in harmony[20] – though difficulties for this theory are posed by languages such as German which involve a strange mixture of different typological characteristics. In German, objects are placed after verbs in main clauses, but before them in subordinate clauses. It is possible – though not definite – that German is in a state of transition, and will eventually end up, like most other European languages, with objects consistently placed after the verb.

There is even less agreement as to the order in which the harmonizing occurs. At one time, it was suggested that the first event was a switch over of the order of verb and object, which in turn dragged round all the related constructions. This has turned out to be wrong. In ancient Greek, at least, the reordering of verb and object occurred relatively late in the chain of events involved in the switch over.[21] In several languages, among them Greek, Latin, perhaps English, Mandarin Chinese and certain Niger-Congo languages, the earliest changes seem to have involved a switching round of complex sentences – sentences with more than one clause – then later affected simple sentences and the order of verbs and objects.[22]

All we can perhaps conclude at this time is that we appear to have a series of linked changes which are reminiscent of a drag chain, though the exact nature of these links remains a question for the future.

Summary of language change causes

Let us now summarize our conclusions on the causes of language change.

Change is likely to be triggered by social factors, such as fashion, foreign influence and social need. However, these factors cannot take effect unless the language is 'ready' for a particular change. They simply make use of inherent tendencies which reside in the physical and mental make-up of human beings. Causality needs therefore to be explored on a number of different levels. The immediate trigger must be looked at alongside the underlying propensities of the language concerned, and of human languages in general.

A language never allows disruptive changes to destroy the system. In response to disruptions, therapeutic changes are likely to intervene and restore the broken patterns – though in certain circumstances therapeutic changes can themselves cause further disruptions by setting off a chain of changes which may last for centuries.

Above all, anyone who attempts to study the causes of language change must be aware of the multiplicity of factors involved. It is essential to realize that language is both a social and a mental phenomenon in which sociolinguistic and psycholinguistic factors are likely to be inextricably entwined. 'Nothing is simple' might be a useful motto for historical linguists to hang in their studies, as one researcher aptly remarked.[23]

Part 4
Beginnings and endings

14 Language birth
How languages begin

> Language was born in the courting days of mankind – the
> first utterances of speech I fancy to myself like something
> between the nightly love-lyrics of puss upon the tiles and
> the melodious love-songs of the nightingale.
>
> Otto Jespersen, *Language, its nature, development*
> *and origin* (1922)

Introduction

This chapter considers how languages begin. It outlines how
pidgins, embryo languages, start out, and then how they evolve
into creoles, full languages. Pidgins are simpler than full languages;
they have fewer vocabulary items, fewer sounds and relatively little
morphology or syntax. But a creole gradually acquires vocabulary,
word endings, and syntax. Eventually, it is indistinguishable from
a 'full' language. This chapter outlines how it all happens.

Most people are quite puzzled about how languages might come
into being. When they think about language birth, their thoughts
are led inevitably to the fascinating problem of the ultimate origin
of language. Various bizarre hypotheses have been put forward
over the past hundred years or so. The 'ding-dong' theory claimed
that the earliest words were imitations of natural sounds such as
bang!, *cuckoo*, *splash!*, *moo*. The 'pooh-pooh' theory suggested that
language arose from cries and gasps of emotion. The 'yo-he-ho'
theory proposed that language was ultimately based on communal
effort, with essential instructions such as *Heave!* and *Haul!* being the
first words spoken, and numerous other speculative ideas were put
forward.[1] For example, the Danish linguist Otto Jespersen argued
that 'We must imagine primitive language as consisting (chiefly at
least) of very long words, full of difficult sounds, and sung rather
than spoken . . .'[2] His musings on 'the courting days of mankind'
are given in the quote at the top of the chapter.

Eccentric speculations led to widespread disapproval. In 1866, a ban on papers about language origin was issued by the Linguistic Society of Paris, the foremost linguistic society of the time. In 1893, the linguist William Dwight Whitney commented that: 'The greater part of what is said and written upon it is mere windy talk.'[3] Serious scholars mostly avoided the topic, which was regarded as a playground for cranks. Yet language evolved by normal evolutionary mechanisms, as has recently been widely recognized. The topic has finally become respectable, and a huge quantity of publications has erupted.[4]

This chapter will outline recent ideas on language origin. It will then discuss the birth of pidgins, restricted language systems which cater for essential common needs when people speaking different languages come into contact. Finally, it will show how pidgins may, in certain cirumstances, become elaborated, and grow into creoles, which are potential 'full' languages.

The origin of human language

Africa was probably the homeland of modern humans, and also of human language.[5] An 'East-side story' provides a plausible backdrop. Several hundred thousand years ago, we and our chimp cousins were spread across Africa. Then a major earthquake created the Great Rift Valley, splitting Africa into lush forest in the west and relatively dry savannah in the east. Future humans were stranded in the arid east. Their desiccated territory became even drier, and they were forced to adapt, or die. They supplemented their meagre diet by scavenging for meat, which aided brain growth. They started to walk upright, partly in order to minimize the heat of the sun on their bodies. An upright stance promoted the production of clear sounds.

These physical developments were supplemented by mental advances. Primates – the animal order to which humans belong, alongside chimps, gorillas and others – are social animals. They have strong family ties, they interact with other group members, and they have a well-defined ranking order. Language may have developed as part of this extensive interaction. Perhaps 'grooming talking' – social chit-chat – supplemented, then largely replaced, manual grooming, the gentle picking out of each other's nits.

The ability to deceive provided a further incentive. True deception requires an animal to see things from another's point of view. This enabled humans to develop a 'naming insight', an understanding that an object may have a 'name', a symbol which can replace it. Chimps, incidentally, can easily label an object such as *banana* when they are requesting one to eat, but they rarely use such names at other times.

These underpinnings – clear sounds and the naming insight – possibly led to a heaping up of dozens, even hundreds, of vocabulary items.

From words to grammar

Numerous words led to the need for some kind of word order, and inbuilt predilections probably paved the way.

Humans have certain basic biases when they view the world, such as a tendency to place references to animate beings, especially humans, before other words. They also usually position verbs next to the objects involved in a verbal action. So words which meant, say, 'I killed a turtle' might come in a probable order *me kill turtle*, or *me turtle kill*. At first such an order might be variable. But later it might firm up: preferences become habits, then habits may became 'rules'.

This 'grammaticalization' tendency seems to be a firm characteristic of the speech of human beings. We see it happening in day-to-day language (Chapter 9). We also observe it happening in the development of pidgins, embryo languages.

How pidgins arise

A pidgin is frequently described as a 'marginal' language, used by people who need to communicate for certain restricted purposes. For this reason, pidgins tend to arise on trade routes, for example along the coast of West Africa, in the Caribbean and on Pacific islands. We have records of a pidgin formed by Russian traders and Norwegian fishermen in north Norway,[6] and another between American-Indians in northwest USA and Canada.[7] The origin of the term *pidgin*[8] is also disputed, and a number of explanations have been put forward. The most popular theory is that it comes from

Chinese Pidgin English, where the word *pidgin* means 'business', as in *gospidgin man* (literally *god-business-man*) 'a man who has a god as his business, a priest'. Another theory is that it is derived from a Hebrew word *pidjom* 'barter' – though at least five other origins have been claimed for the word. It is possible that similar terms arose independently in different places, and then reinforced one another, coalescing in the common term 'pidgin'.

A pidgin takes one or more already existing language(s) as its point of origin. Many Pacific and West African pidgins are based on English, while a number of those found in the Caribbean are French-based.

Consider Tok Pisin, the English-based pidgin found in Papua New Guinea, which is also known as New Guinea Pidgin. It has now been in existence for about a century.[9] Here we find the word *mi* for 'I' and 'me' and the word *yu* for 'you', as in:

mi go	'I go'
yu go	'you go'
mi lukim yu	'I see you'
yu lukim mi	'you see me'

The plural of 'I' and 'you' is formed by adding the ending *pela* (from English *fellow*), so we get:

mipela go	'we go'
yupela go	'you (plural) go'

The English possessive 'my', 'your', 'our' and so on is expressed by using the word *bilong* 'of ' (from English *belong*), so we find phrases such as:

papa bilong mi	'my father'
haus bilong mipela	'our house'
gras bilong het	'hair' (from 'grass of head')
gras bilong pisin	'bird feathers' (from 'grass of pigeon')
gras bilong solwara	'seaweed' (from 'grass of salt-water')
sit bilong paia	'ash' (from 'residue (shit) of fire')
sit bilong lam	'soot' (from 'residue (shit) of lamp')
papa bilong yu	'your father'
haus bilong yupela	'your (plural) house'

Faced with such superficially bizarre adaptations of the base language, some older writers condemned pidgins as 'crudely distorted by false ideas of simplification' and dismissed them as 'broken language' or a 'bastard blend', unworthy of serious study.[10] Hugo Schuchardt, one of the few scholars who considered them worthy of attention in the nineteenth century, was warned by a senior colleague that if he wished to further his academic career he should abandon this foolish study of funny dialects, and work on Old French – a warning repeated as late as the 1950s to Robert Hall, an American pioneer in the field.[11] So pervasive was this attitude that only in recent years have pidgins received their fair share of attention. The result of this neglect is that the formation of most pidgins went unrecorded, and the exact process by which pidginization occurred has been lost in the snowdrifts of time. Instead of accurate observation, there are a number of conflicting theories about the steps by which these restricted languages come into being.

The earliest theory, commonly found in the first half of the nineteenth century, was based on the false assumption that European languages are too sophisticated and complex to be learnt by supposedly primitive 'natives', who therefore simplified these advanced languages down to their own level: 'It is clear,' commented one writer in 1849, 'that people used to expressing themselves with a rather simple language cannot easily elevate their intelligence to the genius of a European language . . . it was necessary that the varied expressions acquired during so many centuries of civilization dropped their perfection, to adapt to ideas being born and to barbarous forms of language of half-savage peoples.'[12] This arrogant and naive viewpoint is no longer thought to be relevant.

It is a mistake to think that societies which lack Western technology have primitive languages. A Stone Age culture may well possess less sophisticated vocabulary items, but the language's essential structure is likely to be as complex as that of any other language.

Today, there are four commonly held theories of pidgin origin which are not necessarily mutually exclusive.[13]

The first theory is that of imperfect learning. According to this viewpoint, a pidgin represents the best attempt of a people to learn a language quite unlike their own. In so doing, they produce a simplified form of speech comparable with that produced by children learning to speak for the first time. This becomes petrified when the speakers are no longer in contact with the base language. This may well be partially correct. It cannot, however, be the sole source of the pidgins of the world, because we have evidence that the Portuguese-based pidgin spoken in West Africa around 1500 was developed by the Portuguese, who taught it to the Africans.[14]

The second theory, therefore, suggests that a pidgin represents attempts by native speakers of the base language to simplify it in ways that might make it easier for non-native speakers to learn. Such a view regards a pidgin as a regularized form of 'foreigner talk', the sort of broken speech Londoners sometimes use if a foreign tourist asks them how to get to the zoo. This viewpoint was put forward by the famous American linguist Leonard Bloomfield, and is found in a number of subsequent textbooks. Bloomfield claims, without giving any evidence, that such 'foreigner talk' is based primarily on imitation of learners' errors:

> Speakers of a lower language may make so little progress in learning the dominant speech, that the masters, in communicating with them, resort to 'baby-talk'. This 'baby-talk' is the masters' imitation of the subjects' incorrect speech . . . The subjects in turn, deprived of the correct model, can do no better now than acquire the simplified 'baby-talk' version of the upper language. The result may be a conventionalised jargon.[15]

The 'foreigner talk' theory has a number of supporters, although it is unlikely that such talk is based on imitation of learners' errors. There is no evidence that speakers of the base language ever listen critically or attentively to non-native speakers. 'Foreigner talk', therefore, has its source mainly in the preconceived notions of people who *think* they are imitating foreigners, but are in fact spontaneously creating the simplified talk themselves.

Both the imperfect learning and the foreigner talk theories leave one major problem unsolved. They do not account for the fact that many pidgins share certain features. These shared characteristics have given rise to the suggestion that the pidgins of the world ultimately derive from one common source. The main candidate is a Portuguese-based pidgin which was widespread along the trade routes of the world in the fifteenth and sixteenth centuries at a time when Portugal was at the height of its economic power as a trading nation. Supporters of this theory point to Portuguese-based words which are found in a large number of pidgins, such as *save* or *savvy* for 'know', from Portuguese *saber* 'know', and *pikinini* or *pikin* for 'child', from Portuguese *pequeno* 'little'. Two problems arise from this monogenetic ('single birth') theory: first, it cannot be proved; secondly, there seem to be pidgin languages with pidgin characteristics based on non-European languages in places unlikely to have been influenced by Portuguese pidgin.

The difficulties of the single birth theory, combined with the observation that all pidgins have common features, have led other scholars to a fourth 'universalist' viewpoint.[16] They suggest that universal language structures automatically surface when anyone tries to build a simple language, and that any shared features will be universal features. Yet the similarities between pidgins seem to be enormously vague ones, and there is very little that can be said about common language universals beyond the fact that pidgins tend to follow the maxim 'one form per unit of meaning' (Chapter 12) to a greater extent than fully developed languages. A major problem is that any structural universals which might be trying to surface are often obscured by common features shared by the base and the substratum languages. If such a shared feature exists, it is highly likely to appear in the pidgin, even if it is a characteristic which is otherwise rare in the languages of the world. This is shown by 'Chinook jargon', a pidgin probably developed by American-Indians in the northwest USA and Canada before the arrival of Europeans. It contained a number of highly idiosyncratic features, by the standards of the rest of the world, but these all occur in the American-Indian languages of the region.[17]

While scholars argue the merits of these four theories, considerable light has been shed on the origins of Tok Pisin.[18] It was a product of the particular socio-economic conditions prevalent in the Pacific. In its formation, all the above processes may have played a part.

In the nineteenth century, there were extensive coconut and cocoa plantations on Samoa, for which the German owners had considerable difficulty finding adequate labour. Workers were therefore recruited in large numbers from the surrounding Pacific islands. Trading records show, for example, that in the last decade of the century, numerous labourers were shipped from New Guinea and the surrounding islands. Approximately a quarter of them died away from home, but the survivors were eventually repatriated. Altogether around 6,000 labourers had a spell of several years on Samoa.

It seems likely that these workers were exposed to a jargonized form of English on the recruiting vessels taking them to Samoa. This broken English probably utilized conventions which had existed in trading circles for some time, such as the Portuguese-based *pikinini* 'child', and *save* 'know', mentioned earlier. Once on Samoa, this jargon seems to have been developed and stabilized. It was the means by which workers speaking a variety of different languages communicated with each other and with their masters.

Governor Solf's diary for 1895 includes a number of relevant comments on this:

> It is a well-known fact that almost everyone of the various native islands of the blacks in the South Seas possesses not only one but a whole number of different languages . . . Thus, in what way do the workers from such different places and islands communicate, when thrown together in Samoa? They use that Volapuk of the South Seas, which has become international among whites and coloureds: pidgeon English . . . The words *belong* and *fellow* are especially important. The former used with nouns and pronouns indicates property, *house belong me*, *horse belong me* 'my house', 'my horse' . . . The latter is added to all numbers, without regard to the gender of the following noun, *three fellow woman* 'three women', *two fellow horse* 'two horses'. It is incredible how quickly all blacks learn this lingua franca . . . [19]

Once repatriated, the labourers retained the pidgin they had learnt in Samoa in order to communicate with each other, which was otherwise impossible owing to the estimated 700 languages which are spoken in what is now Papua New Guinea. Whereas the pidgin on Samoa died out as soon as recruiting for the plantations ended at the time of the First World War, the pidgin in New Guinea expanded as it was gradually used for more purposes, particularly administrative and mission ones. At first it was a subsidiary language used when communicating with strangers. Eventually, with increasing mobility of the population, and the growth in importance of towns, it became the first language for children of mixed marriages. At this point it is no longer a pidgin – a subsidiary language used for certain restricted purposes – but a **creole**, an almost fully fledged language.

Embryo languages

A pidgin is, as it were, a language in embryo. Let us consider its essential characteristics.[20]

First of all, a genuine pidgin must not be confused with broken English, as frequently happens in popular usage. For example, when the popular singer Paul McCartney was imprisoned briefly in Japan, he claimed that he communicated with the other prisoners in pidgin English, meaning that he used some type of broken English.

A true pidgin has consistent rules. No one can make them up on the spur of the moment. In Papua New Guinea, there is a type of English known as Tok Masta, which is the broken English of certain Europeans who think they are speaking Tok Pisin, but who are in fact merely simplifying English in their own idiosyncratic way.[21] One cannot talk Tok Pisin by simply adding *bilong* and *-pela* randomly between English words, as is sometimes believed.

A pidgin is not made up exclusively from elements of the base language. Vocabulary items are incorporated from native languages spoken in the area, and from others further afield as well. Tok Pisin vocabulary includes, for example, *kaikai* 'food, meal', a word of Polynesian origin, *susu*, an Austronesian word for 'milk', and *rausim* 'throw out', from the German *heraus* 'outside'. Constructions are also imported from other sources, particularly the languages spoken in the area.[22] Tok Pisin, unlike English, has two forms of the pronoun 'we': *mipela*, meaning 'we excluding you', and *yumi*, which means 'we including you', a distinction found in a number of other languages in the Pacific area. Again unlike English, Tok Pisin distinguishes between the form of intransitive verbs (verbs which do not take an object) and transitive verbs (verbs which do), as in the following example using the word *bagarap* 'break down' (from English *bugger up* though with no obscene overtones) and *bagarapim* 'smash up': *ka bilong mi i bagarap* 'my car broke down' (intransitive verb, no ending); *em i bagarapim ka bilong mi* 'he smashed up my car' (transitive verb, ending *-im*). Note also the use of the particle *i*, which often precedes verbs. These examples show that speakers of the base language cannot simply make up a pidgin; its rules have to be learnt. Just as the rules of chess cannot be predicted from looking at the old Indian game from which it was adapted, so the rules of an English-based pidgin cannot be deduced from the standard version of the English language. The pidgin is a separate system, with an identity of its own.

A pidgin is, however, relatively easy to learn. Compared with most fully fledged languages, it is both impoverished and simpler. It is impoverished in that it has a smaller number of elements. There are fewer sounds, fewer words, fewer constructions. This becomes clear when Tok Pisin is compared with its base language, English. Most varieties of English have a large number of vowels, whereas Tok Pisin has five: [a], [e], [i], [o], [u]. So the words *slip* 'sleep' and *sip* 'ship' rhyme, and so do *tok* 'talk' and *wok* 'work' – and to avoid confusion the word for 'walk' is *wokabout*. Tok Pisin does not distinguish between [p] and [f], so *lap* 'laugh' and *kap* 'cup' rhyme, and so do *lip* 'leaf' and *slip* 'sleep'. Nor does it distinguish between the consonants [s], [ʃ] and [tʃ], so *sua* means both 'shore' and 'sore'. 'Watch' is *was*, and to avoid confusion 'wash' becomes *waswas*. 'Ship' becomes *sip* and 'sheep' is *sipsip*. Consonant clusters are mostly avoided, so 'salt' and 'shoulder' become *sol*, and 'cold' becomes *kol*. 'Six' becomes *sikis*, and 'spear', in many areas, is *supia*.

There are relatively few vocabulary items, so the same word can mean a number of different things depending on the context. Take the words *pikinini* 'child', *han* 'hand', and *haus* 'house'. *Pikinini man* is 'son', and *pikinini meri* is 'daughter' (from 'child woman'; the word *meri* derives from the name 'Mary', possibly reinforced by the word 'marry'). *Pikinini dok* is 'puppy', and *pikinini pik* is 'piglet'. *Pikinini bilong diwai*, literally 'child of tree', is the fruit of a tree. *Karim pikinini* is therefore either 'to give birth to a child', or 'to bear fruit'. *Han bilong dok* are the front legs of a dog, and *han bilong pik* is a shoulder of pork. *Han bilong pisin* is a bird's wing, *han bilong diwai* is the branch of a tree, while *han wara*, literally 'hand water', is the tributary of a river. *Plantihan* 'plenty hands' is a centipede. *Haus sik* is a hospital, and *haus pepa* 'house paper' is an office. *Haus bilong pik* is a pigsty, and *haus bilong spaida* is a spider's web.

Tok Pisin not only has relatively few vocabulary items, it also has only very limited means for expressing the relationship of one item to another, and of binding them together. For example, English often expresses the relationship between words by means of prepositions, *to, for, by, up, down*, and so on. Tok Pisin makes do with only three prepositions, *bilong* 'of', *long* 'to', 'for', 'from', and *wantaim* 'with'.

The time of an action is not normally specified, since verbs do not distinguish between tenses, though an adverb can be added if required, as in *Asde dispela man i stilim pik* 'Yesterday this man stole a pig.'

In true pidgins, there is little or no embedding. (Embedding is the combination of two potential sentences by inserting one into the other.) Take the statements: *This man smashed up your car. He is my brother*. In English, these would be combined into a single sentence by means of an introductory word such as *who, that*: *This man who smashed up your car is my brother*. In a pidgin, the two statements would simply be juxtaposed: *Dispela man i bagarapim ka bilong yu, em i brata bilong mi*, literally 'This man smash up your car, he is my brother.'

A pidgin is simpler than a mature language because it is more transparent (see Chapter 10), in that it is nearer to the ideal of one form per unit of meaning, with systematic and easily detectable rules governing the alternations, as in the forms *mi* 'I, me', *yu* 'you', *mipela* 'I plural' = 'we', *yupela* 'you plural'.

The low number of elements and the transparency might make a pidgin seem like a linguist's dream – a near-perfect language. It certainly makes it an easily learnable tool for elementary communication purposes. Unfortunately, such simplicity brings its own problems. One of these is ambiguity. With a meagre sound system and a limited number of vocabulary items, the opportunities for confusion are multiplied. The word *hat*, for example, can mean 'hot', 'hard', 'hat' or, less usually, 'heart'. The phrase *bel bilong mi i pas* 'My stomach/heart is closed up/fast' may mean, depending on the area or the circumstance, 'I am depressed', 'I am using a contraceptive', 'I am barren', or 'I am constipated.'

A second problem is that of length. In order to express quite ordinary concepts, a quite inefficient number of words are required.

A hymn, for example, is *singsing bilong haus lotu* 'song of a house worship', and a fertile woman is *meri i save karim planti pikinini* 'a woman (who) is accustomed / knows how to bear plenty of children'. Furthermore, the absence of adequate means of joining sentences together creates extraordinarily long strings of juxtaposed phrases, as well as frequent ambiguity.

In brief, true simplicity in a language system is gained at a high cost, such a high cost that it is only feasible in subsidiary, restricted languages. Once a pidgin becomes used for a wide variety of functions, it is forced to expand. It becomes first of all an extended pidgin – a pidgin which utilizes extra linguistic devices and vocabulary items, and which is halfway to being a full language. Eventually, when children of mixed marriages learn a pidgin as their first language, it becomes by definition a **creole**. At this point it expands still further. Let us now go on to consider by what means this expansion comes about.

Creoles as new-born languages

A pidgin is a language in embryo, a foetus with the potential to become a full language, but not yet capable of fulfilling the entire communication needs of a human. Some pidgins exist for a limited amount of time, and then die out. Others get progressively more complex as the purposes for which they are used expand. Eventually a pidgin may be learnt by someone as a first language. At this point it has become a creole, from the French *créole* 'indigenous', borrowed in turn from the Spanish *criollo* 'native'. The most widely accepted definition of a creole is that it is a one-time pidgin which has become the mother tongue of a speech community: 'A pidgin is no one's first language, whereas a creole is.'[23]

From the point of view of structure, it is difficult to know where a pidgin ends and a creole begins, since one can merge into the other. A pidgin must undergo fairly massive changes in order to be viable as a full language, but we cannot pinpoint the stage at which it is mature. All we can say is that around the time of its 'birth' as a creole, it grows rapidly and extensively. Some of the changes seem to occur before it is acquired as a first language, others are initiated by the new native speakers.

Let us look at the kind of maturation which a pidgin undergoes when it turns into a creole. The examples below come from Tok Pisin,[24] which is now the first language for an estimated 10,000 speakers in Papua New Guinea, the commonest reason being inter-marriage between speakers of different languages who can communicate only by means of Tok Pisin.

Let us look briefly at four different types of alteration and expansion. The first involves the speed of speech; the second lexical expansion; the third the development of tenses; and finally, the development of relative clauses.

People for whom a pidgin is a second, subsidiary language speak it slowly, one word at a time. When Tok Pisin is learnt as a first language, the rate of speech speeds up remarkably. This in turn has a dramatic effect on the phonology. Words are telescoped, and endings omitted. For example, rarely do native Tok Pisin speakers say the word *bilong*, like the older generation. Instead they say *blo*. So *man bilong mi* 'my husband' sounds like [mamblomi]. The word *long* 'to' is shortened to *lo*, and *save* 'to be accustomed to' is shortened to *sa*. So whereas an older speaker might say *mi save go long lotu* 'I am accustomed to go to church', a native Tok Pisin speaker would say *mi sa go lo lotu*. To an outsider, the speech of the older generation, the non-native speakers, is fairly clear, but creolized Tok Pisin, on the other hand, sounds just like any other foreign language, an allegro ra-ta-tat of speeding words and syllables.

In the realm of vocabulary, a number of cumbersome phrases are being replaced by new, shorter words. For example, the old phrase *bel bilong mi i hat* 'my stomach/heart is hot' meaning 'I am angry' now exists alongside *mi belhat* 'I am stomach/heart hot' with the same meaning. The old phrase expressing a person's aptitude for something by the words *man bilong . . .*, as in *em i man bilong pait* 'he is a man of fight, he is a fighter', now exists alongside a shortened form, *em i paitman* 'he is a fightman/fighter'. In addition, technical, political and medical terms are being imported from other languages, particularly English.

Meanwhile, it is becoming relatively normal to mark the time of an utterance, even when this is clear from the context. *Bin*, from the English *been*, is now used in some areas to mark past time, even when it is quite obvious that the action took place in the past, as in *Asde mi bin go lo(ng) taun* 'Yesterday I (past) went to town'. The same is happening with the future. *Baimbai* from English *by and by* was once used as an optional adverb, as in the government advertisement for peanuts:

> Sapos yu kaikai planti pinat, *baimbai* yu kamap strong olsem Phantom.
> 'If you eat plenty of peanuts, you will become strong like Phantom.'
> (Phantom is a popular cartoon figure).

Baimbai has now been shortened to *bai*. It is now often used even when it is obvious that an event will take place in the future, as in:

> *Bai* mi stori long wanem?
> FUT I narrate about what
> 'What shall I talk about?'

But the position of *bai* fluctuates.[25] Mostly it comes before the first pronoun, as above. But with *em* 'he, she, it', it often comes after, perhaps to stop *bai* + *em* coalescing into a single word:

> Em *bai* tokim liklik brata bilongen
> 'She will/would talk to her little brother.'

Time only will tell how this fluctuation will resolve itself.

Other types of wavering are found. *Bin*, a particle indicating the past, is firmly placed between a noun phrase and a verb, as in:

> faia *bin* kukim mi
> 'The fire cooked/burned me.'

Yet this also is seesawing, though in a different way. In some parts of Papua New Guinea, *pinis* from English 'finish' is used for PAST:

> oi, wanpela mi kikim *pinis*[26]
> hey, one I kick PAST
> 'Hey, I kicked one' (a crocodile).

But in areas which use *bin* for pastness, *pinis* has changed to meaning 'after':

> mi sa skinim banana *pinis*, orait, mi kisim kokonat
> 'After I've peeled the banana, I take a coconut.'

This fluctuation, and also the tendency to find new uses for redundant words, show that changes in pidgins are ordinary changes, of the type found everywhere in languages.

And further similarities with full languages are emerging – *bin* can now be combined with other particles, as in:

> mi no *bin sa* go klas
> I not PAST CUSTOMARILY go class
> 'I habitually didn't go to school.'

This described how a pupil did not go to school for a long time, during an illness.

Tok Pisin, then, is twisting and turning English words into syntax of its own, as shown further below.

Almost there

The English word *like* appears in Tok Pisin as *laik*:[27]

> mi *laik* toktok long dispela
> 'I would like to talk about this.'

Alongside this meaning, another polysemous layered meaning (Chapter 9) is taking place: *laik* sometimes now means 'to be about to', at first via ambiguous usages:

> mi smelim kaikai, mi *laik* troaut tasol
> 'If I smelled food, I wanted to / felt as if I was about to throw up'
> mi *laik* pundaun tasol
> 'I was on the point of fainting' (lit. falling down)
> wanpela big woa i *laik* kamap
> 'A big war is about to occur.'

Laik is therefore showing the layered behaviour typical of grammaticalization. In its most grammaticalized usages, it has become a true **proximative**, a grammatical structure found in various languages, meaning 'almost', 'nearly', 'to be about to'.

But *laik* is still competing with or, perhaps, learning to live with, its older rival *klostu* 'almost' (from 'close to'):

> *Klostu* em *laik* paitim dispela sista hia
> 'Almost she was on the point of striking this nurse.'

Time will tell whether these will continue to combine, or whether *klostu* will fade away, or acquire a different meaning.

Who and where

Tok Pisin is also developing complex sentences – sentences with more than one clause.[28] Since creolized Tok Pisin is not yet fully standardized, different areas have developed these clauses in different ways. The following is a method of forming relative clauses (clauses introduced by 'who', 'which', 'that') which is found among a group of relatives originally from Goroka, a town in the Highlands of Papua New Guinea. In their speech the word *we* 'where' is also used to mean 'which'. The usage possibly developed through ambiguous sentences, sentences in which the word *we* could mean either 'where', its original meaning, or 'which'. One speaker, Henni, for example, spoke of the big hospital where / to which all people in Morobe Province go. But in another sentence uttered a few minutes later, she used *we* in a way that could only mean 'which'. She spoke of *sista we wok* 'the sister who was working', meaning 'the sister on duty in the hospital'. Her cousin Betty also used *we* in this way. Henni is a strong character who dominates those around her, who talks a lot, and whom other people tend to imitate. It is possible that her use of *we* will spread to others in the hostel where she lives, girls who come from different areas – and Henni herself may have picked up this usage from friends and relatives.

Time only will tell whether this particular method of forming relative clauses will catch on in Tok Pisin as a whole, or whether it will remain restricted to a limited geographical area, and then die out. At the moment, there are several independent means of making relative clauses in creolized Tok Pisin, depending on the area. When, or if, Tok Pisin becomes standardized, one of them will win out over the others. Clauses introduced by *we*, as described above, have a good chance of being the 'winner', since this construction appears to be used in other areas in the Papua New Guinea region, for example Manus in the New Hebrides. Note, incidentally, that relative clauses beginning with the word 'where' are not an exclusively Tok Pisin phenomenon, since they have also reputedly been found in other parts of the world – for example, West African Pidgin, and certain German dialects.

These changes illustrate how Tok Pisin is developing from a pidgin with limited resources into a full language.

A creole is a full language in the sense that it is often the only language of those who learn it as their mother tongue. It therefore has to be capable of dealing with a greater range of communication needs than a pidgin. The language is likely to develop fast during the first two generations of creole speakers. Later, its rate of growth will slow down, as it becomes a fully mature language and takes its place among the thousands of others spoken in the world.

Some of today's best-known languages may have started out as creolized pidgins. It has even been suggested that the Germanic branch of the Indo-European language family, which includes English, German and Dutch, started out as a pidginized version of Indo-European. This theory is not generally accepted. But it does emphasize the fact that in the long run there is no way of distinguishing one-time pidgins and creoles from any other language.

In conclusion, the stages by which pidgins develop into creoles seem to be normal processes of change. More of the changes may happen simultaneously, and often faster, than in a full language. This makes pidgins and creoles valuable 'laboratories' for the observation of change.

15 Language death
How languages end

I am always sorry when any language is lost, because
languages are the pedigree of nations.

Samuel Johnson, *Tour to the Hebrides* (1773)

Introduction

This chapter considers ways in which languages may disappear.
In some cases, forms are imported from a related, socially dominant
language in the region, so that effectively the original language
ceases to be used by its original speakers. This I have labelled language suicide. In other cases, languages at the lower end of the
social scale cease to be used, because there is simply no obvious use
for them, as the dominant language takes over. This I have labelled
language murder.

In the nineteenth century, scholars frequently talked about languages as if they were organic entities, like plants, which went
through a predictable life cycle of birth, infancy, maturation, then
gradual decay and death. In 1827, the German scholar Franz Bopp
claimed that 'Languages are to be considered organic natural bodies, which are formed according to fixed laws, develop as possessing
an inner principle of life, and gradually die out because they do
not understand themselves any longer, and therefore cast off or
mutilate their members or forms.'[1]

Nowadays, we no longer have this simple belief that languages
behave like beans or chrysanthemums, living out their alloted life,
and fading away in due course. It is, however, a fact that languages
sometimes die out. This is the process which we shall be discussing
in this chapter.

When we talk about languages dying, we are not referring to
languages which gradually alter their form over the centuries, and
in so doing possibly change their names. Latin, for example, is
sometimes spoken of as a 'dead' language, because nobody today

speaks it. But it did not really die, it merely changed its appearance and name, since French, Spanish, Italian and Sardinian are all direct descendants of Latin and are in a sense the same language. By language death, then, we do not simply mean this gradual alteration over time. We are referring to a more dramatic and less usual event, the total disappearance of a language.

Human beings never stop talking. How then can a language die out? When a language dies, it is not because a community has forgotten how to speak, but because another language has gradually ousted the old one as the dominant language, for political and social reasons. Typically, a younger generation will learn an 'old' language from their parents as a mother tongue, but will be exposed from a young age to another more fashionable and socially useful language at school.

In this situation, one of two things is liable to happen. The first possibility is that speakers of the old language will continue speaking it, but will gradually import forms and constructions from the socially dominant language, until the old one is no longer identifiable as a separate language. This is in reality an extreme form of borrowing. The language concerned seems to commit suicide. It slowly demolishes itself by bringing in more and more forms from the prestige language, until it destroys its own identity.

The second possibility is more dramatic. In some circumstances, the old language simply disappears. We are dealing not with the natural passing away of a language, but rather with a case of murder – murder by the dominant language as it gradually suppresses and ousts the subsidiary one. Let us look at these two phenomena.

Language suicide

Language suicide occurs most commonly when two languages are fairly similar to one another. In this situation, it is extremely easy for the less prestigious one to borrow vocabulary, constructions and sounds from the one with greater social approval. In the long run, it may obliterate itself entirely in the process.

The best-known cases of language suicide are those in which a developing language, a creole, gets devoured by its parent. A creole is often situated geographically in an area where people still speak the **lexifier** language, the one which provided most of the creole's vocabulary. This dominant language is usually one with social prestige. Consequently, social pressure tends to move the creole in its direction. This process is known as **decreolization**.[2]

Decreolization begins, as with other cases of borrowing, in constructions and sounds in which there is an overlap between the lexifier and the creole, and, like all language change, it occurs in a series of small steps.

Consider the changes which occurred in Bushlot, a Guyanan village with approximately 1,500 inhabitants of east Indian origin.[3] These were the descendants of labourers brought from India in the nineteenth century, who had learnt a pidgin English from African field-hands, which developed into what is today known as Guyanan Creole. This creole is gradually becoming decreolized as it moves back towards English in a series of step-by-step changes.

For example, among 'deep-creole' speakers, the word *fi* or *fu* is used where English would use *to*:

> Tshap no noo wa *fu* du
> chap not know what to do
> 'The fellow didn't know what to do.'

In less deep creole the word *tu* was used:

> Faama na noo wat *tu* duu
> farmer not know what to do
> 'The farmer didn't know what to do.'

At first sight, the alteration between *fu* and *tu* seemed to be chaotic, since both forms could occur in one person's speech in the same conversation. Closer inspection showed that, where *tu* was replacing *fu*, it was doing so in an orderly fashion, working through the verb system in three stages. At each step, there was fluctuation between *fu* and *tu*, with *tu* gradually winning out. First, *tu* was introduced after ordinary verbs, such as *ron* 'run', *kom* 'come', *wok* 'work', as in:

> Jan *wok tu* mek moni
> 'John works to make money.'

As a second stage, it began to occur after verbs expressing wanting or desire (desiderative verbs):

Jan *won tu* mek moni
'John wants to make money.'

Finally, it spread to verbs meaning 'start' or 'begin' (inceptive verbs), as in:

Jan *staat tu* mek moni
'John started to make money.'

This change, then, moved onwards and outward, like other linguistic changes, saturating each linguistic environment in turn.

Decreolization is also occurring in urban varieties of Tok Pisin.[4] In Papua New Guinea towns, English is the language of instruction used in universities, and the language of commerce and business establishments such as banks. In these environments, Tok Pisin is being increasingly swamped by English words and constructions – a fact sometimes resented by rural speakers. In a letter to *Wantok*, a Tok Pisin newspaper, one rural dweller complained bitterly about this happening: 'Nongut yumi hambak nambaut na bagarapim tokples bilong yumi olsem' – 'We must not [literally, 'It is no good for us to'] mess around and ruin the language of our country in this way.'[5]

Massive vocabulary borrowing is the most superficially noticeable aspect of decreolization in Tok Pisin. Since many existing pidgin words are based on English ones, the mechanisms of adaptation are well understood by the speakers, and hundreds more can easily infiltrate, particularly in situations in which Tok Pisin lacks sufficient vocabulary of its own. For example, Tok Pisin is now the official language of parliamentary transactions in the House of Assembly in the capital, Port Moresby. Political crises require heavy borrowing from English, since Tok Pisin does not have the technical terms to cope. The following is an extract from a radio broadcast describing a change of government:[6]

Lida bilong oposisen bipo, Mista Iambakey Okuk, i kirap na go muvim dispela mosin ov nou konfidens long praim minista, Mista Somare. Tasol memba bilong Menyama, Mista Neville Bourne, i singaut long point ov oda na tokim palamen olsem dispela mosin i no bihainim gud standing oda bilong palamen na konstitusin bilong kantri.

The previous leader of the opposition, Mr Iambakey Okuk, stood up and proceeded to move this motion of no confidence in the prime minister, Mr Somare. But the member for Menyama, Mr Neville Bourne, called out on a point of order and told parliament that this motion was not in accordance with the standing orders of parliament and the constitution of the country.

In the passage above, English structures are imported, as well as English words and phrases, as in *na tokim palamen olsem* 'and told parliament that'.

Advertisements, which often advocate Australian products, also tend to be direct translations of English ones:

Bilong lukautim gud gras long hed bilong yu na rausim ol laus, traim Pretty Hair. Pastaim tru, wasim gras long wara, bihain putim Pretty Hair pauda. Usim wanpela liklik paket Pretty Hair olsem tede, wet inap de bihain long tumora, na usim gen.[7]

To look after your hair properly and get rid of the lice, try Pretty Hair. First of all, wet your hair with water, then apply Pretty Hair powder. Use one little packet of Pretty Hair in this way today, wait until the day after tomorrow, and use it again.

Rural pidgin would have a number of differences. For example, it would probably use the pidgin word *haptumora* instead of the English-based *de bihain long tumora* 'day after tomorrow'.

Expressions of time, such as the one above, are the aspect of English which has most obviously influenced urban pidgin. Many English phrases crop up, even when speakers are convinced that they are speaking 'pure' pidgin. This is a continuation of a movement which has been going on in pidgin for some time. Nowadays, even rural speakers tend to say *foa klok, hapas tri*, 'four o'clock', 'half-past three', and so on, instead of the more cumbersome pidgin phrases which describe the position of the sun or the amount of natural light, as in *taim bilong san i godaun* 'the time of the sun going down', which is around six o'clock in the evening.

In addition, for dates, the English system of weeks and months has been imported. The days of the week are derived from the English ones: *Sande, Mande, Tunde* 'Sunday, Monday, Tuesday', and so on; and so are the words *wik* 'week' and *yia* 'year'. In these circumstances, it is easy for more English words and phrases to creep in, especially as most urban speakers have a reasonable knowledge of English. So we find expressions such as *fes yia* 'first year' instead of the older *namba wan yia*, beside an already existing pidgin *las yia* 'last year'. The pidgin *sampela taim* 'sometimes' tends to be shortened to the English-based *samtaim(s)*. Phrases and words such as *next morning, weekend, late, early, ten o'clock* (instead of *ten klok*) frequently creep into conversations. As in all language change, there is considerable fluctuation. On one day a person might use an English phrase, on another day a Tok Pisin one. Sometimes English and Tok Pisin forms of the same word occur in a single sentence, as in *Sampela taim mipela goaut o samtaims mipela stap na stori* 'Sometimes we go out, or *sometimes* we stay in and chat.'

At other times, Tok Pisin and English phrases get mixed together. The Tok Pisin for 'first . . . then' is *pastaim . . . bihain* (as in the Pretty Hair advertisement quoted above, 'First . . . wet your hair . . . then apply Pretty Hair'). One informant was completely inconsistent over this. Sometimes she used the expected *pastaim . . . bihain*, at other times the English *fest . . . afte* 'first . . . after'. Sometimes she mixed the two, as in *Fest mi boilim pitpit . . . bihain mi putim banana insait* '*First* I boil the pitpit . . . *then* I put the banana in.' This girl also once confused *pastaim* and *fest* into a single word, producing the hybrid *festaim*: *Festaim mipela go kisim paiawut* '*First* we go and get firewood.'

In some sentences, the English and Tok Pisin are so inextricably mixed that it is hard to tell which language is being spoken, as in *Krismas bilong mi, em eighteen years old* 'My Christmases, it's eighteen years old'. The true Tok Pisin form would have been *Mi gat wanpela ten et krismas*, or literally 'I have one ten and eight Christmases'.

These expressions of time represent more than the importation of isolated vocabulary items. Many of them have a more insidious effect. For example, Tok Pisin does not normally alter the form of a word when it is plural. Instead a numeral is added to the front, as in *tripela pik, planti pik* 'three pigs', 'many pigs', or the 'pluralizer' *ol, ol pik* 'pigs'. But in expressions of time, English *-s* is frequently added, as in *tu wiks moa* 'two weeks more', *tri des* 'three days', *wan an haf* *auas* 'one and a half hours', *wikends* 'weekends'. This creeping in of -*s* plurals may represent the first stages of a much wider change in the formation of plurals.

Expressions of time are also having an effect on the sound patterns of the language. For example, the increasing use of the words *after* and *afternoon* means that many people now feel *ft* to be a normal combination of sounds in the middle of a word, even though previously it did not exist, as is shown by the pidgin word *apinun* 'evening' (from the word 'afternoon').

Time expressions are not the only portion of English which is infiltrating the speech of the average urban speaker, though they are perhaps the most pervasive. Numerous other aspects of English life are making their way into Tok Pisin, and disrupting its structures and vocabulary. For example, most shops and businesses are structured in accordance with the meal breaks in a standard Australian day, so pidgin speakers talk about *hevim brekfas, lunch, tea, dinner*, and so on. This, incidentally, sometimes angers older speakers who boast that in their youth they used to work all day without stopping to eat.

Western foods are being introduced alongside the traditional root vegetables such as yam, taro, sweet potato, which used to comprise the total diet of many Papua New Guineans. So people now talk about *mekim sandwich, bread*, as in *Favourite kaikai bilong mi, em bread, toasted bread* 'My favourite food is bread, toasted bread', *kiau na bread slice* 'eggs and a slice of bread'. This is another area in which Western words and phrases have become intermeshed with Tok Pisin ones.

The interweaving of English and Tok Pisin occurs not only in single sentences, but also in conversation. One person may ask a question in English, and the other reply in Tok Pisin:

Speaker A   Have you seen our brush?
Speaker B   Mi no lukim. ('No, I haven't seen it.')
Speaker C   It might be in the bathroom.
Speaker A   Yes, em i stap. ('Yes, here it is.')

The fact that this mixture is totally natural, and not an attempt to be clever or funny, is shown by the fact that it happens in situations where the participants are concentrating on what they are doing, and are not consciously paying attention to their speech. Rugby football is a game in which emotions run high, and the surrounding crowd is continually yelling encouragement or abuse, in an inextricable mixture of English and Tok Pisin. *Come on, boys! Autim!* 'Pass it out!', *Em nau!* 'That's it!', *Some more of that! Some more, Brothers!* (Brothers is the name of a football team), *Maski namba tu!* 'Don't pay any attention to number two!', *Good work, Jumbo. Gerim low!* 'Get him low' (English words with Tok Pisin pronunciation of [r] for [t] as in *wara* 'water'), *Don't let them put a try! Ah, em i putim trai!* 'Ah, he scored a try.'

The examples of decreolization discussed show the way the process occurs. Phrases from the base language are borrowed in particular situations, usually where there is a strong overlap between the creole and the base language, and/or where the creole is lacking or cumbersome. The borrowed words and phrases, though seemingly isolated and innocuous, tend to have a more pernicious and far-reaching effect than is obvious at first sight. The base language spreads in all directions, like an octopus entwining its tentacles round all parts of an animal before it eventually kills it.

Language murder

Language murder is more dramatic than language suicide. The old language is slaughtered by the new. How does this happen?

The first stage is a decrease in the number of people who speak the language. Typically, only isolated pockets of rural speakers remain. If these isolated groups come into close contact with a more socially or economically useful language, then bilingualism becomes essential for survival. The 500 or so Kwegu in Ethiopia, for example, lived along the banks of the Omo River, and mainly hunted hippopotamus.[8] They also kept bees. Honey is extremely popular in the Ethiopian Highlands because of its intoxicating properties when converted into mead by mixing it with water and yeast. The Kwegu existed partly by selling honey to the more numerous and powerful Mursi and Bodi who surrounded them. The Kwegu therefore spoke either Mursi or Bodi, but the Mursi and Bodi did not usually speak Kwegu. Mursi and Bodi men married Kwegu girls, who were absorbed into their husbands' lives. But the reverse did not happen. Consequently, the acquisition of Kwegu as a first language decreased.

The first generation of bilinguals is often fluent in both languages. But the next generation down becomes less proficient in the dying language, partly through lack of practice. The old language is therefore spoken mainly by the old people. As one of the few remaining speakers of Arvanítika (an Albanian dialect spoken in Greece) noted: 'We don't speak it with the children; with old folks like ourselves.' And if they did address the younger generation in Arvanítika, the latter were likely to respond in Greek.[9]

The younger generation lacked practice, mainly because the old language was used on fewer and fewer occasions, to talk about fewer and fewer topics. Consider the gradual contraction of German in a trilingual community in Sauris, a small village in northeast Italy.[10] Its inhabitants were once German speakers. Then the 800 or so villagers started to use three languages, Italian, Friulian and German. Italian was the official language, used in church and school. Friulian was the local dialect, which was used in bars and for everyday conversation round the village. German, once the main language, was gradually ousted by the other two. In the course of the twentieth century it gradually retreated, and became used in fewer and fewer circumstances. Eventually, it was spoken almost exclusively in the home, as the language of intimacy between family members. Now even this function is dying out, as many parents feel that it is better for their children's future to converse with them in Italian, and German-speaking families have even begun to meet with some criticism: 'Poor child, he doesn't even speak Friulian'[11] was a remark made by the mayor's mother about a child whose family still addressed it in German. From this viewpoint, languages simply die out because there is no need for them: 'Languages at the lower end of the prestige scale retreat . . . until there is nothing left for them appropriately to be used about.'[12]

Finally, the few remaining speakers are 'semi-speakers'. They can still converse after a fashion, but they forget the words for things, get endings wrong, and use a limited number of sentence patterns. This phenomenon is reported fairly frequently in the literature. A typical example is Bloomfield's (1924) description of the speech of White Thunder, one of the last remaining speakers of the American-Indian language Menomini: 'His Menomini is atrocious. His vocabulary is small; his inflections are often barbarous; he constructs sentences on a few threadbare models.'[13]

One of the earliest detailed studies of language death was by Nancy Dorian, an American linguist who studied the demise of Scottish Gaelic, which is a receding language throughout Highland Scotland.[14]

Dorian looked in particular at isolated pockets of Gaelic speakers in three fishing villages, Brora, Golspie and Embo. These villages are situated on the eastern coast in the far north of Scotland, an area in which Gaelic had practically died out apart from in the villages under discussion. In Brora and Golspie there were a number of 70–80-year-olds who were taught Gaelic as their first language, and in Embo, a more isolated village, it was possible to find people in their early forties who regarded Gaelic as their mother tongue. These residual Gaelic speakers were bilingual, and a number of them spoke English better than Gaelic. Most of them were aware that their Gaelic was inferior to that spoken by their parents and grandparents, and were particularly conscious of gaps in their vocabulary, explaining that their elders had many more 'words for things' than they have themselves.

Dorian's study showed the messiness of language death. Although general trends could be discerned, the old language did not fade away neatly. Isolated words retained their Gaelic inflections right up to the end. As she noted: 'Gaelic can be said to be dying . . . with its morphological boots on.'[15]

In the next stage, the younger generation would recognize only a few scattered Gaelic words, usually plants, foods, or town names. At this stage, the language could be said to have died, or, more appropriately, to have been murdered by the influx of another socially and politically dominant language.

Language death is a social phenomenon, and triggered by social needs. There is no evidence that there was anything wrong with the dead language itself: its essential structure was no better and no worse than that of any other language. It faded away because it did not fulfil the social needs of the community who spoke it.

So many doors

'Death hath so many doors to let out life,' said John Fletcher in the seventeenth century.[16] And this is certainly true of language death. As more and more dying languages are explored, numerous variants of the scenarios outlined above have been found.[17]

In particular, sociolinguistic work on **code-switching** indicates how dying languages can be intertwined with healthy ones.[18] Bilingual speakers often 'switch codes', that is, move from one language to another and back again in the course of conversations. Sometimes, it is unclear which one they are speaking at any particular point. The process may result in language mixing. But in most cases, one of the languages wins out, and the other is demoted to subsidiary status.

Children exposed to two languages can shed light on this switching and mixing. A child who was a fluent speaker of Hebrew moved from Israel to the USA at the age of two and a half.[19] At around the age of three, she could speak both Hebrew and English. Soon after, she started to use defective Hebrew verb forms, and sometimes she inserted these into an English frame:

> I'm *menagev*-ing myself. I want to *inagev* myself
> 'I'm *drying* myself. I want to *dry* myself.'

Eventually, Hebrew verbs faded away.

Diminishing numbers

A language finally dies when no one speaks it, and this can happen suddenly. The last speaker of Kasabe, a Cameroon language, died on 5 November one year. By 6 November, Kasabe was an extinct language.[20] And such extinctions are happening at an ever-increasing rate.

Around 6,000 languages exist, according to one count. Of these, half may be moribund: they are no longer learned as a first language by a new generation of speakers. A further 2,400 are in a danger zone: they have fewer than 100,000 speakers. This leaves only around 600, 10 per cent of the current total, in the safe category.[21]

Of course, new dialects, sometimes new languages, are constantly emerging, as existing languages split apart: English has already divided into many Englishes – American English, British English, Australian English, Indian English, and so on.[22] But the structural diversity of the world's languages will undoubtedly be diminished, something most people regret. 'Just as the extinction of any animal species diminishes our world, so does the extinction of any language.'[23] 'With every language that dies, another precious source of data about the nature of the human language faculty is lost.'[24]

So what can be done? The answer, perhaps, is to ensure that people are aware of the value of their first-learned language. Only they, the speakers, can preserve it. And they can succeed, if they want to – as Hebrew and, to a lesser extent, Welsh have shown. Both have been significantly revived in recent years.

Perhaps, in an ideal world, everyone would speak two, three or even multiple languages. In Papua New Guinea, which is reputed to have more languages crammed into its small space than any other part of the world, numerous people are multilingual.[25] When I admitted that I spoke only English fluently, my informants were puzzled: 'But how do you then talk to your relatives who live in a different place?'

16 Progress or decay?
Assessing the situation

> If you can look into the seeds of time,
> And say which grain will grow and which will not
> > William Shakespeare, *Macbeth* (1606)

Introduction

This chapter summarizes the conclusion reached in this book on the question raised in the title, as to whether language change is progress or decay. The answer is neither. Disruptive and therapeutic tendencies vie with one another in a perpetual stalemate. There is no evidence that language is evolving in any particular direction. Activists who try to control language are unlikely to be successful. Standardization can be useful, but cannot be imposed legally. At the most, we should try and recognize attempts to manipulate language, and avoid being affected by them.

Predicting the future depends on understanding the present. The majority of self-proclaimed 'experts' who argue that language is disintegrating have not considered the complexity of the factors involved in language change. They are giving voice to a purely emotional expression of their hopes and fears.

A closer look at language change has indicated that it is natural, inevitable and continuous, and involves interwoven sociolinguistic and psycholinguistic factors which cannot easily be disentangled from one another. It is triggered by social factors, but these social factors make use of existing cracks and gaps in the language structure. In the circumstances, the true direction of a change is not obvious to a superficial observer. Sometimes alterations are disruptive, as with the increasing loss of *t* in British English, where the utilization of a natural tendency to alter or omit final consonants may end up destroying a previously stable stop system. At other times, modifications can be viewed as therapy, as in the loss of *h* in some types of English, which is wiping out an exception in the otherwise symmetrical organization of fricatives.

However, whether changes disrupt the language system, or repair it, the most important point is this: it is in no sense wrong for human language to change, any more than it is wrong for humpback whales to alter their songs every year.[1] In fact, there are some surprising parallels between the two species. All the humpback whales sing the same song one year, the next year they all sing a new one. But the yearly differences are not random. The songs seem to be evolving. The songs of consecutive years are more alike than those that are separated by several years. When it was first discovered that the songs of humpbacks changed from year to year, a simple explanation seemed likely. Since the whales only sing during the breeding season, and since their song is complex, it was assumed that they simply forgot the song between seasons, and then tried to reconstruct it the next year from fragments which remained in their memory. But when researchers organized a long-term study of humpback whales off Hawaii, they got a surprise. The song that the whales were singing at the beginning of the new breeding season turned out to be identical to the one used at the end of the previous season. Between breeding seasons, the song had seemingly been kept in cold storage, without change. The songs were gradually modified as the season proceeded. For example, new sequences were sometimes created by joining the beginning and end of consecutive phrases and omitting the middle part – a procedure not unlike certain human language changes.

Both whales and humans, then, are constantly changing their communication system, and are the only two species in which this has been proved to happen – though some birds are now thought to alter their song in certain ways. Rather than castigating one of these species for allowing change to occur, it seems best to admit that humans are probably programmed by nature to behave in this way. As a character in John Wyndham's novel *Web* says: 'Man is a product of nature . . . Whatever he does, it must be part of his nature to do – or he could not do it. He is not, and cannot be *un*natural. He, with his capacities, is as much the product of nature as were the dinosaurs with theirs. He is an *instrument* of natural processes.'

A consideration of the naturalness and inevitability of change leads us to the three final questions which need to be discussed in this book. First, is it still relevant to speak of progress or decay? Secondly, irrespective of whether the move is a forwards or backwards one, are human languages evolving in any detectable direction? Thirdly, even though language change is not wrong in the moral sense, is it socially undesirable, and, if so, can we control it? Let us consider these matters.

Forwards or backwards?

'Once, twice, thrice upon a time, there lived a jungle. This particular jungle started at the bottom and went upwards till it reached the monkeys, who had been waiting years for the trees to reach them, and as soon as they did, the monkeys invented climbing down.' The opening paragraph of Spike Milligan's fable *The story of the bald twit lion* indicates how easy it is to make facts fit one's preferred theory.

This tendency is particularly apparent in past interpretations of the direction of change, where opinions about progress or decay in language have tended to reflect the religious or philosophical preconceptions of their proponents, rather than a detached analysis of the evidence. Let us briefly deal with these preconceptions before looking at the issue itself.

Many nineteenth-century scholars were imbued with sentimental ideas about the 'noble savage', and assumed that the current generation was by comparison a race of decadent sinners. They therefore took it for granted that language had declined from a former state of perfection. Restoring this early perfection was viewed as one of the principal goals of comparative historical linguistics. 'A principal goal of this science is to reconstruct the full, pure forms of an original stage from the variously disfigured and mutilated forms which are attested in the individual languages,' said one scholar.[2]

This quasi-religious conviction of gradual decline has never entirely died out. But from the mid nineteenth century onward, a second, opposing viewpoint came into existence alongside the earlier one. Darwin's doctrine of the survival of the fittest and ensuing belief in inevitable progress gradually grew in popularity. 'Progress, therefore, is not an accident, but a necessity . . . It is a part of nature,'[3] claimed one nineteenth-century enthusiast. Darwin himself believed that in language 'the better, the shorter, the easier forms are constantly gaining the upper hand, and they owe their success to their inherent virtue'.[4]

The doctrine of the survival of the fittest, in its crudest version, implies that those forms and languages which survive are inevitably better than those which die out. This is unfortunate, since it confuses the notions of progress and decay in language with expansion and decline. As we have seen, expansion and decline reflect political and social situations, not the intrinsic merit or decadence of a language. Today, it is a historical accident that English is so widely spoken in the world. Throughout history, quite different types of language – Latin, Turkish, Chinese, for example – have spread over wide areas. This popularity reflects the military and political strength of these nations, not the worth of their speech. Similarly, Gaelic is dying out because it is being ousted by English, a language with social and political prestige. It is not collapsing because it has got too complicated or strange for people to speak, as has occasionally been maintained.

In order to assess the possible direction of language, then, we need to put aside both quasi-religious beliefs and Darwinian assumptions. The former lead to an illogical idealization of the past, and the latter to the confusion of progress and decay with expansion and decline.

Leaving aside these false trails, we are left with a crucial question: What might we mean by 'progress' within language?

The term 'progress' implies a movement towards some desired endpoint. What could this be, in terms of linguistic excellence? A number of linguists are in no doubt. They endorse the view of Jespersen, who maintained that 'that language ranks highest which goes farthest in the art of accomplishing much with little means, or, in other words, which is able to express the greatest amount of meaning with the simplest mechanism'.[5]

If this criterion were taken seriously, we would be obliged to rank pidgins as the most advanced languages. As we have already noted, true simplicity seems to be counterbalanced by ambiguity and cumbersomeness. Darwin's confident belief in the 'inherent virtue' of shorter and easier forms must be set beside the realization that such forms often result in confusing homonyms, as in the Tok Pisin *hat* for 'hot', 'hard', 'hat' and 'heart'.

A straightforward simplicity measure then will not necessarily pinpoint the 'best' language. A considerable number of other factors must be taken into account, and it is not yet clear which they are, and how they should be assessed. In brief, linguists have been unable to decide on any clear measure of excellence, even though the majority are of the opinion that a language with numerous irregularities should be less highly ranked than one which is economical and transparent. However, preliminary attempts to rank languages in this way have run into a further problem.

A language which is simple and regular in one respect is likely to be complex and confusing in others. There seems to be a trading relationship between the different parts of the grammar which we do not fully understand. This has come out clearly in the work of one researcher who compared the progress of Turkish and Serbo-Croatian children as they acquired their respective languages.[6] Turkish children find it exceptionally easy to learn the inflections of their language, which are remarkably straightforward, and they master the entire system by the age of two. But the youngsters struggle with relative clauses (the equivalent of English clauses beginning with *who, which, that*) until around the age of five. Serbo-Croatian children, on the other hand, have great problems with the inflectional system of their language, which is 'a classic Indo-European synthetic muddle', and they are not competent at manipulating it until around the age of five. Yet they have no problems with Serbo-Croatian relative clauses, which they can normally cope with by the age of two.

Overall, we cannot yet specify satisfactorily just what we mean by a 'perfect' language, except in a very broad sense. The most we can do is to note that a certain part of one language may be simpler and therefore perhaps 'better' than that of another.

Meanwhile, even if all agreed that a perfectly regular language was the 'best', there is no evidence that languages are progressing towards this ultimate goal. Instead, there is a continuous pull between the disruption and the restoration of patterns. In this perpetual ebb and flow, it would be a mistake to regard pattern neatening and regularization as a step forwards. Such an occurrence may be no more progressive than the tidying up of a cluttered office. Reorganization simply restores the room to a workable state. Similarly, it would be misleading to assume that pattern disruption was necessarily a backward step. Structural dislocation may be the result of extending the language in some useful way.

We must conclude therefore that language is ebbing and flowing like the tide, but neither progressing nor decaying, as far as we can tell. Disruptive and therapeutic tendencies vie with one another, with neither one totally winning or losing, resulting in a perpetual stalemate. As the famous Russian linguist Roman Jakobson said over fifty years ago: 'The spirit of equilibrium and the simultaneous tendency towards its rupture constitute the indispensable properties of that whole that is language.'[7]

Are languages evolving?

Leaving aside notions of progress and decay, we need to ask one further question. Is there any evidence that languages as a whole are moving in any particular direction in their intrinsic structure? Are they, for example, moving towards a fixed word order, as has sometimes been claimed?

It is clear that languages, even if they are evolving in some identifiable way, are doing so very slowly – otherwise all languages would be rather more similar than they in fact are. However, unfortunately for those who would like to identify some overall drift, the languages of the world seem to be moving in different, often opposite, directions. For example, over the past 2,000 years or so, most Indo-European languages have moved from being SOV (subject–object–verb) languages, to SVO (subject–verb–object) ones. As we noted earlier, certain Niger-Congo languages seem to be following a similar path. Yet we cannot regard this as an overall trend, since Mandarin Chinese may be undergoing a change in the opposite direction, from SVO to SOV.[8]

During the same period, English and a number of other Indo-European languages have gradually lost their inflections, and moved over to a fixed word order. However, this direction is not inevitable, since Wappo, a Californian Indian language, appears to be doing the reverse, and moving from a system in which grammatical relationships are expressed by word order to one in which they are marked by case endings.[9]

A similar variety is seen in the realm of phonology. For example, English, French and Hindi had the same common ancestor. Nowadays, Hindi has sixteen stop consonants and ten vowels, according to one count. French, on the other hand, has sixteen vowels and six stops. English, meanwhile, has acquired more fricatives than either of these two languages, some of which speakers of French and Hindi find exceptionally difficult to pronounce. Many more such examples could be found.

Overall, then, we must conclude that 'the evolution of language as such has never been demonstrated, and the inherent equality of all languages must be maintained on present evidence'.[10]

Is language change socially undesirable?

Let us now turn to the last question, which has two parts. Is language change undesirable? If so, is it controllable?

Social undesirability and moral turpitude are often confused. Yet the two questions can quite often be kept distinct. For example, it is certainly not 'wrong' to sleep out in the open. Nevertheless, it is fairly socially inconvenient to have people bedding down wherever they want to, and therefore laws have been passed forbidding people to camp out in, say, Trafalgar Square or Hyde Park in London.

Language change is, we have seen, in no sense wrong. But is it socially undesirable? It is only undesirable when communication gets disrupted. If different groups change a previously unified language in different directions, or if one group alters its speech more radically than another, mutual intelligibility may be impaired or even destroyed. In Tok Pisin, for example, speakers from rural areas have difficulty in understanding the urbanized varieties. This is an unhappy and socially inconvenient state of affairs.

In England, on the other hand, the problem is minimal. There are relatively few speakers of British English who cannot understand one another. This is because most people speak the same basic dialect, in the sense that the rules underlying their utterances and vocabulary are fairly much the same. They are likely, however, to speak this single dialect with different accents. There is nothing wrong with this, as long as people can communicate satisfactorily with one another. An accent which differs markedly from those around may be hard for others to comprehend, and is therefore likely to be a disadvantage in job-hunting situations. But a mild degree of regional variation is probably a mark of individuality to be encouraged rather than stamped out.

A number of people censure the variety of regional accents in England, maintaining that the accent that was originally of one particular area, London and the southeast, is 'better' than the others. In fact, speakers from this locality sometimes claim that they speak English *without* an accent, something which is actually impossible. It may be socially useful in England to be able to speak the accent of so-called Southern British English, an accent sometimes spoken of as Received Pronunciation (RP), which has spread to the educated classes throughout the country. But there is no logical reason behind the disapproval of regional accents. Moreover, such objections are by no means universal. Some people regard regional accents as a sign of 'genuineness'. And in America, a regional accent is simply a mark of where you are from, with no stigma attached, for the most part.

Accent differences, then, are not a matter of great concern. More worrying are instances where differing dialects cause unintelligibility, or misunderstandings. In the past, this often used to be the case in England. William Caxton, writing in the fifteenth century, noted that 'comyn englysshe that is spoken in one shyre varyeth from another'.[11] To illustrate his point, he narrated an episode concerning a ship which was stranded in the Thames for lack of wind, and put into shore for refreshment. One of the merchants on board went to a nearby house, and asked, in English, for meat and eggs. The lady of the house, much to this gentleman's indignation, replied that she could not speak French! In Caxton's words, the merchant 'cam in to an hows and axed for mete and specyally he axyd after eggys. And the good wyf answerde that she coude speke no frenshe. And the merchaunt was angry for he also coude speke no frenshe, but wolde haue hadde egges and she vnderstode hym not.' The problem in this case was that a 'new' Norse word *egges* 'eggs' was in the process of replacing the Old English word *eyren*, but was not yet generally understood.

Unfortunately, such misunderstandings did not disappear with the fifteenth century. Even though, in both America and England, the majority of speakers are mutually intelligible, worrying misunderstandings still occur through dialect differences. Consider the conversation between Samuel, a five-year-old black boy from West Philadelphia, and Paul, a white psychologist who had been working in Samuel's school for six months:

Samuel	I been know your name.
Paul	What?
Samuel	I been know your name.
Paul	You better know my name?
Samuel	I *been* know your name.[12]

Paul failed to realize that in Philadelphia's black community *been* meant 'for a long time'. Samuel meant 'I have known your name for a long time.' In some circumstances, this use of *been* could be misleading to a white speaker. A black Philadelphian who said *I been married* would in fact mean 'I have been married for a long time.' But a white speaker would normally interpret the sentence as meaning 'I have been married, but I am not married any longer.'

Is it possible to do anything about situations where differences caused by language change threaten to disrupt the mutual comprehension and cohesion of a population? Should language change be stopped?

If legislators decide that something is socially inconvenient, then their next task is to decide whether it is possible to take effective action against it. If we attempted to halt language change by law, would the result be as effective as forbidding people to camp in Trafalgar Square? Or would it be as useless as telling the pigeons there not to congregate around the fountains? Judging by the experience of the French, who have an academy, the Académie Française, which adjudicates over matters of linguistic usage, and whose findings have been made law in some cases, the result is a waste of time. Even though there may be some limited effect on the written language, spoken French appears not to have responded in any noticeable way.

If legal sanctions are impractical, how can mutual comprehension be brought about or maintained? The answer is not to attempt to limit change, which is probably impossible, but to ensure that all members of the population have at least one common language, and one common variety of that language, which they can mutually use. The standard language may be the only one spoken by certain people. Others will retain their own regional dialect or language alongside the standard one. This is the situation in the British Isles, where some Londoners, for example, speak only Standard British English. In Wales, however, there are a number of people who are equally fluent in Welsh and English.

The imposition of a standard language cannot be brought about by force. Sometimes it occurs spontaneously, as has happened in England. At other times, conscious intervention is required. Such social planning requires tact and skill. In order for a policy to achieve acceptance, a population must *want* to speak a particular language or particular variety of it. A branch of sociolinguistics known as 'language planning' or, more recently, 'language engineering', is attempting to solve the practical and theoretical problems involved in such attempts.[13]

Once standardization has occurred, and a whole population has accepted one particular variety as standard, it becomes a strong unifying force and often a source of national pride and a symbol of independence.

Great Permitters

Perhaps we need one final comment about 'Great Permitters' – a term coined by the late William Safire, who wrote a column about language for the *New York Times*.[14] These are intelligent, determined people, often writers, who 'care about clarity and precision, who detest fuzziness of expression that reveals sloppiness or laziness of thought'. They want to give any changes which occur 'a shove in the direction of freshness and precision', and are 'willing to struggle to preserve the clarity and color in the language'. In other words, they are prepared to accept new usages which they regard as advantageous, and are prepared to battle against those which seem sloppy or pointless.

Such an aim is admirable. An influential writer–journalist can clearly make interesting suggestions, and provide models for others to follow. Two points need to be made, however. First, however hard a 'linguistic activist' (as Safire called himself) works, s/he is unlikely to reverse a strong trend, however much s/he would like to. Safire, for example, gave up his fight against the word *hopefully*, and also against *viable*, which, he regretfully admitted, 'cannot be killed'. Secondly, and perhaps more importantly, we need to realize how personal and how idiosyncratic are judgments as to what is 'good' and what is 'bad', even when they are made by a careful and knowledgeable writer, as became clear from the often furious letters which followed Safire's pronouncements in the *New York Times*. Even Safire fans admitted that he held a number of opinions which were based on nothing more than a subjective feeling about the words in question. Why, for example, did he give up the struggle against *hopefully*, but continue to wage war on *clearly*? As one of his correspondents noted, 'Your grudge against clearly is unclear to me.' Similarly, Safire attacked ex-President Carter's 'needless substitution of encrypt for encode', but was sharply reminded by a reader that 'the words "encrypt" and "encode" have very distinct meanings for a cryptographer'. These, and other similar examples, show that attempts of caring persons to look after a language can mean no more than the preservation of personal preferences which may not agree with the views of others.

Linguistic activists of the Safire type are laudable in one sense, in that they are aware of language and pay attention to it. But, it has been suggested, they may overall be harmful, in that they divert attention away from more important linguistic issues. The manipulation of people's lives by skilful use of language is something which happens in numerous parts of the world. 'Nukespeak', language which is used to refer to nuclear devices, is one much-publicized example.[15] We do not nowadays hear very much about *nuclear bombs* or *nuclear weapons*. Politicians tend to refer to them as *nuclear deterrents* or *nuclear shields*. Other deadly weapons have been referred to as *assets*.[16] Whether or not these devices are useful possessions is not the issue here. The important point is that their potential danger may not be realized by many people because of the soothing language intentionally used to describe them. In the long run, it may be more important to detect manipulation of this type, than to worry about whether the word *media* should be treated as singular or plural.

Conclusion

Continual language change is natural and inevitable, and is due to a combination of psycholinguistic and sociolinguistic factors.

Once we have stripped away religious and philosophical preconceptions, there is no evidence that language is either progressing or decaying. Disruption and therapy seem to balance one another in a perpetual stalemate. These two opposing pulls are an essential characteristic of language.

Furthermore, there is no evidence that languages are moving in any particular direction from the point of view of language structure – several are moving in contrary directions.

Language change is in no sense wrong, but it may, in certain circumstances, be socially undesirable. Minor variations in pronunciation from region to region are unimportant, but change which disrupts the mutual intelligibility of a community can be socially and politically inconvenient. If this happens, it may be useful to encourage standardization – the adoption of a standard variety of one particular language which everybody will be able to use, alongside the existing regional dialects or languages. Such a situation must be brought about gradually, with tact and care, since a population will only adopt a language or dialect it *wants* to speak.

Finally, it is always possible that language is developing in some mysterious fashion that linguists have not yet identified. Only time and further research will tell.

But we may finish on a note of optimism. We no longer, like Caxton in the fifteenth century, attribute language change to the domination of man's affairs by the moon:

> And certaynly our language now vsed varyeth ferre from that which was vsed and spoken whan I was borne. For we englysshe men ben borne vnder the domynacyon of the mone, which is neuer stedfaste but euer wauerynge wexynge one season and waneth and dycreaseth another season.[17]

Instead, step by step, we are coming to an understanding of the social and psychological factors underlying language change. As the years go by, we hope gradually to increase this knowledge. In the words of the nineteenth-century poet Alfred Lord Tennyson:

> Science moves, but slowly slowly, creeping on from point to point.

Optional questions

This book has been written for people who are interested in language change, and enjoy reading about it. It is NOT written primarily for people who want to be tested on the topic in essays or exams. However, I have been told that some people have requested possible questions which might help them to see how much of the book they have remembered. So here, chapter by chapter, are some suggestions.

Chapter 1

Q.1.1 Why in the eighteenth and nineteenth centuries were people so worried about language change?

Q.1.2 Explain what is meant by the word 'grammar'.

Q.1.3 What is the difference between a prescriptive and a descriptive grammar?

Chapter 2

Q.2.1 Suggest at least three types of clue which might help linguists to reconstruct the pronunciation of speakers in past centuries.

Q.2.2 Outline two basic assumptions of comparative historical linguistics.

Q.2.3 Name two other types of reconstruction, and explain what they involve.

Chapter 3

Q.3.1 Distinguish between real time and apparent time and explain why this distinction is important to historical linguists.

Q.3.2 What are linguistic variables, and why are they important in language change?

Q.3.3 What are participant observers, and why are they useful in the study of ongoing change?

Chapter 4

Q.4.1 What is hypercorrection, and what can it tell us about language change?

Q.4.2 What is a curvilinear pattern, and what information can it provide for those studying ongoing change?

Q.4.3 Suggest overlapping stages which might characterize the spread of a change.

Chapter 5

Q.5.1 Outline at least one situation in which social pressures can cause linguistic conflict.

Q.5.2 What is meant by 'accommodation', and what is its relevance to language change?

Q.5.3 In what way might the language of new immigrants be altered as they encounter a novel (to them) linguistic situation, even though they might be speaking the same language?

Chapter 6

Q.6.1 What is the typical pattern of a sound change?

Q.6.2 What type of words might get affected early in a sound change?

Q.6.3 How reliable are speakers in their implementation of a change?

Chapter 7

Q.7.1 In what way are syntactic variants relevant to syntactic change?

Q.7.2 Why are ambiguous structures important in syntactic change?

Q.7.3 Discuss the speed of change. Do changes happen fast, or gradually?

Chapter 8

Q.8.1 Explain the term 'grammaticalization'.

Q.8.2 What types of change are typically associated with grammaticalization?

Q.8.3 What is meant by the term 'rebus', and why is it relevant to text messaging?

Chapter 9

Q.9.1 What is polysemy?

Q.9.2 How is polysemy relevant to meaning change?

Q.9.3 What is prototype theory, and why is it important for language change?

Chapter 10

Q.10.1 Why is meaning change unlikely to be due to random fluctuation?

Q.10.2 What is substratum theory, and how is it relevant to language change?

Q.10.3 Outline some characteristics of language borrowing.

Chapter 11

Q.11.1 Explain why the human vocal organs might cause language change.

Q.11.2 Suggest some natural tendencies in language which might affect word order.

Q.11.3 What is iconicity, and how is it relevant to linguistic change?

Chapter 12

Q.12.1 What is meant by therapeutic change?

Q.12.2 Give at least two examples of pattern neatening.

Q.12.3 Suggest some general tendencies which underlie pattern neatening.

Chapter 13

Q.13.1 What do you understand by chain reaction changes?

Q.13.2 Distinguish between drag chains and push chains, and explain why one is likely to be more usual than the other.

Q.13.3 Give examples of some ongoing changes in *either* British English diphthongs *or* Northern American vowels, and explain in what way(s) they might cause problems in understanding.

Chapter 14

Q.14.1 What are pidgins and creoles?

Q.14.2 How do pidgins begin?

Q.14.3 How do pidgins change into creoles?

Chapter 15

Q.15.1 Why might a language die? Give at least two reasons.

Q.15.2 What is meant by decreolization? Give an example or examples of this process.

Q.15.3 What are semi-speakers, and how do they handle the language of which they are semi-speakers?

Chapter 16

Q.16.1 In what way are the communication systems of whales similar to those of humans?

Q.16.2 Why is the notion of progress problematic?

Q.16.3 Why is it unlikely that human language is evolving in any particular direction?

Notes and suggestions for further reading

1 The ever-whirling wheel

1 In Lehmann, 1967: 63.
2 In Fisher & Bornstein, 1974: 77. *Disours* and *seggers* are public reciters, *harpours* are harpers.
3 *Troylus and Criseyde* II, 22–6.
4 Saussure, 1915/1959: 77.
5 Spike Hughes, *Daily Telegraph*, 26 April 1968.
6 Anthony Lejeune, *Daily Telegraph*, 7 May 1971.
7 Mary Stott, *Guardian*, 9 September 1968.
8 Douglas Bush, Polluting our language, *American Scholar*, Spring 1972: 244.
9 David Holloway, *Daily Telegraph*, 7 July 1978.
10 Richard Gilman, *Decadence*, London: Secker & Warburg, 1979.
11 Philip Howard, *Words fail me*, London: Hamish Hamilton, 1980.
12 Reuben Glass, *Guardian*, 13 July 1982.
13 Val Hume, *Evening Standard*, 22 July 1986.
14 Edward Pearce, *The Sunday Times*, 16 October 1988.
15 Kingsley Amis, They can't even say it properly now, in Ricks & Michaels, 1990: 458. On laments about language in general, Crystal (1981, 1984) lists some common complaints about English usage, and points out that several of them have been around for centuries. The topic is a popular one: Aitchison (1997), R. W. Bailey (1992), Bex & Watts (1999), Tony Crowley (1989), Hitchings (2011), Langer & Nesse (2012), Milroy & Milroy (1998) all discuss purism and 'the complaint tradition'.
16 Philip Norman, *The Sunday Times*, 14 February 1999.
17 Humphrys, 2004.
18 Humphrys, 2004: 4–5.

19 John Humphrys, *Daily Mail*, 28 September 2007, in Crystal, 2008: 9.
20 Anthony Lejeune, *Daily Telegraph*, 7 May 1971.
21 Val Hume, *Evening Standard*, 22 July 1986.
22 In Jespersen, 1922: 322.
23 Jespersen, 1922: 263.
24 Vendryès, 1923/1925: 359.
25 In Hyman, 1975: 131.
26 In Wilkinson, 1967: 18–19.
27 In Jespersen, 1922: 42.
28 Jonathan Swift, A proposal for correcting, improving, and ascertaining the English tongue, reprinted in Bolton (1966).
29 Lowth, 1762/1967: i, ix.
30 Sapir, 1921: 124.
31 Samuel Johnson, *The Rambler*, 15 January 1752.
32 Pyles, 1971: 224.
33 Lowth, 1762/1967: 127–8.
34 Tieken-Boon van Ostade, 2011: 93.
35 Lowth, 1762/1967: xii–xiii, quoted in Tieken-Boon van Ostade, 2011: 55.
36 Lowth, 1762/1967: ix, quoted in Tieken-Boon van Ostade, 2011: 95–6.
37 Lowth, 1762/1967: 127–8.
38 *Canterbury tales*, Prologue, 70–3.
39 Collected by Guy Bailey.
40 Trench, 1855: 18–19.
41 Trench, 1856: 5.
42 John Wallis, in Jespersen, 1942: II, 161.
43 Lowth, 1762/1967: x.
44 See Aitchison (2010) for a brief introduction to linguistics, with further reading suggestions.
45 Lakoff, 1975: 28.

2   Collecting up clues

1 Kuper, 1977.
2 Saussure, 1915/1959: 51.
3 Conan Doyle, *A case of identity*.
4 Shakespeare, *A midsummer night's dream*, II, ii, 9–12.
5 Shakespeare, *Twelfth night*, I, iii, 97ff.
6 Shakespeare, *The merchant of Venice*, IV, i, 123–4.
7 Cicero, *De divinatione*, ii, 84, in Allen, 1978: 98.

8 Allen, 1974: 67. Allen (1974) on ancient Greek, and Allen (1978) on Latin, are clear and comprehensive accounts of how to reconstruct the pronunciation of 'dead' languages. See Gimson & Cruttenden (1994: 68f.) for English. See also Hock & Joseph (1996: ch. 3).

9 Catullus, *Carmina*, 84.

10 *Pickwick papers*, ch. 34.

11 Allen, 1978: 34.

12 John Hart, in Danielsson, 1955: 190.

13 'F litteram imum labrum superis imprimentes dentibus, reflexa ad palati fastigium lingua, leni spiramine proferemus.' Marius Victorinus K, vi, 34, partially quoted in Allen (1978: 34).

14 Iris Murdoch, *The nice and the good*, Harmondsworth: Penguin, 1965/1978.

15 On Indo-European, see Baldi (1983), Beekes (2011), Clackson (2007), Mallory & Adams (2006). The homeland of the Indo-Europeans is discussed in Thième (1964), Mallory & Adams (2006).

16 On the comparative method, see Fox (1995). Also Anttila (1989), Bynon (1977), Campbell (2003), Terry Crowley (1997), A. Harris & Campbell (1995), Harrison (2003), Hock (1991), Hock & Joseph (1996), Joseph & Janda (2003), W. P. Lehmann (1992), Rankin (2003), Trask (1996). Durie & Ross (1996) is a book of readings which discusses the limitations and potential of reconstruction. See also Aikhenvald & Dixon (2001), Harrison (2003), Lass (1993). McMahon & McMahon (1995) explore the problems of handling American-Indian languages, where it is unclear how many languages are involved. Most books deal with the Indo-European language family, but see Campbell (1997) on American-Indian languages, Terry Crowley (1997) on Polynesian languages, Dimmendaal (2011) on African languages.

17 Thomason & Kaufman (1988), Thomason (2001) explain why comparisons break down in mixed-language situations.

18 Unreliable resemblances are discussed in Campbell (2003).

19 *Papa, mama*, Jakobson, 1941/1968.

20 Statistical calculations on chance, Ringe, 1992.

21 Polynesian examples, Terry Crowley, 1997.

22 Grace, 1990.

23 Nichols, 1992, 2003.

24 Aitchison, 2000.

25 The word *Nostratic* was probably coined by Holger Pedersen in the first decade of the twentieth century, though it became more widely known via his later work (1931/1962).

26 On Nostratic, see Dolgopolsky (1998) and Salmons & Joseph (1998). Kaiser (1997) and Peiros (1997) have good discussions of the problems of the reconstruction of macro-families.

27 Stress and accent reconstruction, Halle, 1997.

28 Reconstruction of formulae, Watkins, 1989, 1995.

29 Iroquoian 'and', Mithun, 1992.

30 Several textbooks provide a good overview of internal reconstruction, and useful further references. See: Anttila (1989), Bynon (1977), Campbell (1998), Terry Crowley (1997) with an example from Samoan, Fox (1995), Hock (1991), Jeffers & Lehiste (1979), Ringe (2003). See Hogg (1992) for the historical facts underlying the English examples of internal reconstruction discussed in this section.

31 On typological reconstruction, see Hock (1986: ch. 19), Comrie (1989: ch. 10; 1993). Hawkins (1983) contains a fairly detailed attempt to set up typological probabilities among the world's languages, and is perhaps best approached via reviews, e.g. Aitchison (1986).

32 Hock (1991) and Gamkrelidze & Ivanov (1990) contain brief summaries of the 'glottalic theory' of Indo-European sounds. The original book on the topic (in Russian) by Gamkrelidze & Ivanov (1984) has now been translated (Gamkrelidze & Ivanov, 1994–5a, 1994–5b). For clear reviews, see Garrett (1991), Hayward (1989) and Vine (1988).

33 Diffusion studies, Chen, 1976; Ogura, 1990, 1995.

34 Population typology, Nichols, 1992.

35 Nichols, 2003.

36 For a list of computerized corpora, see Leech (1991).

37 Rissanen, 1991.

3   Charting the changes

1 Bloomfield, 1933: 347.

2 Hockett, 1958: 439.

3 Saussure, 1915/1959: 17.

4 Saussure, 1915/1959: 125. But see Aitchison (2012b) on newer views of diachrony vs synchrony.

5 Joos, 1961.

6 Lakoff, 1975: 26.

7 Sapir, 1921: 38. See also comments by C.-J. N. Bailey (1982), on the false neatness imposed by many linguists.

8 Chambers, 1995: 147.

9 G. Bailey, 2002; Chambers, 2002: 358.

10 Hubbell, 1950: 48.
11 Labov, 1972a: 43. Labov (1972a) is a valuable book of papers which contains most of the work by Labov quoted in this chapter. Later work by Labov will be discussed in later chapters.
12 Labov, 1972a: 47.
13 This study was carried out by Fowler (1986), and is reported in Labov (1994).
14 Labov, 1972a: 85–6.
15 Labov, 1972a: 93.
16 Labov, 1972a: 94.
17 Labov, 1972a: 90.
18 Labov, 1972a: 89.
19 Labov, 1972a: 92.
20 Labov, 1972a: 91.
21 Labov, 1972a: 114.
22 Romaine, 1982.
23 Labov, 2001: 38.
24 J. Milroy & L. Milroy, 1978; L. Milroy, 1987a. L. Milroy (1987a) contains the basic information on network analysis. For a general survey of techniques for analysing variation, see L. Milroy (1987b). See also L. Milroy & J. Milroy (1992), J. Milroy & L. Milroy (1993), L. Milroy (2002).
25 L. Milroy, 1987a: 54.
26 L. Milroy, 1987a: 89.
27 L. Milroy, 1987a: 60.

4   Spreading the word

 1 Sturtevant, 1917/1961: 82.
 2 Labov, 1972a: 123. Labov (1972a) contains both of the studies (New York *r* and Martha's Vineyard) mentioned in this chapter.
 3 Labov, 1972a: 132.
 4 Labov, 1972a: 136.
 5 Hubbell, 1950: 48.
 6 From Labov, 1972a: 114.
 7 Labov, 1972a: 115.
 8 Labov, 1972a: 24.
 9 Labov, 1972a: 141.
10 Labov, 1972a: 145.
11 Sturtevant, 1917/1961: 26.
12 Sturtevant, 1917/1961: 77.

13 Labov, 1972a: 317.
14 Labov, 1972a: 1ff.
15 Labov, 1972a: 28.
16 Pope et al., 2007: 615.
17 Labov, 1972a: 29.
18 Labov, 1972a: 32.
19 Blake & Joseph, 2003.
20 Pope et al., 2007.
21 Labov, 2001.
22 Labov, 2001: 31–2.

5 Conflicting loyalties

1 Labov, 1972a: 226.
2 Opie & Opie, 1951: 294.
3 A. A. Wood, in Trudgill, 1974: 9.
4 Trudgill (1974) describes the Norwich changes.
5 Pyles & Algeo, 1982: 179.
6 Diagram from table in Trudgill (1974: 94).
7 Trudgill, 1972; 1974: 94. J. Coates (1993) provides a useful overall survey of sex differences in language.
8 J. Milroy & L. Milroy, 1978, 1985; L. Milroy, 1987a. L. Milroy (1987a) is an accessible account of the Belfast inner-city changes. Further information about Belfast is in J. Harris (1985), L. Milroy & J. Milroy (1992).
9 Patterson, 1860.
10 J. Milroy & L. Milroy, 1985.
11 Coupland, 1984.
12 Trudgill, 1986. This book contains an account of accommodation theory, and discusses its relevance to change.
13 J. Milroy & L. Milroy, 1985. This paper discusses the importance of 'weak links' in the spread of change.
14 Cheshire, 1978, 1982. These papers contain the basic information on the Reading teenagers. Other linguistic conflicts are discussed in Chambers (1995), Labov (1994).
15 Eckert, 1989, 2000.
16 Eckert, 2000: 58–9.
17 Eckert, 2000: 234.
18 Eckert, 2000: 211–12.
19 Chambers, 1992/1998.
20 G. Bailey et al., 1993.

6 Catching on and taking off

1 Sapir, 1921: 178.
2 Osthoff & Brugmann, 1878. Translation (slightly different from mine) in Lehmann (1967: 204). Clear accounts of the Neogrammarian 'regularity hypothesis' occur in Bynon (1977), Hock (1991).
3 Meillet, quoted by Vendryès, in Keiler, 1972: 109.
4 Labov, 1994. See also note 20.
5 J. Harris, 1989.
6 Labov, 1972a: 148.
7 Labov, 1972a: 20.
8 Hooper, 1976b: 1,978.
9 Unstressed first syllables, Fidelholtz, 1975.
10 Dravidian *r*, Krishnamurti, 1978.
11 Labov, 1972a: 19.
12 Belfast [a] → [e], J. Milroy & L. Milroy, 1985.
13 Fidelholtz, 1975: 208.
14 Wang (1969), Chen (1972), Chen & Wang (1975), Chen (1976), Wang (1977), Ogura (1990) and Wang & Lien (1993) all provide clear accounts of lexical diffusion.
15 Welsh *chw-*, Sommerfelt, in Chen, 1972.
16 Stress shift in English bisyllabic nouns, Chen & Wang, 1975.
17 S-curve, from Chen, 1972: 47.
18 Croft, 2000: 183.
19 Chambers, 2002: 361.
20 French nasals, Chen & Wang, 1975: 276; Chen, 1976: 215.
21 Shuang-Feng changes, Chen, 1972: 474.
22 The Neogrammarian vs lexical diffusion viewpoints are outlined in Hock & Joseph (1996), and discussed in Labov (1994). See also Guy (2003).
23 Kiparsky, 1995, reprinted in Joseph & Janda, 2003. Kiparsky's statement is particularly clear. But the insight that sound change and analogy are similar has been suggested in a number of places in recent years, e.g. Aitchison (1990).
24 The tadpole, cuckoo and multiple-births viewpoints are discussed in Aitchison (1995).
25 Guy, 2003.

7 Caught in the web

1 Labov, 1972b: 65.
2 Chaucer, *Canterbury tales*, Prologue 9.

3 Middle English *kan*, in Bynon, 1985: 114.

4 Shakespeare, *As you like it*, III, v, 81, and Marlowe, *Hero and Leander*, First Sestiad 167.

5 Cheshire, 1987.

6 Delhi acceptability, Sahgal & Agnihotri, 1985.

7 *Richard III*, III, iv, 74.

8 *King Lear*, I, iv, 163.

9 Old changes which involve variation, Romaine, 1982; Fischer & van der Leek, 1983.

10 Negation in Indian vs British English, Aitchison & Agnihotri, 1985.

11 French 'at home', Mougeon, Beniak & Valois, 1985.

12 English verbal nouns, van der Wurff, 1993.

13 Brazilian Portuguese word endings, Naro, 1981.

14 Naro, 1981: 97.

15 English *can*, Bynon, 1985.

16 Tok Pisin *save*, Aitchison, 1989, 2000.

17 Old English examples from D. Denison (1993), where impersonal verbs are discussed. See also Fischer & van der Leek (1983, 1987) and Fischer (1992). For a discussion of 'sneaking in' involving infinitival constructions in English, see Fischer (1990, 1992).

18 Chaucer, *Canterbury tales*, Prologue 240; Prologue 45–6; Prologue to Sir Thopas 729.

19 Cole, Harbert, Hermon & Sridhar, 1980; Butler, 1977.

20 Joseph, 1992: 140.

21 Reading teenagers, Cheshire, 1978, 1982.

22 Tok Pisin plurals, Aitchison, 1990; Mühlhäusler, 1980a.

23 French negatives, Ashby, 1981.

24 Los Angeles Spanish, Silva-Corvalán, 1986.

25 Cheshire, 1978, 1982.

26 Aitchison, 1990.

27 Ashby, 1981.

28 English modals, Lightfoot, 1979; Aitchison, 1980; Fischer & van der Leek, 1981. On *do*, see Stein (1990), D. Denison (1993).

29 *Othello*, III, iii, 177.

30 *Hamlet*, III, iii, 19.

31 Huddleston & Pullum, 2002: 800.

32 On the progressive, Potter, 1969.

33 *Antony and Cleopatra*, IV, xiii, 18.

34 *Antony and Cleopatra*, IV, xii, 50.

35 *Hamlet*, II, ii, 193.

36 English -*ing*, Potter, 1969: 121; D. Denison, 1998.

37 *Hackney Echo*, 12 April 1989.
38 *Measure for measure*, III, ii, 241.
39 Potter, 1969: 121.
40 Kroch, 1989; Pintzuk, 2003.

8   The wheels of language

1 John Horne Tooke's *The diversions of Purley* was originally published in 1786. This quotation is from an extract of a later edition, in R. Harris & Taylor (1997: 163).
2 Hopper, 1994.
3 Hopper & Traugott, 2003: 7.
4 Heine, Claudi & Hünnemeyer, 1991: 5.
5 Meillet, 1912/1948: 131.
6 Meillet, 1912/1948: 133.
7 Croft, 2000: 156.
8 Hopper, 1991.
9 Hopper, 1991: 22.
10 Hopper & Traugott, 2003: 10f.
11 Greek *tha*, Meillet, 1912/1948.
12 Sapir, 1921: 150, 155.
13 Heine, Claudi & Hünnemeyer, 1991.
14 Traugott, 2003.
15 *The Chambers Dictionary* (new edition), 1998.
16 Joseph & Janda, 1988; Janda, 1995; Tabor & Traugott, 1998.
17 Heine, 1997: 153; also Heine, 2003.
18 Haspelmath, 1999b.
19 For discussion of the grammaticalization of the grammatical morphemes ('grams') associated with verbs, see J. L. Bybee et al. (1994).
20 From *Sir Gawain and the Green Knight*, 1.2, 157, quoted in J. Bybee, 1988.
21 Heine, 2003.
22 Traugott, 1992: 237.
23 See Heine (1997, 2001) for a summary of various clines.
24 Langacker, 1977: 106.
25 Hopper, 1996.
26 Hudson, 2006.
27 Langacker, 1977; Traugott, 2003.
28 Givón, 1979: 209.
29 Traugott, 2003.
30 Lewis, 1999.

31 Traugott, 1989.
32 Fischer, 1997.
33 Fischer, 1997: 174.
34 Traugott & Heine, 1991a; Mithun, 1991.
35 Jackendoff, 1997; Kay and Fillmore, 1999; Nunberg, Sag & Wasow, 1994.
36 *Longman Dictionary of the English Language* (1984).
37 Bombaugh's poem is in Crystal, 2010: 114.
38 Crystal, 2008; John with Blake, 2001.
39 Kesseler and Bergs, 2003.
40 Quoted in Crystal, 2008: 8.
41 Crystal, 2008: 175.
42 Emma Passmore, *Guardian*, 14 November 2002.
43 Crystal, 2008.
44 Ayto, 2006.
45 Baron, 2000.
46 Baron, 2003.
47 Baron, 2003: 93.
48 Crystal, 2001: 242.

9   Spinning away

1 The quotation at the top of the chapter is from David Lehman, *Signs of the times*, London: Deutsch, 1991. The comment by Humpty Dumpty is in L. Carroll, *Through the looking-glass,* in *The complete works of Lewis Carroll*, London: Penguin, 1872/1982, p. 196.
2 Thucydides III: lxxxii.
3 Trench, 1855: 41.
4 Trench, 1855: 42.
5 Trench, 1856: 192.
6 George Orwell, *Nineteen eighty-four*, London: Penguin, 1949/1954, p. 32.
7 Orwell, 1949/1954: 17.
8 Hughes, 1988: 14.
9 Hock & Joseph, 1996: 252.
10 Michel Bréal, quoted in Ullmann, 1962: 6.
11 Bréal, 1883/1897.
12 This list is from Burchfield, 1985.
13 Ayto, 1990.
14 Ullmann, 1962: 197.
15 Meillet, 1905–6/1948.

16 *L'Autre* 'the devil', Ullmann, 1962: 205; words for 'die', Ayto, 1993.
17 The patchwork quilt idea was particularly associated with the 'lexical fields' of Trier (1931). See Ullmann (1962) for a useful outline account.
18 The haunch–hip–thigh changes are summarized in Ullmann, 1962: 242. The original research was carried out by W. von Wartburg.
19 On the linguistic treatment of emotions, see Aitchison (1992a).
20 On *tabby*, see Ayto (1990).
21 Paul, 1880/1920.
22 Warren (1992) provides a useful account of some sense developments in English.
23 Miller & Fellbaum, 1991/1992: 214, who give the totals as 43,636 different nouns, and 14,190 different verbs.
24 Miller & Fellbaum, 1991/1992: 214.
25 Greenough & Kittredge, 1902: 217.
26 On the origins of prototype theory, see Rosch (1975); for an overview, see Aitchison (2012a), Taylor (1995) and Ungerer & Schmid (1996).
27 Fillmore, 1982; also summarized in Aitchison (2012a) and Taylor (1995).
28 Aitchison, 2012a.
29 Gabelentz, 1891, summarized in Hopper & Traugott, 1993: 19–20.
30 Hopper & Traugott, 1993: 100. See also Aitchison (2012a: ch. 15); Nerlich et al. (2003); Pustejovsky (1995); Pustejovsky & Boguraev (1996); Ravin and Leacock (2000).
31 *New Oxford Dictionary of English*, 1998.
32 On *disaster*, see Aitchison & Lewis (2003a).
33 Otto Jespersen in 1925, quoted in Warren (1992: 125).
34 Aitchison, 1996a/2000.
35 Heine, 1997: 153.
36 Heine, 1997; Sweetser, 1990.

10   The reason why

1 Ohala, 1974b: 269.
2 H. Collitz, in Jespersen, 1922: 257.
3 Jespersen, 1922: 257.
4 Bloomfield, 1933: 385.
5 King, 1969a: 189.
6 J. W. Harris, 1969: 550.
7 Postal, 1968: 283.
8 Hockett, 1958: 440.

9 Hockett, 1958: 441.

10 Hockett, 1958: 443–5.

11 Labov, 1972a: 171.

12 Kupwar situation, Gumperz & Wilson, 1971. On linguistic contact in general, Bynon (1977), Jeffers & Lehiste (1979), Hock (1991), Thomason (2001) all contain useful sections. Weinreich (1953) is a linguistic classic which initiated much serious work on the topic. Lehiste (1988) provides a useful modern overview. Thomason & Kaufman (1988) is an exploration of various contact situations. For recent work, see Thomason (2001).

13 Ma'a, Thomason, 1983b; Thomason & Kaufman, 1988; Thomason, 2000, 2001.

14 Far East tones, Henderson, 1965.

15 African clicks, Guthrie, 1967–71.

16 India as a linguistic area, Emeneau, 1956, 1980; Masica, 1976.

17 Balkan linguistic area, Schaller, 1975; Joseph, 1983; Thomason, 2001.

18 Meso-America as a linguistic area, Campbell, Kaufman & Smith-Stark, 1986.

19 Thomason & Kaufman, 1988; Thomason, 2001.

20 Yiddish, Rayfield, 1970.

21 Lexical borrowing in Australia, Heath, 1981.

22 English loans in Russian, David Bonavia, *The Times*, 21 June 1971.

23 English loans in Swahili, Whiteley, 1967.

24 Deirdre Wilson, unpublished research notes on French dialects.

25 Bickerton, 1973: 644.

26 Greek in Turkey, Dawkins, 1916: 198; Thomason & Kaufman, 1988.

27 Bickerton, 1973, 1981.

28 Ayto, 1999.

29 Ayto & Simpson, 2010.

30 *Sunday Times*, 14 June 2009.

31 Laurie Colwin, *Happy all the time*, London: Chatto & Windus, 1979.

32 C. Sandberg, in *The treasury of humorous quotations*, London: Dent, 1962.

33 Baron, 1974.

34 Labov, 1972a: 234.

35 Politeness phenomena leading to change, P. Brown & Levinson, 1978/1987.

36 Pronouns, usage and change, R. Brown & Gilman, 1964/1970; P. Brown & Levinson, 1978/1987; Mühlhäusler & Harré, 1990.

37 Du Bois, 1987. For other papers on discourse as a source of change, see Hopper & Thompson (1980, 1984) and Givón (1983).

11   Doing what comes naturally

1 Quoted by Macdonald Critchley in Goodglass & Blumstein, 1973: 64.
2 Loss of nasals, Chen & Wang, 1975; Ohala, 1975; Ruhlen, 1978.
3 See Reetz & Jongman (2009) for a comprehensive modern overview.
4 Chen & Wang, 1975.
5 Chen & Wang, 1975.
6 O'Connor, 1973: 251.
7 Ohala, 1993.
8 Ohala, 1993, 2001; Donegan, 1993.
9 Intrusive sounds, Ohala, 1974a. Natural change, Hooper, 1976a; Stampe, 1979.
10 Dark *l*, Ohala, 1974b; Wells, 1982: 258–9.
11 Reetz & Jongman, 2009.
12 Tonogenesis, Hombert, Ohala & Ewan, 1979; Hombert & Ohala, 1982.
13 Stockholm [d], Janson, in Chen & Wang, 1975.
14 American past tenses, Twaddell, 1935.
15 Martinet, 1960/1964: 214; Akamatsu, 1967.
16 Horace, *Epistles*, x. 24: 'Naturam expellas furca, tamen usque recurret.'
17 See Hyman (1975), Pullum (1977), Mithun (1984) and Tomlin (1986) for verb–object closeness.
18 Smith & Wilson, 1979: 48.
19 Ancient Greek, Aitchison, 1979.
20 Niger-Congo change, Hyman, 1975.
21 Haiman, 1985a, 1985b. Other treatments of 'natural syntax' and iconicity are J. Bybee (1985a), Tomlin (1986), Nänny & Fischer (1999).
22 J. Bybee, 1985b.

12   Repairing the patterns

1 Antoine de Saint-Exupéry, *Le petit prince*, Paris: Gallimard, 1946.
2 Alford, 1864: 40, quoted in Mugglestone, 1995: 117.
3 Romance changes, Elcock, 1960. Pattern neatening in sound changes tends to come under the heading of 'economy', a concept particularly associated with the work of Martinet (1955).
4 R. Coates, 1987: 320.
5 For an outline account of the history of English morphology, see Baugh & Cable (1993), which provides information on further reading. See also Hogg (1992) and Blake (1992).

6 Sweet, in Jespersen, 1922: 161.
7 Andersen, 1978: 21.
8 Bybee and Slobin, 1982.
9 Itkonen, 1982.
10 English impersonals, D. Denison, 1993; Fischer & van der Leek, 1983; Lightfoot, 1979.
11 French negatives, Ashby, 1981.
12 Texas *be*, G. Bailey & Maynor, 1988.
13 Texas *be*, further work, G. Bailey, 1993; Cukor-Avila & Bailey, 1995.
14 Exaptation, Lass, 1990.

13   Pushing and pulling

1 Grimm's Law, Bammesberger, 1992.
2 Great Vowel Shift, Baugh & Cable (1993), which also provides further references.
3 Drag chains and push chains, original work in Martinet, 1955.
4 High German Consonant Shift. Good summary in Bynon, 1977.
5 Chinese *s*, Chen, 1976.
6 Yiddish in Poland, Herzog in King, 1969a.
7 Doubts on push chains, King, 1969a, 1969b.
8 Late Middle Chinese Great Vowel Shift, Chen, 1976.
9 Lass, 1976; Ogura, 1990. The latter presents an account of the diffusion of the Great Vowel Shift in space, as well as time.
10 The name 'Estuary English' was coined by David Rosewarne in 1984, and has since been widely adopted. See also Rosewarne (1994a, 1994b, 1996).
11 Cockney accent, Wells, 1982, vol. II.
12 The vowels in the words *mean* and *moon* are most usually transcribed as [i:] [u:] for the sake of simplicity, yet they are in fact diphthongs. The difference can be heard immediately when compared with some genuinely simple vowels, as in French *lit* [li:t] 'bed', *vous* [vu:] 'you'. The phonetic transcription of the other vowels has been slightly simplified for the sake of clarity. See Gimson & Cruttenden (1994), Wells (1982), vol. II.
13 See Gimson & Cruttenden (1994), Wells (1982), for a more detailed account.
14 *Sunday Times*, 7 June 1998.
15 Labov, 1994: 194.
16 Labov, 1994: 178.
17 Labov, 1994: 178.

18 Labov, 1994: 178.
19 Typological harmony. Early proposals, Greenberg, 1963/1966. Further discussion in Aitchison, 2003a, 2003b; Comrie, 1989; Croft, 2003; Dryer, 1992; Hawkins, 1983, 1988.
20 Kuno, 1974; Vincent, 1976; Hawkins, 1983, 1988.
21 Aitchison, 1979.
22 Li & Thompson, 1974 – but see Sun & Givón, 1985; Vincent, 1976; Aitchison, 1979.
23 Moulton, 1985: 687. For a general view of causation different from that found in this book, see Lightfoot (1999); also review by Haspelmath (1999a).

14   Language birth

1 Language origin theories, Jespersen, 1922; Hewes, 1977.
2 Jespersen, 1922: 421. The quote at the top of the chapter is from Jespersen (1922: 434).
3 Whitney, 1893: 279.
4 Pinker & Bloom (1990) was a 'landmark' article on language origin. After that a flood of books and articles emerged, for example Aitchison (1996a/2000), Degraff (1999), Heine and Kuteva (2007), Hurford (2011), Hurford et al. (1998), Jablonski and Aiello (1998), Jackendoff (2002), Knight et al. (2000), Larson et al. (2010), Tallerman (2005), Wray (2002).
5 Coppens, 1994.
6 On Russenorsk, see Broch & Jahr (1984); Jahr & Broch (1996).
7 Chinook jargon, Thomason, 1983a. A number of other pidgins are outlined in Arends et al. (1995) which provides a useful overview.
8 Origin of word *pidgin*, Hancock, 1979.
9 On Tok Pisin as a pidgin mainly from Dutton, 1973; Mihalic, 1971; Mühlhäusler, 1979a; Wurm & Mühlhäusler, 1985; Verhaar, 1995.
10 'crudely distorted' French, in Hall, 1966: 107; 'bastard blend' in Edward Marriott, *The lost tribe*, London: Picador, 1996, p. 74.
11 Hall, 1966. For Schuchardt's work, see Gilbert (1980).
12 M. Bertrand-Boconde, in Meijer & Muysken, 1977: 22.
13 Theories of pidgin origin, Valdman, 1977; Naro, 1978; Thomason & Kaufman, 1988; Thomason, 2001; McWhorter, 2005.
14 Naro, 1978.
15 Bloomfield, 1933: 472.
16 Kay & Sankoff, 1974.
17 Thomason, 1983b.

18 Mühlhäusler, 1978, 1979a; Mosel & Mühlhäusler, 1982.
19 General Solf's diary, quoted in Mühlhäusler, 1978: 72.
20 On pidgin and creole characteristics, see Arends et al. (1995); Holm (1988, 1989); McWhorter (2005); Mufwene (1995); Mühlhäusler (1986, 1997); Romaine (1988); Thomason (2001); Todd (1990); Wurm & Mühlhäusler (1985).
21 Mühlhäusler, 1979a, 1979b.
22 Keesing, 1988; Singler, 1988.
23 Todd, 1990: 4.
24 Information on creolization in Tok Pisin from my own recordings and observations, partially published in Aitchison (1989, 1990, 1992b, 1996b). See also Degraff (1999); McWhorter (2005); Mühlhäusler (1980b, 1986); Romaine (1988); Sankoff (1977); Thomason (2001); Todd (1990); Wurm & Mühlhäusler (1985).
25 Aitchison, 1989.
26 Laycock, 1970: 55.
27 On Tok Pisin *laik*, see Romaine (1999). Most of the examples I have used are from my own data.
28 Aitchison, 1992b.

15 Language death

1 Bopp, 1827, in Jespersen, 1922: 65.
2 Decreolization, Bickerton, 1971, 1973; Rickford, 1987; McWhorter, 2005.
3 Guyanan Creole, Bickerton, 1971.
4 Examples of decreolization in Tok Pisin are from my own recordings and observations.
5 Mühlhäusler, 1979a: 51.
6 NBC radio broadcast, March 1980.
7 NBC radio advertisement, March 1980.
8 Kwegu, Dimmendaal, 1989.
9 On Arvanítika, see Tsitsipis, 1989.
10 Sauris, N. Denison, 1972, 1977, 1980.
11 N. Denison, 1972: 68.
12 N. Denison, 1977: 21.
13 Bloomfield, 1927/1970: 154.
14 Scottish Gaelic, Dorian, 1973, 1978, 1981. See also Schmidt (1985), on Dyirbal in Australia.
15 Dorian, 1978: 608.
16 John Fletcher (1579–1625), *The custom of the country*, II. ii.

17 Grenoble & Whaley, 1998; Robins & Uhlenbeck, 1991; Schilling-Estes & Wolfram, 1999; Schmidt, 1985; Seliger & Vago, 1991.
18 Code-switching, Myers-Scotton, 1993, 1998.
19 Kaufman & Aronoff, 1991: 182.
20 Crystal, 1999. On language death in general, see Crystal (2000); Thomason (2001).
21 Hale et al., 1992.
22 McArthur, 1998.
23 Hale et al., 1992: 8.
24 Crystal, 1999: 58.
25 Ladefoged, 1992: 811.

16   Progress or decay?

 1 Whales, Payne, 1979.
 2 Curtius, 1877, in Kiparsky, 1972: 35; cf. views of Trench (Chapter 1).
 3 Herbert Spencer, *Social statics* (1850), Part 2, ch. 17, sect. 4.
 4 Darwin, 1871, in Labov, 1972a: 273.
 5 Mühlhäusler, 1979a: 151.
 6 Slobin, 1977.
 7 Jakobson, 1949: 336. Translation in Keiler, 1972.
 8 Li & Thompson, 1974. The claim that Mandarin is changing to SOV is disputed by Sun & Givón (1985).
 9 Li & Thompson, 1976.
10 Greenberg, 1957: 65.
11 Caxton, preface to *Erydos* (1490).
12 Labov, 1972b: 62.
13 On language planning, see Cooper (1982), Fasold (1984), Lowenberg (1988). Bex & Watts (1999) and J. Milroy & L. Milroy (1998) discuss the notion of standard language.
14 Safire, 1980, from whom the quotations in this section are taken. For a professional viewpoint on 'good' English, see Greenbaum (1988), especially 11–12, where the word *hopefully* is discussed.
15 'Nukespeak', Aubrey, 1982; Chilton, 1985/1988; Hilgartner, Bell & O'Connor, 1983.
16 Ayto, 1989.
17 Caxton, preface to *Erydos* (1490).

References

Aijmer, K. & Altenberg, B. (eds.) (1991). *English corpus linguistics.* London: Longman.

Aikhenvald, A. Y. & Dixon, R. M. W. (2001). *Areal diffusion and genetic inheritance: Problems in comparative linguistics.* Oxford University Press.

Aitchison, J. (1979). The order of word order change. *Transactions of the Philological Society* 43–65.

(1980). Review of D. Lightfoot (1979) *Principles of diachronic syntax. Linguistics* 17, 137–46.

(1983a). On roots of language. *Language and Communication* 3, 83–97.

(1983b). Review of S. Romaine (1982) *Socio-historical linguistics. Linguistics* 21, 629–44.

(1986). Review of J. Hawkins (1983) *Word order universals. Lingua* 70, 191–7.

(1989). Spaghetti junctions and recurrent routes: some preferred pathways in language evolution. *Lingua* 77, 151–71.

(1990). The missing link: the role of the lexicon. In J. Fisiak (ed.), *Historical linguistics and philology.* Berlin: Walter de Gruyter.

(1992a). Chains, nets or boxes? The linguistic capture of love, anger and fear. In W. G. Busse (ed.), *Anglistentag 1991 Düsseldorf, Proceedings.* Berlin: Mouton de Gruyter.

(1992b). Relative clauses in Tok Pisin: is there a natural pathway? In Gerritsen & Stein (1992).

(1995). Tadpoles, cuckoos and multiple births: language contact and models of change. In J. Fisiak (ed.), *Linguistic change under contact conditions.* Berlin: Mouton de Gruyter.

(1996a/2000). *The seeds of speech: Language origin and evolution.* Cambridge University Press.

(1996b). Small steps or large leaps? Under-generalization and overgeneralization in creole acquisition. In H. Wekker (ed.), *Creole languages and language acquisition.* Berlin: Mouton de Gruyter.

(1997). *The language web: The power and problem of words.* Cambridge University Press.

(2000). *The seeds of speech: Language origin and evolution.* Canto edition. Cambridge University Press.

(2003a). Psycholinguistic perspectives on language change. In Joseph & Janda (2003).

(2003b). From Armageddon to war: the vocabulary of terrorism. In Aitchison & Lewis (2003b).

(2011a). *The articulate mammal: An introduction to psycholinguistics.* London: Routledge Classics Edition.

(2011b). *Aitchison's Linguistics.* 7th edn. of *Linguistics.* London: Hodder & Stoughton Teach Yourself Books.

(2012a). *Words in the mind: An introduction to the mental lexicon.* 4th edn. Oxford: Blackwell.

(2012b). Diachrony and synchrony: the complementary evolution of two (ir)reconcilable dimensions. In Hernandez-Campoy & Conde-Silvestre (2012).

Aitchison, J. & Agnihotri, R. K. (1985). 'I deny that I'm incapable of not working all night': divergence of negative structures in British and Indian English. In R. Eaton, O. Fischer, W. Koopman & F. Van der Leek (eds.), *Papers from the 4th International Conference on English Historical Linguistics.* Amsterdam: John Benjamins.

Aitchison, J. & Lewis, D. M. (2003a). Polysemy and bleaching. In B. Nerlich, V. Herman, Z. Todd & D. Clarke (eds.), *Polysemy: Patterns of meaning in mind and language.* Berlin: Mouton de Gruyter.

(eds.) (2003b). *New media language.* London: Routledge.

Akamatsu, T. (1967). Quelques statistiques sur la fréquence d'utilisation des voyelles nasales françaises. *La linguistique* 1, 75–80.

Alford, H. (1864). *A plea for the Queen's English: Stray notes on speaking and spelling.* 2nd edn. London: Strahan.

Allen, W. S. (1974). *Vox Graeca: A guide to the pronunciation of Classical Greek.* 2nd edn. Cambridge University Press.

(1978). *Vox Latina: A guide to the pronunciation of Classical Latin.* 2nd edn. Cambridge University Press.

Andersen, H. (1978). Perceptual and conceptual factors in abductive innovations. In Fisiak (1978).

Anderson, J. M. & Jones, C. (eds.) (1974). *Historical linguistics.* Amsterdam: North-Holland.

Anttila, R. (1989). *Historical and comparative linguistics.* 2nd edn. Amsterdam: John Benjamins.

Arends, J., Muysken, P. & Smith, N. (1995). *Pidgins and creoles: An intro-duction*. Amsterdam: John Benjamins.

Ashby, W. J. (1981). The loss of the negative particle NE in French: a syntactic change in progress. *Language* 57, 674–7.

Aubrey, C. (1982). *Nukespeak: The media and the bomb*. London: Comedia Publishing Group.

Ayto, J. (1989). *The Longman register of new words*. Vol. I. London: Longman.
    (1990). *Dictionary of word origins*. London: Bloomsbury.
    (1993). *Euphemisms: Over 3,000 ways to avoid being rude or giving offence*. London: Bloomsbury.
    (1999). *Twentieth century words*. Oxford University Press.
    (2006). *Movers and shakers: A chronology of words that shaped our age*. Oxford University Press.

Ayto, J. & Simpson, J. (2010). *Oxford dictionary of modern slang*. 2nd edn. Oxford University Press.

Bailey, C.-J. N. (1982). The garden path that historical linguists went astray on. *Language and Communication* 2, 151–60.

Bailey, G. (1993). A perspective on African-American English. In D. R. Preston (ed.), *American dialect research*. Amsterdam: John Benjamins.
    (2002). Real and apparent time. In Chambers et al. (2002).

Bailey, G. & Maynor, N. (1988). Decreolization? *Language in Society* 16, 449–73.

Bailey, G., Wikle, T., Tillery, J. & Sand, L. (1993). Some patterns of lexical diffusion. *Language Variation and Change* 5, 359–90.

Bailey, R. W. (1992). *Images of English*. Cambridge University Press.

Baldi, P. (1983). *An introduction to the Indo-European languages*. Carbondale, IL: Southern Illinois University Press.

Bammesberger, A. (1992). The place of English in Germanic and Indo-European. In Hogg (1992).

Baron, N. (1974). Functional motivation for age grading in linguistic inno-vation. In Anderson & Jones (1974).
    (2000). *Alphabet to email*. London: Routledge.
    (2003). Why email looks like speech: proofreading, pedagogy and public face. In Aitchison & Lewis (2003b).

Baugh, A. C. & Cable, T. (1993). *A history of the English language*. 4th edn. London: Routledge.

Beekes, R. S. P. (2011). *Comparative Indo-European linguistics: An introduc-tion*. 2nd edn. Revised and corrected by M. de Vaan. Amsterdam: John Benjamins.

Bex, T. & Watts, R. J. (eds.) (1999). *Standard English: The widening debate*. London: Routledge.

Bickerton, D. (1971). Inherent variability and variable rules. *Foundations of Language* 7, 457–92.

(1973). The nature of a creole continuum. *Language* 49, 640–69.

(1981). *The roots of language*. Ann Arbor, MI: Karoma.

Blake, N. F. (ed.) (1992). *The Cambridge history of the English language. Vol. II: The Middle English period, 1066–1476*. Cambridge University Press.

Blake, R. & Joseph, M. (2003). The /ay/ diphthong in a Martha's Vineyard community: what can we say 40 years after Labov? *Language in Society* 32, 451–85.

Bloomfield, L. (1927/1970). Literate and illiterate speech. *American Speech* 2, 432–9. Also in C. F. Hockett (ed.), *A Leonard Bloomfield anthology*. Bloomington, IN: Indiana University Press.

(1933). *Language*. New York: Holt, Rinehart, Winston.

Bolton, W. F. (1966). *The English language: Essays by English and American men of letters 1490–1839*. Cambridge University Press.

Bréal, M. (1883/1897). Les lois intellectuelles du langage. In his *Essai de sémantique*. Paris: Hachette.

Broch, I. & Jahr, E. H. (1984). Russenorsk: a new look at the Russo-Norwegian pidgin in Northern Norway. In P. S. Ureland & I. Clarkson (eds.), *Scandinavian language contacts*. Cambridge University Press.

Brown, P. & Levinson, S. C. (1978/1987). *Politeness: Some universals in language usage*. Cambridge University Press.

Brown, R. & Gilman, A. (1964/1970). Pronouns of power and solidarity. In R. Brown (ed.), *Psycholinguistics: Selected papers*. New York: Free Press.

Burchfield, R. (1985). *The English language*. Oxford University Press.

Butler, M. C. (1977). The reanalysis of object as subject in Middle English impersonal constructions. *Glossa* 11, 155–70.

Bybee, J. (1985a). Diagrammatic iconicity in stem-inflection relations. In Haiman (1985a).

(1985b). *Morphology*. Amsterdam: John Benjamins.

(1988). The diachronic dimension in explanation. In Hawkins (1988).

Bybee, J. & Slobin, D. I. (1982). Why small children cannot change language on their own: suggestions from the English past tense. In A. Ahlqvist (ed.), *Papers from the 5th International Conference on Historical Linguistics*. Amsterdam: John Benjamins.

Bybee, J. L., Perkins, R. D. & Pagliuca, W. (1994). *The evolution of grammar: Tense, aspect and modality in the languages of the world*. University of Chicago Press.

Bynon, T. (1977). *Historical linguistics.* Cambridge University Press.

(1985). Serial verbs and grammaticalisation. In U. Pieper & G. Stickel (eds.), *Studia linguistica diachronica et synchronica.* Berlin: Mouton.

Campbell, L. (1997). *American Indian languages: The historical linguistics of Native America.* Oxford University Press.

(1998). *Historical linguistics: An introduction.* Edinburgh University Press.

(2003). How to show languages are related: methods for distant genetic relationship. In Joseph & Janda (2003).

(2004). *Historical linguistics: An introduction.* 2nd edn. Edinburgh University Press.

Campbell, L., Kaufman, T. & Smith-Stark, T. (1986). Meso-America as a linguistic area. *Language* 62, 530–71.

Chambers, J. K. (1992). Dialect acquisition. *Language* 68, 673–705. Also in Trudgill & Cheshire (1998).

(1995). *Sociolinguistic theory: Linguistic variation and its social significance.* Oxford: Blackwell.

(2002). Patterns of variation including change. In Chambers et al. (2002).

Chambers, J. K. & Trudgill, P. (1980). *Dialectology.* Cambridge University Press.

Chambers, J. K., Trudgill, P. & Schilling-Estes, N. (2002). *The handbook of language variation and change.* Oxford: Blackwell.

Chen, M. (1972). The time dimension: contribution toward a theory of sound change. *Foundations of Language* 8, 457–98.

(1976). Relative chronology: three methods of reconstruction. *Journal of Linguistics* 12, 209–58.

Chen, M. & Wang, W. (1975). Sound change: actuation and implementation. *Language* 51, 255–81.

Cheshire, J. (1978). Present tense verbs in Reading English. In Trudgill (1978).

(1982). *Variation in an English dialect: A sociolinguistic study.* Cambridge University Press.

(1987). Syntactic variation, the linguistic variable, and sociolinguistic theory. *Linguistics* 25, 257–82.

Chilton, P. (1985/1988). *Language and the nuclear arms debate: Nukespeak today.* London: Cassell.

Clackson, J. (2007). *Indo-European linguistics: An introduction.* Cambridge University Press.

Coates, J. (1993). *Women, men and language.* 2nd edn. London: Longman.

Coates, R. (1987). Pragmatic sources of analogical reformation. *Journal of Linguistics* 23, 319–40.

Cole, P., Harbert, W., Hermon, G. & Sridhar, S. N. (1980). The acquisition of subjecthood. *Language* 56, 719–43.

Comrie, B. (1989). *Language universals and linguistic typology: Syntax and morphology.* 2nd edn. Oxford: Blackwell.

(1993). Typology and reconstruction. In Jones (1993).

Cooper, R. L. (1982). *Language spread: Studies in diffusion and social change.* Bloomington, IN: Indiana University Press.

Coppens, Y. (1994). East Side story: the origin of humankind. *Scientific American* 270 (5), 62–79.

Coupland, N. (1984). Accommodation at work. *International Journal of the Sociology of Language* 4–6, 49–70.

Croft, W. (2000). *Explaining language change: An evolutionary approach.* London: Longman.

(2003). *Typology and universals.* Cambridge University Press.

Crowley, Terry (1997). *An introduction to historical linguistics.* 3rd edn. Oxford University Press.

Crowley, Tony (1989). *The politics of discourse: The standard language question in British cultural debates.* London: Macmillan. Published in the USA under the title *Standard English and the politics of language.* Urbana: University of Illinois.

Crystal, D. (1981). Language on the air – has it degenerated? *Listener,* 9 July 1981.

(1984). *Who cares about English usage?* Harmondsworth: Penguin.

(1999). The death of language. *Prospect,* November, 56–8.

(2000). *Language death.* Cambridge University Press.

(2001). *Language and the internet.* Cambridge University Press.

(2008). *Txting: The gr8 db8.* Oxford University Press.

(2010). *Evolving English: One language, many voices.* London: British Library.

Cukor-Avila, P. & Bailey, G. (1995). Grammaticalization in AAVE. *Proceedings of the Berkeley Linguistics Society* 21, 401–13.

Danielsson, B. (1955). *John Hart's works on English orthography and pronunciation. Part I.* Stockholm: Almqvist & Wiksell.

Davis, G. W. & Iverson, G. K. (eds.) (1992). *Explanation in historical linguistics.* Amsterdam: John Benjamins.

Dawkins, R. M. (1916). *Modern Greek in Asia Minor.* Cambridge University Press.

DeGraff, M. (ed.) (1999). *Language creation and language change: Creolization, diachrony and development.* Cambridge, MA: MIT Press.

Denison, D. (1993). *English historical syntax: Verbal constructions*. London: Longman.

   (1998). Syntax. In S. Romaine (ed.), *The Cambridge history of the English language*. Vol. IV: *1776–1997*. Cambridge University Press.

Denison, N. (1972). Some observations on language variety and plurilingualism. In J. B. Pride & J. Holmes (eds.), *Sociolinguistics*. Harmondsworth: Penguin.

   (1977). Language death or language suicide? *Linguistics* 191, 13–22.

   (1980). Sauris: a case study of language shift in progress. In P. H. Nelde (ed.), *Languages in conflict*. Wiesbaden: Franz Steiner Verlag.

Dimmendaal, G. J. (2011). *Historical linguistics and the comparative study of African languages*. Amsterdam: John Benjamins.

   (1989). On language death in eastern Africa. In Dorian (1989).

Dolgopolsky, A. (1998). *The nostratic macrofamily and linguistic palaeontology*. Cambridge, MA: McDonald Institute for Archaeological Research.

Donegan, P. (1993). On the phonetic basis of phonological change. In Jones (1993).

Dorian, N. C. (1973). Grammatical change in a dying dialect. *Language* 49, 413–38.

   (1978). The fate of morphological complexity in language death. *Language* 54, 590–609.

   (1981). *Language death: The life cycle of a Scottish Gaelic dialect*. Philadelphia, PA: University of Pennsylvania Press.

   (ed.) (1989). *Investigating obsolescence: Studies in language contraction and death*. Cambridge University Press.

Drachman, G. (1978). Child language and language change: a conjecture and some refutations. In Fisiak (1978).

Dryer, M. S. (1992). The Greenbergian word order correlations. *Language* 68, 81–138.

Du Bois, J. W. (1987). The discourse basis of ergativity. *Language* 63, 805–55.

Durie, M. & Ross, M. (eds.) (1996). *The comparative method reviewed: Regularity and irregularity in language change*. Oxford University Press.

Dutton, T. E. (1973). *Conversational New Guinea Pidgin*. Pacific Linguistics D-12. Canberra: Australian National University.

Eckert, P. (1989). *Jocks and Burnouts: Social categories and identity in the high school*. New York: Teachers College Press.

   (2000). *Linguistic variation as social practice*. Oxford: Blackwell.

Elcock, W. D. (1960). *The Romance languages*. London: Faber & Faber.

Embleton, S. (1992). Historical linguistics: mathematical concepts. In W. Bright (ed.), *International encyclopaedia of linguistics* (4 vols.), vol. II. Oxford University Press.

Emeneau, M. B. (1956). India as a linguistic area. *Language* 32, 3–16.

(1980). *Language and linguistic area: Essays.* Stanford University Press.

Fasold, R. (1984). *The sociolinguistics of society.* Oxford: Basil Blackwell.

Fidelholtz, J. L. (1975). Word frequency and vowel reduction in English. *Chicago Linguistic Society* 11, 200–13.

Fillmore, C. J. (1982). Frame semantics. In Linguistic Society of Korea (ed.), *Linguistics in the morning calm.* Seoul: Hanshin.

Fischer, O. C. M. (1990). *Syntactic change and causation: Developments in infinitival constructions in English.* Amsterdam Studies in Generative Grammar 2. University of Amsterdam.

(1992). Syntax. In Blake (1992).

(1997). On the status of grammaticalisation and the diachronic dimension in explanation. *Transactions of the Philological Society* 95.2, 149–87.

Fischer, O. C. M. & van der Leek, F. C. (1981). Optional vs radical reanalysis: mechanisms of syntactic change. *Lingua* 55, 301–50.

(1983). The demise of the OE impersonal construction. *Journal of Linguistics* 19, 337–68.

(1987). A 'case' for the Old English impersonal. In W. Koopman, F. van der Leek, O. Fischer & R. Eaton (eds.), *Explanation and linguistic change.* Amsterdam: John Benjamins.

Fisher, J. H. & Bornstein, D. (1974). *In forme of speche is chaunge.* Englewood Cliffs, NJ: Prentice-Hall.

Fisiak, J. (ed.) (1978). *Recent developments in historical phonology.* The Hague: Mouton.

Fletcher, P. (1979). The development of the verb phrase. In P. Fletcher & M. Garman (eds.), *Language acquisition: Studies in first language development.* Cambridge University Press.

Fowler, J. (1986). The social stratification of (r) in New York City department stores, 24 years after Labov. New York University ms.

Fox, A. (1995). *Linguistic reconstruction: An introduction to theory and method.* Oxford University Press.

Fromkin, V. A. (ed.) (1973). *Speech errors as linguistic evidence.* The Hague: Mouton.

Gabelentz, G. von der (1891). *Die Sprachwissenschaft. Ihre Aufgaben, Methoden, und bisherigen Ergebnisse.* Leipzig: Weigel.

Gamkrelidze, T. V. & Ivanov, V. V. (1984). *Indoevropejskij jazyk i indoevropejcy (The Indo-European language and the Indo-Europeans)*. Vols. I–II. Tbilisi: Izdatel'stvo Tbilisskogo Universiteta.

   (1990). The early history of Indo-European languages. *Scientific American* 62.3 (March), 82–9.

   (1994–5a). *Indo-European and the Europeans: A reconstruction and historical analysis of a proto-language and a proto-culture. Part 1: The text*. Berlin: Mouton de Gruyter. Translated by Johanna Nichols.

   (1994–5b). *Indo-European and the Europeans: A reconstruction and historical analysis of a proto-language and a proto-culture. Part 2: Bibliography and indexes*. Berlin: Mouton de Gruyter.

Garrett, A. (1991). Indo-European reconstruction and historical methodologies. *Language* 67, 790–804.

Gerritsen, M. & Stein, D. (eds.) (1992). *Internal and external factors in syntactic change*. Berlin: Mouton de Gruyter.

Gilbert, G. G. (ed.) (1980). *Pidgin and creole languages. Selected essays by Hugo Schuchardt*. Cambridge University Press.

Gimson, A. C. & Cruttenden, A. (1994). *Gimson's pronunciation of English*. 5th edn. London: Arnold.

Givón, T. (1979). *On understanding grammar*. New York: Academic Press.

   (ed.) (1983). *Topic continuity in discourse: A quantitative, cross-language study*. Amsterdam: John Benjamins.

Goodglass, H. & Blumstein, S. (1973). *Psycholinguistics and aphasia*. Baltimore: Johns Hopkins University Press.

Goodman, M. (1985). Review of Bickerton (1981). *International Journal of American Linguistics* 51, 109–13.

Grace, G. W. (1990). The 'aberrant' vs 'exemplary' Melanesian languages. In P. Baldi (ed.), *Linguistic change and reconstruction methodology*. Berlin: Mouton de Gruyter.

Green, L. J. (2002). *African American English: A linguistic introduction*. Cambridge University Press.

Greenbaum, S. (1988). *Good English and the grammarian*. London: Longman.

Greenberg, J. (1957). *Essays in linguistics*. Chicago University Press.

   (1963/1966). Some universals of language with particular reference to the order of meaningful elements. In J. Greenberg (ed.), *Universals of language*. 2nd edn. Cambridge, MA: MIT Press.

Greenough, J. & Kittredge, G. (1902). *Words and their ways in English speech*. London: Macmillan.

Grenoble, L. A. & Whaley, L. J. (eds.) (1998). *Endangered languages: Current issues and future prospects*. Cambridge University Press.

Gumperz, J. J. & Wilson, R. (1971). Convergence and creolization: a case from the Indo-Aryan/Dravidian border. In D. Hymes (ed.), *Pidginization and creolization of languages*. Cambridge University Press.

Guthrie, M. (1967–71). *Comparative Bantu: An introduction to the comparative linguistics and prehistory of the Bantu languages*. Farnborough, Hants: Gregg Press.

Guy, G. (2003). Variationist approaches to phonological change. In Joseph & Janda (2003).

Haiman, J. (1985a). *Natural syntax: Iconicity and erosion*. Cambridge University Press.

(ed.) (1985b). *Iconicity in syntax*. Amsterdam: John Benjamins.

Hale, K. (1973). Deep-surface canonical disparities in relation to analysis and change: an Australian example. In T. A. Sebeok (ed.), *Current trends in linguistics.* Vol. II: *Diachronic, areal and typological linguistics*. The Hague: Mouton.

Hale, K., Craig, C., England, N., LaVerne, J., Krauss, M., Watahomigie, L. & Yamamoto, A. (1992). Endangered languages. *Language* 68, 1–42.

Hall, R. A. (1966). *Pidgin and creole languages*. Ithaca, NY: Cornell University Press.

Halle, M. (1962). Phonology in generative grammar. *Word* 18, 54–72.

(1997). On stress and accent in Indo-European. *Language* 73, 275–313.

Hancock, I. F. (1979). On the origins of the term *pidgin*. In I. F. Hancock (ed.), *Readings in creole studies*. Ghent: E. Story-Scienta.

Harris, A. & Campbell, L. (1995). *Historical syntax in cross-linguistic perspective*. Cambridge University Press.

Harris, J. (1985). *Phonological variation and change: Studies in Hiberno-English*. Cambridge University Press.

(1989). Towards a lexical analysis of sound change in progress. *Journal of Linguistics* 25, 35–56.

Harris, J. W. (1969). Sound change in Spanish and the theory of markedness. *Language* 45, 538–52.

Harris, M. (1978). The interrelationship between phonological and grammatical change. In Fisiak (1978).

Harris, R. & Taylor, T. J. (1997). *The Western tradition from Socrates to Saussure*. Vol. I in the series Landmarks of linguistic thought, 2nd edn. Oxford: Routledge.

Harrison, S. (2003). On the limits of the comparative method. In Joseph & Janda (2003).

Haspelmath, M. (1998). Does grammaticalization need reanalysis? *Studies in Language* 22, 49–85.
  (1999a). Are there principles of grammatical change? Review of Lightfoot (1999). *Journal of Linguistics* 35, 579–95.
  (1999b). Why is grammaticalization irreversible? *Linguistics* 37, 1,043–68.

Hawkins, J. A. (1983). *Word order universals*. New York: Academic Press.
  (ed.) (1988). *Explaining language universals*. Oxford: Blackwell.

Hayward, K. (1989). The Indo-European language and the history of its speakers: the theories of Gamkrelidze and Ivanov. *Lingua* 78, 37–86.

Heath, J. (1981). A case of intensive lexical diffusion. *Language* 57, 335–67.

Hegedüs, I., Michalove, P. A. & Manaster-Ramer, A. (eds.) (1997). *Indo-European, Nostratic and beyond*. Journal of Indo-European Studies monographs 22. Washington: Institute for the Study of Man.

Heine, B. (1997). *Cognitive foundations of grammar*. Oxford University Press.
  (2003). Grammaticalization. In Joseph & Janda (2003).

Heine, B., Claudi, U. & Hünnemeyer, F. (1991). *Grammaticalization: A conceptual framework*. University of Chicago Press.

Heine, B. & Kuteva, T. (2007). *The genesis of grammar: A reconstruction*. Oxford University Press.

Henderson, E. J. A. (1965). The topography of certain phonetic and morphological characteristics of South East Asian languages. *Lingua* 15, 400–34.

Hernandez-Campoy, J. M. & Conde-Silvestre, J. C. (2012). *The handbook of historical sociolinguistics*. Oxford: Wiley-Blackwell.

Hewes, G. W. (1977). Language origin theories. In D. M. Rumbaugh (ed.), *Language learning by a chimpanzee: The Lana project*. New York: Academic Press.

Hilgartner, S., Bell, R. C. & O'Connor, R. (1983). *Nukespeak: The selling of nuclear technology in America*. Harmondsworth: Penguin.

Hitchings, H. (2011). *The language wars: A history of proper English*. London: John Murray.

Hock, H. H. (1986). *Principles of historical linguistics*. Berlin: Mouton de Gruyter.
  (1991). *Principles of historical linguistics*. 2nd edn. Berlin: Mouton de Gruyter.

Hock, H. H. & Joseph, B. D. (1996). *Language history, language change and language relationship: An introduction to historical and comparative linguistics.* Berlin: Mouton de Gruyter.

Hockett, C. F. (1958). *A course in modern linguistics.* New York: Macmillan.

Hogg, R. N. (ed.) (1992). *The Cambridge history of the English language.* Vol. I: *The beginnings to 1066.* Cambridge University Press.

Holm, J. A. (1988). *Pidgins and creoles.* Vol. I: *Theory and structure.* Cambridge University Press.

(1989). *Pidgins and creoles.* Vol. II: *Reference survey.* Cambridge University Press.

Hombert, J. M. & Ohala, J. (1982). Historical development of tone patterns. In Maher, Bomhard & Koerner (1982).

Hombert, J. M., Ohala, J. & Ewan, W. (1979). Phonetic explanations for the development of tones. *Language* 55, 37–58.

Hooper, J. (1976a). *An introduction to natural generative phonology.* New York: Academic Press.

(1976b). Word frequency in lexical diffusion and the source of morphophonological change. In W. Christie (ed.), *Proceedings of the Second International Conference on Historical Linguistics.* Amsterdam: North-Holland.

(1978). Constraints on schwa-deletion in American English. In Fisiak (1978).

Hopper, P. J. (1991). On some principles of grammaticalization. In Traugott & Heine (1991a).

(1994). Phonogenesis. In W. Pagliuca (ed.), *Perspectives on grammaticalization.* Amsterdam: John Benjamins.

(1996). Some recent trends in grammaticalization. *Annual Review of Anthropology* 25, 217–36.

(1998). The paradigm at the end of the universe. In Ramat & Hopper (1998).

Hopper, P. J. & Thompson, S. A. (1980). Transitivity in grammar and discourse. *Language* 56, 251–99.

(1984). The discourse basis for lexical categories in universal grammar. *Language* 60, 703–52.

Hopper, P. J. & Traugott, E. C. (2003). *Grammaticalization.* 2nd edn. Cambridge University Press.

Hopper, P. J. & Traugott, E. C. (1993). *Grammaticalization.* 1st edn. Cambridge University Press.

Horne Tooke, J. (1786/1857). *Epea pteroenta; or the diversions of Purley. Part 1.* London: W. Tegg & Co.

Hubbell, A. F. (1950). *The pronunciation of English in New York City*. New York: Columbia University Press.

Huddleston, R. & Pullum, G. K. (2002). *The Cambridge grammar of the English language*. Cambridge University Press.

Hudson, R. (2006). *Wanna* revisited. *Language* 82, 604–27.

Hughes, G. (1988). *Words in time: A social history of English vocabulary*. Oxford: Blackwell.

Humphrys, J. (2004). *Lost for words: The mangling and manipulating of the English language*. London: Hodder.

Hurford, J. (2011). *The origins of grammar: Language in the light of evolution* (3 vols.). Oxford University Press.

Hurford, J., Knight, C. & Studdert Kennedy, M. (eds.) (1998). *Approaches to the evolution of language*. Cambridge University Press.

Hyman, L. (1975). On the change from SOV to SVO: evidence from Niger-Congo. In C. N. Li (ed.), *Word order and word order change*. Austin, TX: University of Texas Press.

Itkonen, E. (1982). Short-term and long-term teleology in linguistic change. In Maher, Bomhard & Koerner (1982).

Jablonski, N. G. & Aiello, L. C. (eds.) (1998). *The origin and diversification of language*. Memoirs of the California Academy of Sciences 24. San Francisco: California Academy of Sciences.

Jackendoff, R. (1997). Twistin' the night away. *Language* 73, 534–59.
    (1999). Possible stages in the evolution of language. *Trends in Cognitive Sciences* 3.7, 272–9.
    (2002). *Foundations of language: Brain, meaning, grammar evolution*. Oxford University Press.

Jahr, E. H. & Broch, I. (eds.) (1996). *Language contact in the Arctic: Northern pidgins and contact languages*. Berlin: Mouton de Gruyter.

Jakobson, R. (1941/1968). *Child language, aphasia and phonological universals*. The Hague: Mouton.
    (1949). Principes de phonologie historique. Appendix in *Principes de phonologie* by N. S. Troubetzkoy. Paris: Klincksieck (1949). English translation by A. R. Keiler in A. R. Keiler (ed.), *A reader in historical and comparative linguistics*. New York: Holt, Rinehart & Winston, 1972.

Janda, R. D. (1995). From agreement affix to subject 'clitic' and bound root: *-mos* > *-nos* vs *(-)nos(-)* and *nos-otros* in New Mexican and other regional Spanish dialects. *Chicago Linguistic Society* 31.1, 118–39.

Janda, R. D. & Joseph, B. D. (2003). On language, change, and language change – or, of history, linguistics and historical linguistics. In Joseph & Janda (2003).

Jeffers, R. J. & Lehiste, I. (1979). *Principles and methods for historical linguistics*. Cambridge, MA: MIT Press.

Jespersen, O. (1922). *Language, its nature, development and origin*. London: Allen & Unwin.

(1942). *A modern English grammar*. Copenhagen: Ejaar Munksgaard.

John, A. with Blake, S. (2001). *The total txtmsg dictionary*. London: Michael O'Mara.

Jones, C. (ed.) (1993). *Historical linguistics: Problems and perspectives*. London: Longman.

Joos, M. (1961). *The five clocks*. New York: Harcourt Brace Jovanovitch.

Joseph, B. D. (1983). *The synchrony and diachrony of the Balkan infinitive: A study in areal, general and historical linguistics*. Cambridge University Press.

(1992). Diachronic explanation: putting speakers back into the picture. In Davis & Iverson (1992).

Joseph, B. D. & Janda, R. D. (1988). The how and why of diachronic morphologization and demorphologization. In M. Hammond & M. Noonan (eds.), *Theoretical morphology: Approaches in modern linguistics*. San Diego: Academic Press.

(eds.) (2003). *The handbook of historical linguistics*. Oxford: Blackwell.

Kaiser, M. (1997). Rigor or vigor: whither distant comparison? In Hegedüs, Michalove & Manaster-Ramer (1997).

Kaufman, D. & Aronoff, M. (1991). Morphological disintegration and reconstruction in first language attrition. In Seliger & Vago (1991).

Kay, P. & Fillmore, C. J. (1999). Grammatical constructions and linguistic generalizations: the What's X doing Y? construction. *Language* 75, 1–33.

Kay, P. & Sankoff, G. (1974). A language-universals approach to pidgins and creoles. In D. Decamp & I. F. Hancock (eds.), *Pidgins and creoles: Current trends and prospects*. Washington, DC: Georgetown University Press.

Keesing, R. (1988). *Melanesian pidgin and the Oceanic substrate*. Stanford University Press.

Keiler, A. R. (ed.) (1972). *A reader in historical and comparative linguistics*. New York: Holt, Rinehart & Winston.

Kennedy, G. (1991). *Between* and *through*. The company they keep and the functions they serve. In Aijmer & Altenberg (1991).

Kerswill, P. (1996). Children, adolescents and language change. *Language Variation and Change* 8.2, 177–202.

Kesseler, A. & Bergs, A. (2003). Literacy and the new media: *vita brevis, lingua brevis*. In Aitchison & Lewis (2003b).

King, R. D. (1969a). *Historical linguistics and generative grammar.* Englewood Cliffs, NJ: Prentice-Hall.

(1969b). Push chains and drag chains. *Glossa* 3, 3–21.

Kiparsky, P. (1968). Linguistic universals and language change. In E. Bach & R. T. Harms (eds.), *Universals in linguistic theory.* New York: Holt, Rinehart & Winston. Also in Keiler (1972).

(1972). From palaeogrammarians to neogrammarians. *York Papers in Linguistics* 2, 33–43.

(1995). The phonological basis of sound change. In J. A. Goldsmith (ed.), *The handbook of phonological theory.* Oxford: Blackwell. Reprinted in Joseph & Janda (2003).

Knight, C., Studdert-Kennedy, M. & Hurford, J. (eds.) (2000). *The evolutionary emergence of language.* Cambridge University Press.

Krishnamurti, B. (1978). Areal and lexical diffusion of sound change: evidence from Dravidian. *Language* 54, 1–20.

Kroch, A. S. (1989). Reflexes of grammar in patterns of language change. *Language Variation and Change* 1, 199–244.

Kuno, S. (1974). The position of relative clauses and conjunctions. *Linguistic Inquiry* 5, 117–36.

Kuper, J. (ed.) (1977). *The anthropologist's cookbook.* London: Routledge & Kegan Paul.

Labov, W. (1972a). *Sociolinguistic patterns.* Philadelphia: University of Pennsylvania Press.

(1972b). Where do grammars stop? In R. W. Shuy (ed.), *Sociolinguistics: Current trends and prospects.* Washington, DC: University of Georgetown Press.

(1994). *Principles of linguistic change.* Vol. 1: *Internal factors.* Oxford: Blackwell.

(2001). *Principles of linguistic change.* Vol. 2: *Social factors.* Oxford: Blackwell.

(2010). *Principles of linguistic change.* Vol. 3: *Cognitive and cultural factors.* Oxford: Blackwell.

Ladefoged, P. (1992). Another view of endangered languages. *Language* 68, 809–11.

Lakoff, R. (1975). *Language and a woman's place.* New York: Harper & Row.

Langacker, R. W. (1977). Syntactic reanalysis. In C. N. Li (ed.), *Mechanisms of syntactic change.* Austin, TX: University of Texas Press.

Langer, N. & Nesse, A. (2012). Linguistic purism. In Hernandez-Campoy & Conde-Silvestre (2012).

Larson, R. K., Deprez, V. & Yamakido, H. (2010). *The evolution of human language: Biolinguistic perspectives.* Cambridge University Press.

Lass, R. (1976). *English phonology and phonological theory: Synchronic and diachronic studies*. Cambridge University Press.

(1990). How to do things with junk: exaptation in language evolution. *Journal of Linguistics* 26, 79–102.

(1993). How real(ist) are reconstructions? In Jones (1993).

Laycock, D. (1970). *Materials in New Guinea Pidgin (Coastal and Lowlands)*. Pacific Linguistics D-5. Canberra: Australian National University.

Leech, G. (1991). The state of the art in corpus linguistics. In Aijmer & Altenberg (1991).

Lehiste, I. (1988). *Lectures on language contact*. Cambridge, MA: MIT Press.

Lehmann, W. P. (ed.) (1967). *A reader in nineteenth-century historical linguistics*. Bloomington, IN: Indiana University Press.

(1992). *Historical linguistics*. 3rd edn. London and New York: Routledge.

Lenneberg, E. H. (ed.) (1967). *Biological foundations of language*. New York: Wiley.

Lewis, D. M. (1999). Rhetorical factors in grammaticalization: some English modal adverbs. Paper presented at International Symposium: New Reflections on Grammaticalization, Potsdam, June 1999.

Li, C. N. & Thompson, S. A. (1974). Historical change of word order: a case study of Chinese and its implications. In Anderson & Jones (1974).

(1976). Strategies for signalling grammatical relations in Wappo. *Chicago Linguistic Society* 12.

Lightfoot, D. (1979). *Principles of diachronic syntax*. Cambridge University Press.

(1999). *The development of language: Acquisition, change and evolution*. Maryland Lectures in Language and Cognition 1. Malden, MA, and Oxford: Blackwell.

Lowenberg, P. H. (ed.) (1988). *Language spread and language policy: Issues, implications and case studies*. Washington, DC: Georgetown University Press.

Lowth, R. (1762/1967). *A short introduction to English grammar*. Menston, England: Scholar Press. Facsimile reprint.

Maher, J. P., Bomhard, A. R. & Koerner, E. F. K. (eds.) (1982). *Papers from the 3rd International Conference on Historical Linguistics*. Amsterdam: John Benjamins.

Mallory, J. P. (1989). *In search of the Indo-Europeans: Language, archaeology and myth*. London: Thames & Hudson.

Mallory, J. P. & Adams, D. Q. (2006). *The Oxford introduction to Proto-Indo-European and the Proto-Indo-European world*. Oxford University Press.

Martinet, A. (1955). *Economie des changements phonétiques*. Berne: A. Francke.

(1960/1964). *Eléments de linguistique générale*. Paris: Armand Colin. English translation by E. Palmer. *Elements of general linguistics*. London: Faber & Faber, 1964.

Masica, C. P. (1976). *Defining a linguistic area*. Chicago University Press.

McArthur, T. (1998). *The English language*. Cambridge University Press.

McMahon, A. M. F. & McMahon, R. (1995). Linguistics, genetics and archeology: internal and external evidence in the Amerind controversy. *Transactions of the Philological Society* 93.2, 125–227.

McWhorter, J. H. (2005). *Defining creole*. Oxford University Press.

Meijer, G. & Muysken, P. (1977). On the beginnings of pidgin and creole studies: Schuchardt and Hesseling. In Valdman (1977).

Meillet, A. (1905–6). Comment les mots changent de sens. *Année Sociologique* 1–38. Reprinted in A. Meillet (1912/1948).

(1912/1948). *Linguistique historique et linguistique générale*. Paris: Champion.

Mihalic, F. (1971). *Jacaranda dictionary and grammar of Melanesian pidgin*. Milton, Queensland, Australia: Jacaranda Press.

Miller, G. A. & Fellbaum, C. (1992). Semantic networks of English. In B. Levin & S. Pinker (eds.), *Lexical and conceptual semantics*. Oxford: Blackwell. Originally published in *Cognition* 41 (1991), 197–229.

Milroy, J. (1992). *Linguistic variation and change: On the historical sociolinguistics of English*. Oxford: Blackwell.

Milroy, J. & Milroy, L. (1978). Belfast: change and variation in an urban vernacular. In Trudgill (1978).

(1985). Linguistic change, social network and speaker innovation. *Journal of Linguistics* 21, 339–84.

(1993). Mechanisms of change in urban dialects: the role of class, social network and gender. *International Journal of Applied Linguistics* 3, 57–78.

(1998). *Authority in language: Investigating standard English*. 3rd edn. London: Routledge.

Milroy, L. (1987a). *Language and social networks*. 2nd edn. Oxford: Basil Blackwell.

(1987b). *Observing and analysing natural language*. Oxford: Blackwell.

(2002). Social networks. In Chambers et al. (2002).

Milroy, L. & Milroy, J. (1992). Social network and social class: toward an integrated sociolinguistic model. *Language in Society* 21, 1–26.

Minett, J. W. & Wang, W. S. Y. (2003). On detecting borrowing: distance-based and character-based methods. *Diachronica* 20, 289–331.

Mithun, M. (1984). The evolution of noun incorporation. *Language* 60, 847–94.

(1991). The role of motivation in the emergence of grammatical categories: the grammaticalization of subjects. In Traugott & Heine (1991b).

(1992). External triggers and internal guidance in syntactic development: coordinating conjunction. In Gerritsen & Stein (1992).

Morpurgo Davies, A. (1989). Discussion. *Transactions of the Philological Society* 87, 166–7.

Mosel, U. & Mühlhäusler, P. (1982). New evidence of a Samoan origin of New Guinea Tok Pisin (New Guinea Pidgin English). *Journal of Pacific History* 17, 166–75.

Mougeon, R., Beniak, E. & Valois, D. (1985). A sociolinguistic study of language contact, shift and change. *Linguistics* 23, 455–87.

Moulton, W. G. (1985). Review of Rauch & Carr (1983). *Language* 61, 680–7.

Mufwene, W. (1995). Creoles and creolization. In J.-O. Östman & J. Blommaerts (eds.), *Handbook of pragmatics*. Amsterdam/Philadelphia: John Benjamins.

Mugglestone, L. (1995). *'Talking proper': The rise of accent as social symbol*. Oxford: Clarendon Press.

Mühlhäusler, P. (1978). Samoan plantation pidgin English and the origin of New Guinea Pidgin. *Papers in Pidgin and Creole Linguistics* 1, 67–119.

(1979a). *Growth and structure of the lexicon of New Guinea Pidgin*. Pacific Linguistics C-52. Canberra: Australian National University.

(1979b). Sociolects in New Guinea Pidgin. In S. A. Wurm (ed.), *New Guinea and neighbouring areas: A sociolinguistic laboratory*. The Hague: Mouton.

(1980a). The development of the category of number in Tok Pisin. In P. Muysken (ed.), *Generative studies in creole languages*. Dordrecht: Foris.

(1980b). Structural expansion and the process of creolization. In A. Valdman & A. Highfield (eds.), *Theoretical orientations in creole studies*. New York: Academic Press.

(1986). *Pidgin and creole linguistics*. Oxford: Basil Blackwell.

(1997). *Pidgin and creole linguistics*. Expanded and revised edn. Westminster Creolistics Series 3. London: University of Westminster Press.

Mühlhäusler, P. & Harré, R. (1990). *Pronouns and people: The linguistic construction of social and personal identity*. Oxford: Blackwell.

Myers-Scotton, C. (1993). *Duelling languages: Grammatical structure in codeswitching*. Oxford University Press.

(1998). A way to dusty death: the Matrix Language turnover hypothesis. In Grenoble & Whaley (1998).

Nänny, M. & Fischer, O. (eds.) (1999). *Form miming meaning: Iconicity in language and literature*. Amsterdam: John Benjamins.

Naro, A. J. (1978). A study on the origins of pidginization. *Language* 54, 314–47.

(1981). The social and structural dimensions of a syntactic change. *Language* 57, 63–98.

Nerlich, B., Herman, V., Todd, Z. & Clarke, D. (eds.), *Polysemy: Patterns of meaning in mind and language*. Berlin: Mouton de Gruyter.

Nettle, D. & Romaine, S. (2000). *Vanishing voices: The extinction of the world's languages*. Oxford University Press.

Nichols, J. (1992). *Linguistic diversity in space and time*. University of Chicago Press.

(2003). Diversity and stability in language. In Joseph & Janda (2003).

Norde, M. (2009). *Degrammaticalization*. Oxford University Press.

Nunberg, G., Sag, I. A. & Wasow, T. (1994). Idioms. *Language* 70, 491–538.

O'Connor, J. D. (1973). *Phonetics*. Harmondsworth: Penguin.

Ogura, M. (1990). *Dynamic dialectology: A study of language in space and time*. Tokyo: Kenkyusha.

(1995). The development of Middle English c and e. *Diachronica* 12.1, 31–53.

Ohala, J. J. (1974a). Experimental historical phonology. In Anderson & Jones (1974).

(1974b). Phonetic explanation in phonology. In *Papers from the Parasession on Natural Phonology*. Chicago Linguistic Society.

(1975). Phonetic explanations for nasal sound patterns. In C. A. Ferguson, L. M. Hyman & J. J. Ohala (eds.), *Nasalfest: Papers on a symposium on nasals and nasalization*. Stanford, CA: Language Universals Project.

(1993). The phonetics of sound change. In Jones (1993).

(2003). Phonetics and historical phonology. In Joseph & Janda (2003).

Opie, I. & Opie, P. (1951). *The Oxford dictionary of nursery rhymes*. Oxford: Clarendon Press.

Orton, H. & Wright, N. (1974). *A word geography of England*. London: Seminar Press.

Osthoff, C. H. & Brugmann, K. (1878). Preface to *Morphologische Untersuchungen auf dem Gebiete der Indogermanischen Sprachen*. Translated in Lehmann (1967).

Patterson, D. (1860). *Provincialisms of Belfast*. Belfast: Boyd.

Paul, H. (1880/1920). *Prinzipien der Sprachgeschichte*. Tübingen: Max Niemeyer.

Payne, R. (1979). Humpbacks: their mysterious songs. *National Geographic* 155.1 (January), 18–25.

Pedersen, H. (1931/1962). *Linguistic science in the nineteenth century: Methods and results*. Cambridge, MA: Harvard University Press. Later published under the title *The discovery of language: Linguistic science in the nineteenth century*. Bloomington, IN: Indiana University Press, 1962.

Peiros, I. (1997). Macro families: can a mistake be detected? In Hegedüs, Michalove & Manaster-Ramer (1997).

Pinker, S. & Bloom, P. (1990). Natural language and natural selection. *Behavioral and Brain Sciences* 13, 707–84.

Pintzuk, S. (2003). Variationist approaches to syntactic change. In Joseph & Janda (2003).

Pope, J., Meyerhoff, M. & Ladd, D. R. (2007). Forty years of language change on Martha's Vineyard. *Language* 83.3, 615–27.

Postal, P. M. (1968). *Aspects of phonological theory*. New York: Harper & Row.

Potter, S. (1969). *Changing English*. London: Deutsch.

Pullum, G. K. (1977). Word order universals and grammatical relations. In P. Cole & J. Saddock (eds.), *Syntax and semantics*. Vol. VIII: *Grammatical relations*. New York: Academic Press.

Pustejovsky, J. (1995). *The generative lexicon*. Cambridge, MA: MIT Press.

Pustejovsky, J. & Boguraev, B. (1996). *Lexical semantics: The problem of polysemy*. Oxford: Clarendon Press.

Pyles, T. (1971). *The origins and development of the English language*. 2nd edn. New York: Harcourt Brace Jovanovich.

Pyles, T. & Algeo, J. (1982). *The origins and development of the English language*. 3rd edn. New York: Harcourt Brace Jovanovich.

Radford, A., Atkinson, M., Britain, D., Clahsen, H. & Spencer, A. (1999). *Linguistics: An introduction*. Cambridge University Press.

Ramat, A. G. & Hopper, P. J. (eds.) (1998). *The limits of grammaticalization*. Amsterdam: John Benjamins.

Rankin, R. L. (2003). The comparative method. In Joseph & Janda (2003).

Rauch, I. & Carr, G. (eds.) (1983). *Language change*. Bloomington, IN: Indiana University Press.

Ravin, Y. & Leacock, C. (2000). *Polysemy: Theoretical and computational approaches*. Oxford University Press.

Rayfield, J. R. (1970). *The languages of a bilingual community*. The Hague: Mouton.

Reetz, H. & Jongman, A. (2009). *Phonetics: Transcription, production, acoustics, and perception*. Oxford: Wiley-Blackman.

Renfrew, C. (1987). *Archaeology and language: The puzzle of Indo-European origins*. London: Jonathan Cape.

Rickford, J. R. (1987). *Dimensions of a creole continuum: History, texts and linguistic analysis of Guyanese Creole*. Stanford University Press.

Ricks, C. & Michaels, I. (eds.) (1990). *The state of the language: 1990 edition*. London: Faber & Faber.

Ringe, D. A. (1992). On calculating the factor of chance in language comparison. *Transactions of the American Philosophical Society* 82.1, 1–110. (2003). Internal reconstruction. In Joseph & Janda (2003).

Rissanen, M. (1991). On the history of *that*/zero as object clause links in English. In Aijmer & Altenberg (1991).

Roberts, J. (1997). Hitting a moving target: acquisition of sound change in progress. *Language Variation and Change* 7.1, 101–12.

Roberts, J. & Labov, W. (1993). Learning to talk Philadelphian: acquisition of short *a* by preschool children. *Language Variation and Change* 9.2, 249–66.

Robins, R. H. & Uhlenbeck, E. M. (eds.) (1991). *Endangered languages*. Oxford: Berg.

Romaine, S. (1982). *Sociohistorical linguistics*. Cambridge University Press. (1988). *Pidgin and creole languages*. London: Longman. (1999). The grammaticalization of the proximative in Tok Pisin. *Language* 75, 322–46.

Rosch, E. (1975). Cognitive representations of semantic categories. *Journal of Experimental Psychology* 104, 192–233.

Rosewarne, D. (1984). Estuary English. *Times Education Supplement*, 19 October 1984. (1994a). Estuary English: tomorrow's RP? *English Today* 10.1 (no. 37, January), 3–8. (1994b). Pronouncing Estuary English. *English Today* 10.4 (no. 40, October), 3–7. (1996). Estuary as a World language? *Modern English Teacher* 5.1, 13–17.

Ruhlen, M. (1978). Nasal vowels. In J. H. Greenberg (ed.), *Universals of human language* (4 vols.). Vol. II. Stanford University Press. (1994). *On the origin of languages: Studies in linguistic taxonomy*. Stanford University Press.

Safire, W. (1980). *On language*. New York: Times Books.

Sahgal, A. & Agnihotri, R. K. (1985). Syntax – the common bond: acceptability of syntactic deviances in Indian English. *English World-Wide* 6, 117–29.

Salmons, J. (1992). A look at the data for a global etymology: **tik* 'finger'. In Davis & Iverson (1992).

Salmons, J. C. & Joseph, B. D. (eds.) (1998). *Nostratic: Sifting the evidence.* Amsterdam: John Benjamins.

Sankoff, G. (1977). Creolization and syntactic change in New Guinea Tok Pisin. In B. Blount & M. Sanches (eds.), *Sociocultural dimensions of language change.* New York: Academic Press.

Sapir, E. (1921). *Language.* New York: Harcourt, Brace and World.

Saussure, F. de (1915/1959). *Cours de linguistique générale.* Paris: Payot. Translated into English by W. Baskin as *Course in general linguistics.* New York: The Philosophical Library. London: Fontana, 1974.

Schaller, H. W. (1975). *Die Balkansprachen.* Heidelberg: Winter.

Schilling-Estes, N. & Wolfram, W. (1999). Alternative models of dialect death: dissipation vs concentration. *Language* 75, 486–521.

Schmandt-Besserat, D. (1992). *Before writing.* Austin, TX: University of Texas Press.

Schmidt, A. (1985). *Young people's Dyirbal: An example of language death from Australia.* Cambridge University Press.

Seliger, H. W. & Vago, R. M. (eds.) (1991). *First language attrition.* Cambridge University Press.

Silva-Corvalán, C. (1986). Bilingualism and language change. *Language* 62, 587–608.

Singler, J. V. (1988). The homogeneity of the substrate as a factor in pidgin/creole genesis. *Language* 64, 27–51.

Slobin, D. I. (1977). Language change in childhood and in history. In J. Macnamara (ed.), *Language learning and thought.* New York: Academic Press.

Smith, N. V. & Wilson, D. (1979). *Modern linguistics: The results of Chomsky's revolution.* Harmondsworth: Penguin.

Stampe, D. (1979). *A dissertation on natural phonology.* New York: Garland.

Stein, D. (1990). *The semantics of syntactic change.* Berlin: Mouton.

Sturtevant, E. H. (1917/1961). *Linguistic change.* Chicago University Press. Phoenix Books edition.

Sun, C.-F. & Givón, T. (1985). On the so-called SOV word order in Mandarin Chinese. *Language* 61, 329–51.

Sweetser, E. E. (1990). *From etymology to pragmatics: Metaphorical and cultural aspects of semantic structure.* Cambridge University Press.

Szemerényi, O. (1989). Concerning Professor Renfrew's views of the Indo-European homeland. *Transactions of the Philological Society* 87, 156–65.

Tabor, W. & Traugott, E. C. (1998). Structural scope expansion and grammaticalization. In Ramat & Hopper (1998).

Tallerman, M. (2005). *Language origins: Perspectives on evolution*. Oxford University Press.

Taylor, J. (1995). *Linguistic categorization: Prototypes in linguistic theory*. 2nd edn. Oxford: Clarendon Press.

Thième, P. (1964). The comparative method for reconstruction in linguistics. In D. Hymes (ed.), *Language in culture and society*. New York: Harper & Row.

Thomason, S. G. (1983a). Chinook jargon in areal and historical context. *Language* 59, 820–70.

   (1983b). Genetic relationship and the case of Ma'a (Mbugu). *Studies in African Linguistics* 14, 195–231.

   (2000). *Contact languages: A wider perspective*. Amsterdam: John Benjamins.

   (2001). *Language contact: An introduction*. Washington, DC: Georgetown University Press.

   (2003). Contact as a source of language change. In Joseph & Janda (2003).

Thomason, S. G. & Kaufman, T. (1988). *Language contact, creolization and genetic linguistics*. Berkeley, CA: University of California Press.

Tieken-Boon van Ostade, I. (2011). *The bishop's grammar: Robert Lowth and the rise of prescriptivism*. Oxford University Press.

Todd, L. (1990). *Pidgins and creoles*. 2nd edn. London: Routledge.

Tomlin, R. S. (1986). *Basic word order: Functional principles*. London: Croom Helm.

Trask, R. L. (1996). *Historical linguistics*. London: Arnold.

Traugott, E. C. (1989). On the rise of epistemic meanings in English: an example of subjectification in semantic change. *Language* 65, 31–55.

   (1992). Syntax. In Hogg (1992).

   (2003). Constructions in grammaticalization. In Joseph & Janda (2003).

Traugott, E. C. & Heine, B. (1991a). *Approaches to grammaticalization* (2 vols.). Vol. I. Amsterdam: John Benjamins.

   (1991b). *Approaches to grammaticalization* (2 vols.). Vol. II. Amsterdam: John Benjamins.

Trench, R. C. (1855). *On the study of words*. 6th edn. London: J. W. Parker.

   (1856). *English past and present*. 3rd, revised, edn. London: J. W. Parker.

Trier, J. (1931). *Der Deutsche Wortschatz im Sinnbezirk des Verstandes*. Heidelberg: Winter.

Trudgill, P. (1972). Sex, covert prestige and linguistic change in the urban British dialect of Norwich. *Language in Society* 1, 179–95.

   (1974). *The social differentiation of English in Norwich*. Cambridge University Press.

(ed.) (1978). *Sociolinguistic patterns in British English*. London: Edward Arnold.

(1983). *On dialect*. Oxford: Basil Blackwell.

(1986). *Dialects in contact*. Oxford: Basil Blackwell.

Trudgill, P. & Cheshire, J. (1998). *The sociolinguistics reader*. Vol. 1: *Multilingualism and bilingualism*. London: Arnold.

Tsitsipis, I. D. (1989). Skewed performance and full performance in language obsolescence. In Dorian (1989).

Twaddell, W. F. (1935). On defining the phoneme. Reprinted in M. Joos (ed.) (1958), *Readings in linguistics*. University of Chicago Press.

Ullmann, S. (1962). *Semantics: An introduction to the science of meaning*. Oxford: Blackwell.

Ungerer, F. & Schmid, H.-J. (1996). *An introduction to cognitive linguistics*. London: Longman.

Valdman, A. (ed.) (1977). *Pidgin and creole linguistics*. Bloomington, IN: Indiana University Press.

Vendryès, J. (1923/1925). *Language*. London: Kegan Paul.

Verhaar, J. W. M. (1995). *Toward a reference grammar of Tok Pisin: An experiment in corpus linguistics*. Honolulu: University of Hawaii Press.

Vincent, N. (1976). Perceptual factors and word order change in Latin. In M. Harris (ed.), *Romance syntax*. University of Salford.

Vine, B. (1988). Review of T. V. Gamkrelidze & V. V. Ivanov (1984). *Language* 64, 396–401.

Wang, W. (1969). Competing changes as a cause of residue. *Language* 45, 9–25.

(ed.) (1977). *The lexicon in phonological change*. The Hague: Mouton.

Wang, W. S.-Y. (1994). Glottochronology, lexicostatistics, and other numerical methods. In R. E. Asher (ed.), *The encyclopaedia of language and linguistics*. Oxford and Aberdeen: Pergamon Press and Aberdeen University Press.

Wang, W. S.-Y. & Lien, C. (1993). Bidirectional diffusion in sound change. In Jones (1993).

Warren, B. (1992). *Sense developments: A contrastive study of the development of slang senses and novel standard senses in English*. Stockholm: Almqvist & Wiksell.

Watkins, C. (1989). New parameters in historical linguistics, philology, and culture history. *Language* 65, 783–99.

(1995). *How to kill a dragon: Aspects of Indo-European philology*. New York: Oxford University Press.

Weinreich, U. (1953). *Languages in contact: Findings and problems*. New York: Publications of the Linguistic Circle of New York.

Wells, J. (1982). *Accents of English* (3 vols.). Cambridge University Press.

Whiteley, W. H. (1967). Swahili nominal classes and English loan words: a preliminary survey. In G. Manessy (ed.), *Classification nominale dans les langues négroafricaines*. Paris: Centre National de la Recherche Scientifique.

Whitney, W. D. (1893). *Oriental and linguistic studies* (2 vols.). Vol. I. New York: Charles Scribner's Sons.

Wilkinson, A. (1967). *In your own words*. London: BBC Publications.

Wray, A. (ed.) (2002). *The transition to language*. Oxford University Press.

Wurff, W. van der (1993). Gerunds and their objects in the Modern English period. In J. van Marle (ed.), *Historical linguistics 1991: Papers from the 10th International Conference on Historical Linguistics*. Amsterdam: John Benjamins.

Wurm, S. A. & Mühlhäusler, P. (eds.) (1985). *Handbook of Tok Pisin (New Guinea Pidgin)*. Pacific Linguistics C-70. Canberra: Australian National University.

Index